New Casebooks

FEMINIST THEATRE
AND THEORY

New Casebooks

New Casebooks

FEMINIST THEATRE AND THEORY

EDITED BY HELENE KEYSSAR

First published 1996 by
MACMILLAN PRESS LTD
Houndmills, Basingstoke, Hampshire RG21 6XS
and London
Companies and representatives
throughout the world

ISBN 0–333–61550–6 hardcover
ISBN 0–333–61551–4 paperback

A catalogue record for this book is available
from the British Library.

10   9   8   7   6   5   4   3   2   1
05   04   03   02   01   00   99   98   97   96

Printed in Malaysia

Contents

Acknowledgements

The editor, Helene Keyssar, wishes to thank Gregory Stephens, Jill McDowell, Martin Coyle and Tracy B. Strong for diverse assistance at moments when help was much needed. She also wishes to thank Martin Coyle for being the perfect 'editor's editor'.

The editor and publishers also wish to thank the following for permission to use copyright material:

Karen Cronacher, for 'Unmasking the Minstrel Mask's Black Magic in Ntozake Shange's *spell #7*', *Theatre Journal*, 44 (1992), 177–93, by permission of The Johns Hopkins University Press; Tracy C. Davis, for '*Extremities and Masterpieces:* A Feminist Paradigm of Art and Politics', *Modern Drama*, 32:1 (March 1989), 89–103, by permission of *Modern Drama*; Jeanie Forte, for 'Realism, Narrative, and the Feminist Playwright – A Problem of Reception', *Modern Drama*, 32:1 (March 1989), 115–27, by permission of *Modern Drama*; Barbara Freedman, for 'Frame-Up: Feminism, Psychoanalysis, Theatre', *Theatre Journal*, 40:3 (October 1989), 375–97 reprinted in *Performing Feminisms: Feminist Critical Theory and Theatre*, ed. Sue-Ellen Case (1990), pp. 54–76, by permission of The Johns Hopkins University Press; Deborah R. Geis, for 'Wordscapes of the Body: Performative Language as Gestus in Marie Irene Fornes's Plays', *Theatre Journal*, 42:3 (October 1990), 291–307, reprinted and extended in Deborah Geis, *Postmodern Theatric(k)s: Monologue in Contemporary American Drama*, The University of Michigan Press, pp. 117–34, by permission of The Johns Hopkins University Press and The University of Michigan Press; Helen Keyssar, for 'Drama and the Dialogic Imagination: Wendy Wasserstein's *The Heidi Chronicles* and Maria Irene Fornes' *Fefu and her Friends*', *Modern Drama*, 34:1 (1991), 88–106, by

vii

permission of *Modern Drama*; Loren Kruger, for 'The Dis-Play's the Thing: Gender and Public Sphere in Contemporary British Theatre', *Theatre Journal*, 42:1 (March 1990), 27–47, by permission of the author; Judith Graves Miller, for 'Contemporary Women's Voices in French Theatre', *Modern Drama*, 32:1 (March 1989), 5–23, revised in Christine P. Makward and Judith G. Miller (eds), *Plays by French and Francophone Women: A Critical Anthology*, The University of Michigan Press, 1–14, by permission of *Modern Drama* and The University of Michigan Press; Janelle Reinelt, for 'Beyond Brecht: Britain's New Feminist Drama', *Theatre Journal*, 38.2 (May 1986), 154–63, reprinted in Sue-Ellen Case (ed.), *Performing Feminisms: Feminist Critical Theory and Theatre* (1990), by permission of the author and The Johns Hopkins University Press; Patricia R. Schroeder, for 'Locked Behind the Proscenium: Feminist Strategies in *Getting Out* and *My Sister in This House*', *Modern Drama* 32:1 (March 1989), 104–14, by permission of *Modern Drama*; Haiping Yan, for 'Male Ideology and Female Identity: Images of Women in Four Modern Chinese Historical Plays', *Journal of Dramatic Theory and Criticism*, 8:1 (Fall 1993), 61–81, by permission of the *Journal of Dramatic Theory and Criticism*; Yvonne Yarbro-Bejarano, for 'Chicanas' Experience in Collective Theatre: Ideology and Form', *Women and Performance: A Journal of Feminist Theory*, 2:2 (1985), 45–58, by permission of the author.

Every effort has been made to trace all the copyright holders but if any have been inadvertently overlooked the publishers will be pleased to make the necessary arrangement at the first opportunity.

General Editors' Preface

The purpose of this series of New Casebooks is to reveal some of the ways in which contemporary criticism has changed our understanding of commonly studied texts and writers and, indeed, of the nature of criticism itself. Central to the series is a concern with modern critical theory and its effect on current approaches to the study of literature. Each New Casebook editor has been asked to select a sequence of essays which will introduce the reader to the new critical approaches to the text or texts being discussed in the volume and also illuminate the rich interchange between critical theory and critical practice that characterises so much current writing about literature.

In this focus on modern critical thinking and practice New Casebooks aim not only to inform but also to stimulate, with volumes seeking to reflect both the controversy and the excitement of current criticism. Because much of this criticism is difficult and often employs an unfamiliar critical language, editors have been asked to give the reader as much help as they feel is appropriate, but without simplifying the essays or the issues they raise. Again, editors have been asked to supply a list of further reading which will enable readers to follow up issues raised by the essays in the volume.

The project of New Casebooks, then, is to bring together in an illuminating way those critics who best illustrate the ways in which contemporary criticism has established new methods of analysing texts and who have reinvigorated the important debate about how we 'read' literature. The hope is, of course, that New Casebooks will not only open up this debate to a wider audience, but will also encourage students to extend their own ideas, and think afresh about their responses to the texts they are studying.

John Peck and Martin Coyle
University of Wales, Cardiff

Introduction

HELENE KEYSSAR

I

In the early eighties, feminist theatre was an emergent cultural form. It had its origins in experimental theatre groups and in the women's movement of the sixties and seventies. It sought a definition and found several: productions and scripts characterised by consciousness of women as women; dramaturgy in which art is inseparable from the condition of women as women;[1] performance (written and acted) that deconstructs sexual difference and thus undermines patriarchal power; scripting and production that present transformation as a structural and ideological replacement for recognition; and the creation of women characters in the 'subject position'.[2] Feminist theatre thrived particularly in Britain and the United States and found its homes primarily in non-commercial spaces in cities and towns. It was exciting because it dared to venture to the stage with such diverse and sometimes surprising representations and explorations of women, of their relationships to each other and to men, that it created a new audience for theatre. Its only assumption was that the domain for feminist theatre was not consecrated ground.

As I write this Introduction, in the mid-nineties, feminist theatre is no longer emergent in the almost naïve way it was ten to fifteen years ago. Some of what has been called feminist theatre is now central to the dominant culture, perhaps more in the United States than in Britain, but to some extent in both. Plays such as Marsha Norman's *'night Mother* (1982) and Wendy Wasserstein's *The Heidi Chronicles* (1990) in the United States, and Mary O'Malley's *Once a Catholic* (1977) and Nell Dunn's *Steaming* (1981) in Britain, are instances of works by and about women that have been produced in mainstream commercial theatres and heralded as feminist dramas by mainstream critics and spectators. Not all critics agree, however, that these and other recent dramas by and about women are, indeed, authentically feminist. That the male critics who dominate the media have praised plays such as *'night Mother* as feminist theatre has been disturbing but not surprising. These works yield the stage to familiar female types, engaged in activities that remind us of conventional modern drama by men.

One good that has come of this commercial success, in addition to whatever fame and fortune has accrued for the writers, actors, producers, directors, and other theatre personnel and investors, is that it has called into question the qualities crucial to an authentic feminist theatre. This, in turn, has inspired a truly astonishing quality and quantity of feminist theatre criticism. Plays by and about women continue to be written and produced, but the most striking development in the domain of gender and drama in the eighties and early nineties has been the emergence of a rich and diverse array of writings in feminist criticism and theory. Evidence of this 'explosion of feminist dramatic criticism', as bibliographer Susan Steadman calls it,[3] can be found in both the regularity with which major journals now publish feminist theatre criticism, history and theory, and the commitment to feminist criticism of entire issues of several major drama journals. Also notable is the establishment of a new journal, *Women and Performance: A Journal of Feminist Theory*, and, most efficaciously, the publication of Susan Steadman's bibliographic book, *Feminist Dramatic Criticism*. My research for this *New Casebook* turned up hundreds of articles in the field of contemporary feminist theatre; conceived in the broadest terms to include performance art and reviews, history, and feminist criticism of classical works such as the plays of Shakespeare or Greek dramas, the total number of pieces of feminist writing on drama published between 1970 and 1994 approaches one thousand.

As remarkable as the quantity of books and articles from Britain and the United States has been the international proliferation of feminist theatre criticism. The articles included in this volume on theatre in China and France suggest the worldwide reach of contemporary feminist thinking in theatre, and they are only a small fraction of the work being done in this domain around the world.

This flowering of criticism has, I think, three roots. First, it is a response to the maturation and continuation of feminist theatre itself. Much like other gestures of the contemporary women's movement, in its early stages, from the late sixties to the early eighties, most writing about feminist theatre was a matter of identification, recognition, definition and contextualisation. Janet Brown's *Feminist Drama: Definition and Critical Analysis* (1979),

Dinah Leavitt's *Feminist Theatre Groups* (1980), and, more broadly cast, Helen Chinoy and Linda Jenkins's *Woman in American Theatre* (1981), as well as a small trickle of articles in the alternative press, announced the existence of the form and its precursors. Arguments occurred from the beginning about the differences between plays written by women and 'true' feminist drama, and these disputes have been carried into the realm of production. For the most part, however, these debates were, in the beginning of the form, secondary to the acknowledgement that there were distinctive new plays by women and new groups of theatre artists particularly concerned with the condition and consciousness of women as women.

Michelene Wandor's *Understudies* (1981) and my *Feminist Theatre* (1984) took up these announcements and augmented them with further historical and analytic work. Wandor's book focused on the emergence from left-wing and lesbian political movements of feminist theatre in Britain as an instance of alternative theatre. My book examined the history of this emerging feminist theatre in both Britain and the United States and took a close look at plays by approximately twenty contemporary American and British women. Wandor and I concurred on the inseparability of feminist theatre from politics, which for each of us has everything to do with process of production and relations of a given production to audience.

To some extent, like the women's movement itself, feminist theatre criticism was first devotedly diverse and welcoming to anyone who wanted to participate. The feminist criticism of the seventies and early eighties was mainly historical, informative and recuperative, and thus mostly uncontentious. History, of course, is always a matter of subjectivity, but these first moments of feminist criticism were concerned more with discovery and celebration than analysis. As more plays have been written, the sheer quantity, diversity and continuity of feminist theatre has occasioned more critical writing. The combination of dramatic and critical work, sustained now over several decades, has made mainstream media attention inevitable. It has also made feminist theatre as a cultural form less fragile and less vulnerable to negative criticism.

The second source of the abundance of critical writing on feminist theatre in the last decade has been the recognition of the need for judgements of particular works and for possibly new, 'feminist' criteria for evaluation. The earliest critical and historical writings on feminist theatre drew their bearings from non-gendered theories and approaches to drama – that is from the Aristotelian traditions of drama criticism, with an occasional use of Brechtian theory and performance theory. By the mid-eighties, however, a contagion occurred between more generalised feminist theories and feminist theatre criticism. The names associated with the approaches that have emerged from these associations are suggestive of the diversity of forms of criticism: they include Marxist-feminism, radical-feminism, cultural-feminism, lesbian-feminism (which for some overlaps with radical), Lacanian psychoanalytic criticism, more traditional Freudian psychoanalytic criticism, and socialist/ materialist feminism. Few of these approaches are rigid, most are plastic, several are hybrid. The student of feminist theatre must be wary of names that have different meanings for different writers. Readers should also know that concern with identity politics – with who one is, especially in terms of race, gender and class – is at the centre of political debate in general and is a significant part of the debate among feminists in this volume.

Within this montage of theories, two sets of conventions or styles do stand out – Realism and Brechtian non-realism. Ironically, more than a decade ago, when I began my book *Feminist Theatre*, I did so with the hypothesis that realism (especially psychological realism) and a resistance to realism presented in several different forms were the keypoles of energy informing the styles and substance of feminist drama. In my hypothesis I took this to represent contrasting commitments to an exploration of women as individuals on the one hand, and, on the other hand, interest in women as social and political forces. Perhaps from a slight apologetic perspective, I thought that American feminist theatre tended towards the realism typified by the plays of Beth Henley and Wendy Wasserstein and that British feminist theatre inclined towards Brechtian epic theatre such as that found in the plays of Carol Churchill and Louise Page. I made no secret to myself at least that I thought realism and the American instances of it in plays that claimed to be feminist to be less powerful, less provocative than dramas that were non-realistic (and, I thought, British) in structure.

By the time I finished my research in 1983, I knew that I was wrong, as I mentioned in the Preface to *Feminist Theatre*. Realism and various alternatives to realism occurred in relatively equal numbers in Britain and the United States, if for different reasons. From the early seventies on, in Britain feminist writers often attempted to conjoin socialist and feminist politics and in so doing turned to a Brechtian style of dramaturgy. Left-wing politics was less frequently a source of dramaturgic impulse in American feminist theatre; rather, non-narrative, unconventionally staged productions drew their inspirations from psychoanalytic understandings of representation and historical models of community theatre, as well as from film and television.

Ironically, a decade and a half later, realism and Brechtian 'epic' conventions, both opposed to each other and combined, now are the key distinguishing marks and rallying cries of much feminist theatre and feminist theatre criticism. The line-up is not, however, as neat as I once thought, and nor is it separated by national borders or cultures. At least in Britain and the United Ststes, defences of realism and invocations of Brecht in theatre criticism are equally abundant.

The case for realism within feminist theatre actually goes back almost a decade to the plays and critical writings of Michelene Wandor. Her idea of 'domestic realism' permeates both her dramas and her criticism. Almost identical in Wandor's writing to naturalism,[4] realism is at once a matter of style and content: it is a representation of recognisable settings, characters and events reaccentuated by the newness of the material to the stage; it is typified by juxtaposition along with continuity of incident from scene to scene, and references to popular culture. Wandor's understanding is initially, in the seventies and early eighties, very much like Catherine Belsey's notion of 'classic realism': texts which carry 'the authority of an apparent familiarity' and which tend 'to efface their own textuality'.[5] Realism encourages us to forget the border between stage and audience; the world of the play could easily be part of our world, and we come to care about it almost as we would about our own lives and communities. Critics hostile to realism argue that realism obliterates or disguises the construction of the world – all appears seamless and 'natural', therefore appropriate. For Wandor, this is potentially a political good: it allows an audience of ordinary working-class and middle-class people to be at ease with the theatre and thus to be more receptive to political and social ideas and behaviours that they might otherwise avoid.

By the early nineties, Wandor saw glimmers of a 'new realism', a style that incorporates historical and didactic messages in conventions similar to those urged by Bertolt Brecht.[6] In the first essay in this *Casebook*, 'Realism, Narrative and the Feminist Playwright –

A Problem of Reception', Jeanie Forte argues similarly to Wandor for a flexible realism that is 'readable' on stage as well as off. Anti-realism, she suggests, can be so alienating that its meanings are entirely lost. Janelle Reinelt, whose essay (2) argues for a modified Brechtian approach to feminist dramaturgy, has struggled elsewhere with the possibility that 'any kind of feminist statement' could be expressed in theatre in 'traditional realistic terms'.[7] Reinelt presents a good, if minimal, working definition of realism as 'a theatrical representation of everyday life embedded in the more general flux of history'.[8] I would augment this with three thoughts. First, that realism can refer to various aspects of a representation, including those not readily seen or felt or heard. Realism is not only a matter of the surface. It can be an expression of 'deep structure'. Second, that 'classic realism', at least, implies a single, indisputable reality; this is an understanding disputed by much postmodernist thinking. Third, that realism is like good sex: you know it when you see it, but it resists conclusive definition.

The most common alternative posed by feminist theatre critics (and playwrights) to realism is something like the 'feminist trans-formation of Brechtian techniques' described by Janelle Reinelt in her essay in this volume: 'Beyond Brecht: Britain's New Feminist Drama'. Reinelt sees the use of Brechtian conventions such as that of the 'gest' – a singular, symbolic gesture associated with each character that controls and articulates the spectator's relation to the actor-as-character – as useful for feminist theatre because it facili-tates revelation of 'relations between the sexes'. Her article examines the use of several Brechtian conventions in three British plays. She first discusses the Red Ladder Theatre company's *Strike While the Iron is Hot,* a collaborative production in which gender and class are explicit forces whose conflicting interests are revealed around issues of equal wages and the value and degendering of domestic work. Reinelt then turns to Clare Luckham's *Trafford Tanzi,* and Carol Churchill's *Vinegar Tom* to discuss exemplary uses of Brechtian techniques. In *Trafford Tanzi,* a much-discussed drama of a working-class family for which wrestling is the central activity, Reinelt finds the wrestling match itself to be a perfect metaphor or Brechtian gest for 'the struggle of women to free them-selves from male oppression both economic and sexual'. Churchill's *Vinegar Tom,* Reinelt urges, uses another of Brecht's notions, that of creating historical allegory for contemporary issues and events. Set in seventeenth-century Britain during the notorious witch hunts,

Vinegar Tom is meant to 'reclaim the history play from women's point of view'. Reinelt argues that both this borrowing of the notion of historicising and other conventions such as the episodic structure of *Vinegar Tom* suggest 'feminist transformations' of Brechtian technique.[9]

In the next essay (3) in this collection, 'The Dis-Play's the Thing: Gender and Public Sphere in Contemporary British Theatre', Loren Kruger argues by contrast that neither discussions of realism nor its Brechtian dramaturgic alternatives suffice as grounds for an authentic feminist theatre. Instead, she argues, feminist theatre critics must 'critique those masculinist strategies of legitimation in the theatre institution that allow for the marginalisation of alternative theatre, and, in particular, certain kinds of feminist theatre practices by dismissing them as illegitimate and therefore improperly "theatre"'.[10] Grounded in commentary on British institutions and the organisation of theatre financing in Britain, Kruger's piece analyses Caryl Churchill's career to illustrate the importance for feminist theatre critics of prioritising the material conditions of theatre. Churchill, she suggests, in terms that will surely incite argument, often only 'titillates' spectators 'with the display of a "concern for gender"'. In contrast to Reinelt (and, explicitly, to my own analysis in *Feminist Theatre*), Kruger offers *Vinegar Tom* as an example of just such a seductive play in which Brechtian devices serve to displace material difference with 'the *display* of a feminist line'.[11] In contrast, Kruger finds Churchill's *Light Shining in Buckinghamshire,* a drama not often viewed as feminist, to be engaging of spectators in a way that is political and materially critical. Informed by the work of Raymond Williams, Kruger's essay broadens the vision of the task of feminist theatre while inviting responses from other voices inside and outside this collection of essays.

Drawing on yet another perspective, that of psychoanalysis, Barbara Freedman in 'Frame-Up: Feminism, Psychoanalysis, Theatre' (essay 4) argues for the potential of theatre to revise representations of gender difference on the stage. Through reference to the writings of the French scholars Julia Kristeva and Jacques Lacan, Freedman suggests how psychoanalysis can claim common grounds with deconstruction, feminism and theatre. Like several of the authors in this collection, Freedman asks if a feminist theatre is possible. She also asks if the notion 'feminist theatre' is 'a contradiction in terms'.[12]

Freedman's discussion of Lacanian psychoanalytic theory sets up the grounds for her introduction of the controversial writings of the

feminist film critics Laura Mulvey and Teresa de Lauretis. Does the
central Lacanian notion of the 'gaze', which Mulvey has famously
applied to film in 'Visual Pleasure and Narrative Cinema'[13] and
which de Lauretis deploys for discussions of the gendered construction of narrative in film, also illuminate the allocations and
designations of gender in theatre? Freedman's response reflects the
complexity of the Lacanian path: if the gaze, as control of language
and symbol, is unalterably male, and if language itself is phallocentric, then even the sentences or dramas which appear to oppose
the hegemony of patriarchy are still inevitably speaking from the
ideology of the dominant male culture. Freedman does not,
however, stop in the face of this seeming obstruction. Instead, she
questions the totalising tendencies in assertions of the Lacanian
gaze and suggests the possibility in theatre of a 'disruptive' gaze
'that never rests secure'.[14] The last part of her essay imagines
possibilities for what this might look like.

Although it is not immediately apparent, much of the thrust of
Freedman's essay is aimed at problematising the tendency, in
various critical circles, to essentialise feminism. Her hesitation to
perceive inversions of gender difference as significant, or at least as
automatically significant, is part of her protest against the essential
feminine. And it is that resistance to essentialising that returns her
thinking to theatre, the locus, Freedman writes, of instability of all
human identity, and, in particular, of gender identity.

My own essay in this *Casebook,* 'Drama and the Dialogic
Imagination: *The Heidi Chronicles* and *Fefu and her Friends*', takes
up Freedman's discourse on identity not through psychoanalysis but
through the lens of the writings of the philosopher-critic Mikhail
Bakhtin. Although, ironically, Bakhtin dismissed drama, except for
folk drama, as monologic, I find his arguments for the value of
what he calls 'dialogism' invaluable in my own attempts to expli-
cate the attributes of drama that I call feminist. Dialogism is a
subtle concept, specific in its origination to Bakhtin's ideas of
certain qualities of the nineteenth-century novel but illuminating of
a much larger domain of human activity. In a dialogic relationship
or a dialogic text, two or more voices interact with each other, con-
tinuously transforming each other such that neither rigid thought
nor essential types of being are possible.[15]

Drawing on Bakhtin's image of a world in continuous transformation due to 'heteroglossia', 'the mingling of different language
groups, cultures and classes',[16] I argue that while most drama

appears to be structured on dialogue, seemingly different voices are often disguised parts of one, authorial voice. I then demonstrate how Bakhtin's differentiation between the monologic and the dialogic text can be used to evaluate drama by analysing Wendy Wasserstein's Pulitzer prize-winning *The Heidi Chronicles* and Maria Irene Fornes' *Fefu and her Friends*. Feminist drama, I claim here, as I have in previous work, is distinguished by its ongoing dialogism and, therefore, its resistance to the resolution of events and the fixing of characters.

II

With my essay on Bakhtin, Wasserstein and Fornes, a slight shift of emphasis occurs in this *Casebook*; whereas the first four essays are primarily concerned with theory and with critical positions, my article on Bakhtin and feminist drama and the subsequent pieces are at least as interested in particular plays and playwrights as they are concerned with problems and general attributes of feminist theatre. This is not to deny the important critical insights about particular works in the first four essays; nor is it to privilege theory over criticism or history. It is to note that in making my selections, it was not only important to represent fairly several of the critical positions in the field but also to present especially provocative readings of feminist dramas, each of which, in turn, contributes something to the genre.

Tracy Davis's '*Extremities* and *Masterpieces*: A Feminist Paradigm of Art and Politics' (essay 6) foregrounds the two plays cited in the title in precisely the way I am suggesting. By contrasting *Masterpieces*, a British play (first produced at the Manchester Royal Exchange in 1983 and subsequently at the Royal Court) written by Sarah Daniels, with *Extremities*, written by the American playwright William Mastrosimone (performed at Rutgers University and on Broadway in 1981), Davis reveals qualities of strategy and structure that can distinguish a feminist play from a conventional sensationalist drama about rape. Davis shows how and why, given two plays with similar subjects, one is feminist and admirable and the other is demeaning and threatening, to women especially, but ultimately to all human beings. Daniels's play is feminist and valuable because it draws the spectator to reject violence as a solution to any problem and problematises power and control; in contrast,

Davis reveals, Mastrosimone's play is anti-feminist, conservative and dangerous in its exploitation of images of women as objects to desecrate and possess. A key to Davis's contrasting readings is her analysis of the role of pornographic 'snuff' film in *Masterpieces*. Davis's comparative analyses of these plays also raise further questions about realism, alienation and fantasy, questions that are at once social and aesthetic.

Patricia Schroeder (essay 7) takes a similar comparative strategy to get to an opposite position from Davis. Schroeder's careful analyses of Marsha Norman's *Getting Out* and Wendy Kesselman's *My Sister in This House* are framed by her hypothesis that what she calls 'formal realism' can well serve feminist interests. For Schroeder 'formal' refers to the basic 'form' of the dramaturgy: within the frame of a realistic style, she urges, an array of innovative and effective gestures may be used. Citing Michelene Wandor on realism, Schroder argues that the power of *Getting Out* and of *My Sister in This House* is in large part a matter of representing two disturbing contexts – prison in the case of *Getting Out,* and an oppressive all-female French bourgeois household in the 1930s in *My Sister in This House* – with realistic sets, three-dimensional characters, chronological plots, and ordinary language. These conventions of realism are intended readily to engage the audience. Within the frame of realism, Schroeder suggests, odd elements are intriguing not alienating: Arlie and Arlene appear as two opposing pieces of one central character in *Getting Out;* in *My Sister in This House* the antagonism between two sets of women – a bourgeois mother and daughter and two sisters who are the former's maids – established through photography, a narrator's voice, and, most potently, silence, augments the fundamental realism of the dramaturgy.

Much as Schroeder's particular criticism speaks directly to Jeanie Forte's discussion of realism earlier in this collection, Deborah Geis's reading (essay 8) of several of Maria Irene Fornes's dramas enriches understanding of what might seem to be the odd pairing of Brechtian conventions with feminism. As Fornes, who began writing drama in the early sixties, has gained respect and prominence in theatre internationally, the feminist qualities of her voice have been heard, claimed and disputed – including by Fornes herself. Geis associates her own emphasis on Brechtian elements of voice in Fornes's work with critic Elin Diamond's 'feminist revaluation of Brecht'.[17] Geis's essay is valuable for the insightful attention it pays to Fornes's dramas as separate pieces that together comprise a body of work characterised by Brechtian elements, especially that of the gestic quality of individual voices. The essay draws attention to the growing recognition of Fornes's achievement as a feminist playwright with a distinctive, disturbing vision and a keen ear for the multi-voicedness that seems to me crucial for feminist theatre.

An emphasis on authentic polyphony in drama is also applauded in 'Unmasking the Minstrel Mask's Black Magic in Ntozake Shange's *spell#7*', by Karen Cronacher (essay 9). Cronacher is concerned with identity as it is discovered in difference. She draws on the languages of postmodernism and psychoanalysis that have occupied a cluster of prominent contemporary feminist critics – Barbara Freedman, Jill Dolan, Laura Mulvey, Sue-Ellen Case and Teresa de Lauretis are key among them. For these critics, the first terms of difference are gender and power and this leads, almost inevitably, to a problem of polarisation and reduction of analysis to binary oppositions. Cronacher, however, creates an intriguing critical hybrid by augmenting the semiotic/symbolic approach as practised by many feminist critics with a historical recuperation of the minstrel tradition. To accomplish this, she makes use of Homi Babba's identification of 'racial stereotype as a discourse of fetishism'.[18] Cronacher then argues, using the work of feminist theorist Hortense Spillers, that Shange reveals the 'absence' for African-American women of a subject position in American society by using the minstrel mask as sign that 'African-Americans are still missing as subjects'.[19] The striking black-face mask suspended upstage above the acting space in productions of *spell#7* recalls the vibrant presence of the enormous fabricated red rose that, singularly, was the set for Shange's *for colored girls who have considered suicide when the rainbow is enuf*. In both shows, one resonant image comprises the set and signifies authorship separate from that of the performers. Cronacher reminds us of the political prescience of Shange's dramatic work and the necessary resistance to dominant cultural forms in the theatre of African-American feminists. Her essay cuts a critical path through race and class as well as gender and highlights the insufficiency of criticism focused on gender alone.

With Shange's dramas and those of most other African-American theatre artists, it is important to note that the most recent 'black'[20] theatre productions have their roots in the Black Arts Movement of the sixties; where African-American theatre is feminist, as in the case of Shange or Adrienne Kennedy or Sonja Sonchez, it is culturally hybrid and polyphonous in its views of history as well as gender. Black theatre, also, notably, has its own history, and within that history, black women playwrights have been writing drama for more than a hundred years. As I have argued elsewhere,[21] while some of this drama can be characterised as social protest theatre, and is thus summarily dismissed by some American critics as narrow in both vision and audience, the conjoining of race, gender and, sometimes, class has produced a powerful and distinctive genre that hauntingly fulfils Raymond Williams's visions of a 'new tragic consciousness'. Among the attributes of that consciousness is 'a struggle against suffering learned in suffering' and 'a total exposure which is also a total involvement'.[22]

Although more recent in its history, the Chicano theatre movement was, even more explicitly than early African-American theatre, a political phenomenon of opposition to dominant material conditions and cultural forms in the United States. The addition of gender consciousness to Chicano theatre has been difficult from the start; as Yvonne Yarbro-Bejarano remarks (in essay 10), 'Chicanas who question traditional gender roles and attempt to organise their desire independently run the risk of being labelled malinchistas (traitors)'.[23] (Coming from different family structures and values, black women, too, have been vulnerable in and outside the theatre, but black women's strength is central to the history of African-Americans, even if met with a mixture of rage and pride by black men.) The existence of a feminist Chicana theatre is therefore an achievement marked by multiple challenges and paradoxes: while the Chicano theatre movement, starting with El Teatro Campesino in the mid-sixties, has been a key voice of opposition to the dominant Anglo-American society, it has also been a voice of celebration of Chicano and Mexican cultural traditions: through song, dance, broad satire, stock characters and, especially notably, the hybridisation of Spanish, colloquial Chicano terms and English language, Chicano theatre has thrived and mainstream arenas have welcomed its contributions. Yarbro-Bejarano's history of the theatre of Chicanas relates the creation in the early eighties of a support group (Women in Teatro) and the founding of all-women Chicana theatre companies which sustained some of the political positions of the Chicano theatre but also gradually created feminist productions that opposed both the dominant Anglo-American culture and the male-dominated Chicano culture. She considers the creation of these Chicana theatre groups to name a historical moment, even if the actual production history of Chicana groups has been erratic. It is to this phenomenon and its meanings that Yarbro-Bejarano turns in her essay 'Chicanas' Experience in Collective Theatre: Ideology and Form'.

III

To listen to Yarbro-Bejano and the voices she has amplified of Chicanas involved with collective theatre, or to hear Shange's voice, as mediated by her characters and subsequently by Karen Cronacher, is to be taken a step outside the arenas in which feminist theatre has come to be best known in the West in the last twenty-five years. Most instances of feminist theatre have at least begun in fringe or collaborative, alternative theatre groups and these have been more prevalent in Britain and the United States than elsewhere. Even the critical and/or commercial successes that have been called feminist theatre, often with some challenge, have their roots in alternative or pre-commercial contexts. In the United States, the Actor's Theater of Louisville, Kentucky, has provided support for women writers for more than two decades through productions of new work and grants for writing and production; three of Marsha Norman's early plays, including *Getting Out* and Beth Henley's Pulitzer-prize winning *Crimes of the Heart,* had first runs in Louisville and then moved to Broadway. Similarly, in Britain, several of Caryl Churchill's plays have begun in alternative theatre companies, then moved to the Royal Court, which itself is situated perhaps deliberately ambiguously between the alternative and dominant theatre scenes in London.

Theatres in the margins, whether in the makeshift venues of London and New York, the storefronts or churches of cities, the universities and rural community centres are still producing the work that, to use Raymond Williams's distinction, is at least alternative and occasionally oppositional.[24] In the United States this means both the long-term uncountable number of feminist productions produced by the Omaha Magic Theater, led by playwright/producer/director Megan Terry and producer/performer/director Jo Ann Schmidman and singular, itinerant productions such as *Quilters,* a production of the Denver Center Theater

Company that made its way to Edinburgh, Los Angeles and Washington DC before its 24-performance run in New York City. Not wholly coincidentally, one of the notable feminist attributes of the Omaha Magic Theater productions has been its occasional use of 'soft sets' constructed out of quilted materials which become tables, chairs, backdrops and beds, cars and doors. In Britain, the Women's Theatre Group has prospered with original, timely, politically progressive productions, and Monstrous Regiment has produced long-running collaborative shows often with independent playwrights including Caryl Churchill, Claire Luckham, Bryony Lavery and Michelene Wandor. I think of these and other local companies that continue on the margins or emerge and disappear in Britain and the United States as the inner frontier of feminist theatre.

At least equally remarkable is the appearance in the last decade of an outer frontier of feminist theatre and criticism. For at the same time that feminist criticism has flourished in Britain and the United States, and that feminist production has maintained a steady but vulnerable position in both countries, feminist theatre has emerged and inspired analysis in a startling number of diverse cultures and nations. Spain, Canada, Northern Ireland, France, Italy, Germany, Russia, and also India, China and Mexico not only have something a feminist critic might interpret as feminist theatre, but these theatres themselves are declaring themselves feminist or woman-centred. Articles in American and British journals and anthologies about these various theatres suggest the recurrence of collectively conceived, politically oriented dramas, as well as dramas written by individual women. Both the critical writings and the dramas described are at once new and familiar. And over and again, we hear familiar reports of the suppression of women's theatre work, of joyful but angry productions, and of resistance from women dramatists and directors to the title feminist for fear of narrowing their audiences. This is not news. What is news is that Dario Fo and Franca Rame are not the only Italians creating gender-conscious theatre that some spectators and critics call feminist: since the late sixties, for example, Italian writer Dacia Maraini has written more than 25 plays, many with an explicit feminist strategy. During this time, in 1973, she also founded a feminist theatre collective called La Maddalena in Rome. Across the Atlantic, there is also, ironically, 'news' in Sandra Messinger Cypess's article in *Theatre Journal* (1989) describing the oppositional plays by Mexican writers Rosario Castelonos (*The Eternal Feminine,* 1974) and Sabina Berman (*Eagle or Sun,* 1982). These plays challenge deeply held understandings of male and female roles.

In France, where neither feminism nor women dramatists are news, there is, nevertheless, a significant departure from traditional theatre in the conjoining of feminism and theatre that has gradually occurred since the early nineteen-seventies. In some ways similar in its history to the emergence of feminist theatre in Britain and the United States, French feminist theatre (as often as not called 'women-centred' rather than feminist by French women) first appeared as the work of alternative collective theatre groups such as La Carmagnole, a group noted for its wit, which dramatised incidents of the patriarchal oppression of women. At the same time, French feminism has had its own peculiar duality: French intellectual feminism, as represented by diverse voices such as those of Julia Kristeva, Hélène Cixous, Monique Wittigue, and Luce Irigaray has been highly regarded and imitated throughout Europe and the United States; French feminist theory has mostly remained sombre and separate, however, from the activities of a group of Frenchwomen who are less well known internationally but have carried the petitions and led the marches that have resulted in major changes in law and practice relevant to women in the last twenty years. Theatre is one of the few places where French feminist theory, popular culture and legally oriented political actions have publicly united.

In the penultimate essay in this volume, Judith Graves Miller describes the array of French feminist theatre productions that have come forth in the last twenty-five years from the theorists and the pragmatists, as well as from the theoretical theatre artists, and from those who would not identify themselves as feminists but whose work is importantly focused on gender. Several Frenchwomen whose work has been understood as feminist in other forms – Marguerite Duras, Hélène Cixous, and Simone Benmussa to name a few – have written feminist dramas and feminist criticisms of drama that have informed and challenged basic understandings of gender and identity so deeply that fragments of their thinking have become unfixed from their origins. I have in mind in particular Cixous's *Portrait of Dora,* a re-presentation of Freud's case history of a woman's 'hysteria'. Graves acknowledges Cixous's *Dora,* which has received serious critical responses in the United States and Britain as well as in France, then turns her attention to less well known productions which she presents in some detail as 'indicators of the future of women's voices in French theatre'.[25] The essay manages to be both cautious and inspiring, an approach accurate to the culture it describes but also exemplary for all of us writing about gender and drama.

If French feminist theatre and the criticism it has engendered is only barely located on what I am calling the outer frontier, the last essay in this *New Casebook,* Haiping Yan's 'Male Ideology and Female Identity: Images of Women in Four Modern Chinese Historical Plays', could be said to describe the cultivation of a particularly challenging frontier for feminist theatre. Yan begins her piece with a brief reminder of the first criticism of traditional Chinese theatre during the May 4th New Culture Movement, then traces the beginnings of 'modern' Chinese theatre in the 1920s through the work of poet/playwright/novelist Guo Mo-ruo. With this tradition and Guo Mo-ruo's oppositional historical drama established in the form of a trilogy named *Three Rebellious Women,* Haiping Yan moves to three post-revolutionary plays – a second play by Guo Mo-ruo which startles the writer and thus the reader because it is more traditional in its gender images than Mo-ruo's earlier play, and two more recent plays, one by Cao Yu and the last by Chen Bai-chen. If we recall that a play was key to the beginning of the Cultural Revolution, we may not be surprised at the ease with which Haiping Yan discusses the importance of political figures such as Zhou Enlai in the themes of recent drama, but there is certainly revelation in her analyses of how these plays, all by male authors, use images of women from historical narratives to 'deconstruct, negotiate, transform and reinscribe' 'male patriarchy'.[26]

Haiping Yan presents us with feminist theatre criticism without a feminist dramatic text; the text that opposes patriarchy more strenuously than did Guo Mo Ruo's of the twenties is in a future she imagines but that has not yet occurred. Haiping Yan's voice appeals to the emphasis I have placed in my own criticism on polyphony and dialogism. In Haiping Yan's vision, as in that of Maria Irene Fornes, dramatic dialogue can be not only polyphonous but authentically dialogic: it neither resolves nor balances understandings of what and how the world is, but continues a conversation that equally empowers all of its characters.

The goal of this *New Casebook* is similar to what I find in *Fefu and her Friends:* a set of intersecting conversations about diverse, often contradictory issues, sometimes revolving around gender, always around life, death and personhood. The name calling that occurs in much feminist writing – such and such is radical feminism or cultural feminism or Marxist feminism or materialist feminism or lesbian feminism or, possibly, queer feminism – may be done by readers of this book, but the intention is not to label types and categories but to applaud the depths and breadths to which feminist theatre criticism has already gone and to encourage it to lead players and spectators alike to yet unknown ways of imagining, and of staging, lives worth living.

NOTES

1. Honor Moore, 'Interview' with Phyllis Mael, *Chrysalis*, 10 (1979), 51.

2. These brief definitions are associated, in order, with Jill Dolan in *The Feminist Spectator and Critic* (Ann Arbor, MI, 1988), pp. 37–40, Helene Keyssar, *Feminist Theatre* (1984) and Sue-Ellen Case, 'From Split Subject to Split Britches' in *Feminine Focus,* ed. Enoch Brater (New York, 1989), pp. 126–7.

3. Susan Steadman, *Dramatic Re-visions* (Chicago, 1991).

4. I remark on this because for some readers naturalism, a term used alternatively with realism by Wandor, refers to a particular class-oriented type of collective, essentialist, anti-rational dramatic approach as compared to the familiar middle-class living rooms and psychologically painted characters of realism.

5. Catherine Belsey, 'Constructing the Subject: Deconstructing the Text', in Judith Newton and Deborah Rosenfelt (eds), *Feminist Criticism and Social Change: Sex, Class and Race in Literature and Culture* (New York, 1985).

6. Michelene Wandor, *Drama Today: A Critical Guide to British Drama 1970–1990* (London, 1993), p. 55.

7. Janelle Reinelt, 'The Politics of Form: Realism, Melodrama and Pam Gems's *Camille*', *Women and Performance,* 4(1989), 96. While this piece was published subsequent to the article, 'Beyond Brecht', in this anthology, Reinelt had actually come to reject the possibilities of realism as a form for feminist theatre while watching a performance of Pam Gems's *Camille* in 1985.

8. Ibid.

9. See Chapter 2 below.

10. See Chapter 3 below.

11. Ibid.

12. See Chapter 4 below.

13. Laura Mulvey, 'Visual Pleasure and Narrative Cinema', *Screen*, 16: 3(1975), 6–18; reprinted in Mulvey, *Visual and Other Pleasures* (Bloomington, IN, 1989), pp. 14–28.

14. See Chapter 4 below.

15. See Chapter 5 below.

16. Ibid.

17. See Chapter 8 below.

18. See Chapter 9 below.

19. Ibid.

20. During the late nineteen-sixties, I taught at Morris Brown College in Atlanta University and heard the terminology change from 'Negro' and 'Afro-American' to 'Black'. The change to 'African-American' is a move of the nineties, and thus not necessarily the appropriate name for work/persons of the sixties, seventies and eighties. I use both African-American and black here as an expression of my ambivalence and of what I see and hear around me.

21. Helene Keyssar, 'The Drama of Black American Women', in *Feminine Focus: The New Women Playwrights,* ed. Enoch Brater (Oxford and New York, 1989), pp. 226–40. Also see H. Keyssar, *The Curtain and the Veil: Strategies in Black Drama* (New York, 1982).

22. Raymond Williams, *Modern Tragedy* (Stanford, CA, 1966), p. 54.

23. See Chapter 10 below.

24. Raymond Williams, *Problems in Materialism and Culture* (London, 1980), p. 41.

25. See Chapter 11 below.

26. See Chapter 12 below.

1

Realism, Narrative, and the Feminist Playwright – A Problem of Reception

JEANIE FORTE

The inquiry into what constitutes a feminist playwriting practice today necessarily involves the critic with the investigation of structures of realism and narrative, structures which are implicated in relation to patriarchal ideology. Concomitantly, the theatrical institution, with its accretions of cultural convention and inscription of a dominant system of representation, operates to inhibit radicality (e.g. feminism) in service of the ideology which supports and informs its tradition. However, theories concerning realism and narrative must be called to account for the specific reception of a play text, must address historical particularity and, in the terms of feminist criticism, political efficacy. Playwriting, in an intricate and complex interweave with site, history, representation, and audience as well as conventions of realism, narrative, and stage practice, emerges as a crucial arena of exploration for contemporary feminism, providing insights into the politics of writing and the possible basis for a feminist theory of reception.

Recent debate in feminist criticism regarding playwriting has focused on the question of whether a realist play could not also be a feminist play – for reasons having to do with the relationship between text and reader within a context of ideology. That is, realism (or, to use Catherine Belsey's term, classic realism)[1] supports the dominant ideology by constructing the reader as a subject (or more correctly, an 'individual') within that ideology. It poses an apparently objective or distanced viewpoint from which both the narrator and the reader can assess the action and ultimate meaning of the text, a pose which makes the operations of ideology covert, since the illusion is created for the reader that he or she is the source of meaning or understanding, unfettered by structures of culture. Belsey's extended definition of classic realism clarifies this relationship:

> Classic realism is characterised by 'illusionism', narrative which leads to 'closure', and a 'hierarchy of discourses' which establishes the 'truth' of the story. 'Illusionism' is, I hope, self-explanatory. The other two defining characteristics of classic realism need some discussion ... Classic realist narrative, as Barthes demonstrates in *S/Z*, turns on the creation of enigma through the precipitation of disorder which throws into disarray the conventional cultural and signifying systems. Among the commonest sources of disorder at the level of plot ... are murder, war, a journey or love. But the story moves inevitably towards closure which is also disclosure, the dissolution of enigma through the re-establishment of order, recognisable as a re-instatement or a development of the order which is understood to have preceded the events of the story itself.[2]

In light of this definition, it becomes evident that classic realism, always a reinscription of the dominant order, could not be useful for feminists interested in the subversion of a patriarchal social structure. Such an understanding of realism coincides with contemporary analyses of narrative which have emerged primarily from feminist film criticism. Laura Mulvey, in 'Visual Pleasure and Narrative Cinema', asserts that '[s]adism demands a story, depends on making something happen, forcing a change in another person, a battle of will and strength, victory/defeat, all occurring in a linear time with a beginning and an end'.[3] Teresa de Lauretis points out the implied reversibility of terms in Mulvey's statement, that 'story demands sadism', sadism thus seen as the causative factor for the movement of narrative.[4] Her argument demonstrates the connection between realist narrative and the oppression of women by revealing Oedipal desire as narrative's motivating force. As de Lauretis notes, narrative is governed by an Oedipal logic because it operates within the system of exchange instituted by the incest prohibition, where Woman functions both as a sign (representation) and a value (object) for that exchange – this system is now common knowledge among poststructuralists, as derived from Lévi-Strauss. De Lauretis further elaborates: woman's role constitutes the fulfilment of the narrative promise (made, in the Freudian model, to the little boy), the reward at the end of the Oedipal journey; a representation which supports the male status of the mythical, culturally constructed subject. As the reader's subjectivity is constructed through positionalities within narrative, so women are necessarily interpellated as object/objective/obstacle by the Oedipal desire governing narrative: this is its sadism, that narrative repeatedly and necessarily positions women in the oppressed subjectivity (which is not Subject, but Object) of femininity.[5]

If we take as a given the ideological project, the self-perpetuation of the dominant system, then we can see the place of literature (narrative) in subtly reinforcing the discourse of ideology, and the way in which the apparent unity, coherence and seamlessness of the classic realist text covertly subjects (and positions, in terms of subjectivity) the reader within that ideology. However, if a writer (or let's say a text) aims to reveal and/or subvert the dominant ideology, as a feminist writer/text might, strategies must be found within the realm of discourse, particularly *vis à vis* narrative, which can operate to deconstruct the imbedded ideology: in other words, which might construct the reading subject differently. In writing practice, then, a refusal to perpetuate the conventions of realism/narrative would presumably not only thwart the illusion of 'real' life, but also would function to threaten the patriarchal ideology imbedded in 'story'. A subversive text would not provide the detached viewpoint, the illusion of seamlessness, the narrative closure, but instead would open up the negotiation of meaning to contradictions, circularity, multiple viewpoints; for feminists, this would relate particularly to gender, but also to issues of class, race, age, sexuality, and the insistence on an alternative articulation of female subjectivity. Whether or not this subversion would give rise to politicised action on the part of the newly constructed reader is another matter for debate, which will be discussed later.

Within the specific context of playwriting and the theories outlined above, let us consider the operations of a well-known realist text and its relationship to a feminist agenda. In Marsha Norman's *'night, Mother*, thirty-seven-year-old Jessie informs her mother Thelma that she will kill herself that evening, after having organised the details of her mother's life and her own death. After much argument, during which time the mother attempts to change the daughter's mind, the suicide happens anyway; the mother is left alone on stage, and the audience leaves the theatre, some obviously in tears. Although touted by some critics as a feminist investigation of the hopelessness and degradation of women's lives in patriarchal society,[6] the play ultimately reinscribes the dominant ideology in its realist form. It is indubitably a narrative built on enigmas and mysteries which are revealed gradually until the final scene of (dis)closure. It steadfastly maintains that illusion of reader-as-subject who shares with the absent narrator the position of know-ingness and ultimate understanding; a coherent, unified text that renders up its pleasure in the satisfaction of catharsis, in the illusion of change without really changing anything. As Brecht noted, 'The theatre as we know it [he calls it illusionism] shows the structure of society (represented on stage) as incapable of being influenced by society (in the auditorium).'[7] Narrative closure reinstates the pre-existing order after instigating its temporary crisis. In what Roland Barthes would call a highly 'readable' text,[8] Jessie and her Mother are thus 'known' fully; they are consumed characters, and the ex-planation for Jessie's suicide is perceived not within social relations (ideology) but in individual failure (or worse, as an heroic act, courageously ending a life that was indeed worthless).

In spite of the apparent inevitability of the ideological apparatus of classic realist narrative, can we identify a feminist writing prac-tice that emulates realism but operates as a different discursive strategy, perhaps a pseudo-realism? One such play might be Terry Baum's and Carolyn Meyer's *Dos Lesbos*. Ostensibly dealing with the lives and struggles of two lesbians, Peg and Gracie, *Dos Lesbos* has realistic elements, but functions more like a revue, utilising short sketches, parody, role-playing, songs and musical sound effects to present various aspects of American lesbian experience. Although on the surface it is very funny, there are also deadly serious moments, such as the scene when Peg describes having been spat on, or the scene after a disastrous dinner with Gracie's parents. In this fashion, *Dos Lesbos* acts as a consciousness-raising play – emulating a practice endemic to feminism in the seventies which emphasised the political implications of everything personal in women's experience. Its ribald humour also endears the audience to the characters, who are then able to communicate some of the not-so-humorous problems for lesbians to a sympathetic audience. More importantly for this discussion, the realistic elements serve to promote enough illusion of 'real experience in the real world', so that the audience can identify (in a manner to which it has been culturally conditioned) with Peg and Gracie as people who are just trying to achieve a measure of happiness – seeking decent jobs, loving relationships, family togetherness, etc. But there is also a sense in which the episodic structure, the songs and the transparency of the text conjure up what classic realism usually renders invisible, which is the society that isn't on stage – in this case, the dominant culture which has excluded lesbians from its texts, its stage practice. An audience is thus implicated, in a heightened consciousness, in Peg and Gracie's oppression, the play motivating the spectators to think about their culture's or their own heterosexism. The text apparently calls for a Brechtian sensibility, since it makes use of the very devices Brecht recommended for achieving critical distance, while simultaneously retaining sufficient 'fable' for establishing a moment in history. However, I think there are other forces at play in the text which are crucial from a feminist standpoint, and which move the play beyond Brechtian considerations.

By transparency of the text, I mean that the apparent realist narrative has gaps or holes, both in between and even during individual scenes – the scenes free-float in a cultural condition, making visible the oppressive society in which Peg and Gracie must move when they are not in the scenes. Within the scenes, Gracie's ambivalence about her coming out and her feelings about sex, or Peg's refusal to 'kill' her best friend Russell in a Utopian vision even though he is a man, give play to a multiplicity of discourses around and about lesbianism or being lesbian that refuse an authoritative position. Thus, in Barthesian terms, the text is more a 'plural' text, wherein 'no single discourse is privileged, and no consistent and coherent plot constrains the free play of the discourses'.[9] Rather than distancing its readers (following Brecht), the text would draw us in, frustrating the kind of closure or catharsis experienced with *'night, Mother*: the fabric of realistic elements have merely provided the framework for a different mode of perception.

In effect, the play masquerades as realism, which is wholly appropriate, since it is a play precisely about masquerade and rejecting masquerade – and, just as Gracie makes the decision to come out in the play, so the play itself begins to emerge from the patterns of classic realism and the ideology imbedded therein, pointing the way toward other discourses, other subjectivities. However, it's also important that it's an incomplete project, as if the text had one foot in and one foot out – Peg says at one point, 'It's pretty tedious, this coming out business'. As Barthes notes, there is no such thing as a wholly plural text; but on a continuum of textual readability versus plurality, the terminology enables a crucial distinction between *'night, Mother* and *Dos Lesbos*.

It is also significant that Gracie the *writer* is the one having difficulty coming out – as Peg notes several times, Gracie wants to turn everything into a story, wants to narrate it – for Gracie, it's painful that life will not bend into a coherent fiction. Similarly, she enjoys their sex best when she can turn it into a poem, and reveals that she still thinks of their relationship within a stereotypical heterosexual model – she can't stand to be possessed by a man, but she loves possessing women. But it is equally significant that the last scene of the play is in bed, the site of sexuality (as Peg says, culture defines homosexuals by who they sleep with), and that it ends with a kiss – Gracie finally physically declares her love relationship with Peg, and the play finally begins coming out, making the sexuality visceral, graphic.

In spite of its identifiable pseudo-realist strategies, it is undoubtedly true that many readers find *Dos Lesbos* somewhat palatable, even if the content disturbs them, precisely because of its relative readability, its quiescent realism. However, some critics argue that the play, rather than pointing the way out of classic realism, ends up falling backwards into it, thus nullifying its own attempts to demonstrate an authentically different practice, either in terms of sexuality or writing. If feminism is a struggle against oppression, then is it really possible for feminist playwrights to communicate the workings of oppressive ideology within the realistic narrative *from* within? Is the structure so powerful and deeply ingrained that to allow virtually any realistic elements constitutes a capitulation to dominant ideology? If so, then realism must be abandoned altogether in the search for a subversive practice.

Adrienne Kennedy's plays of a Black American woman's struggle for identity in a hostile oppressive culture illustrate some of the problems as well as advantages of a totally non-realistic form. In *The Owl Answers*, the central character, a young Black woman named She Who Is Clara Passmore Who Is The Virgin Mary Who Is The Bastard Who Is The Owl, encounters other characters of multiple identities who include her Black mother, a Black stepfather Reverend and wife, her real white father who refuses to claim her as his child, Anne Boleyn, a Dead White Father, a White Bird, a Negro Man, Shakespeare, Chaucer and William the Conqueror. She Who Is (or Clara) travels ambiguously among scenes in a New York subway, the Tower of London, a Harlem hotel room, St Peter's Cathedral, and her past, caught in a deadly struggle with herself and her culture. In this play of shifting subjectivities, a 'terrain in flux',[10] there is no possibility of a fixed, stable identity, either for She or the reader; all the same, we follow the heroine (non-heroine, non-character) as she moves from place to place, person to person, in an effort to locate her identity. Note that the Owl traditionally asks 'Who', that is, a question of identity; and Clara is the Owl, seeking to discover who she is (She who is). The owl is also a solitary bird, a solo traveller, a lonely sound in the forest.[11]

Clara's attempt to construct her subjectivity is made doubly difficult by the fact that she is both female and black; both gender and race conspiring against her in a culture dominated by her opposites. She is powerless to alter these parameters of her search, and doomed to feel estranged from a heritage that she has been taught to desire but that she is prevented from claiming. Heritage in patriarchy is determined by lines of paternity,[12] but Clara is only a bastard, just 'the daughter of somebody who cooked for me'. The play conflates the death of her white father in Georgia with her dead father in London; to attend her white father's funeral would be to claim her white heritage, the one which she traces back to England in the literary and historical heritage of Shakespeare, Chaucer et al., but they know it is not her heritage and keep her from it, locking her up; ironically, they lock her up in the Tower of London, symbolically trapping her inside the very heritage which she desires but cannot have.

The Negro heritage described by the play also fails Clara in her search for subjectivity – inhabited as it is by frustrated and abused women who commit suicide, Negro men who are only interested in colonising her body for their own desire, and a Reverend who is forever reading the Bible (symbol of another colonising force – she identifies with the Virgin Mary who is indelibly white, her pleas to a white God are laughed at or ignored; religion cannot cure her, it rather enforces her bastard position). For Clara, the Negro world is the urban tawdriness and sub-ground hell of the subway, site of shameful seductions, where she is haunted by her desired white heritage, but from which there is no escape. As Herbert Blau notes, Kennedy's use of the term Negro is 'archaic', or 'regressive', as if the revolutions of the fifties and sixties (in language and ideology) never happened: 'her experience is irredeemably Negro experience, the desire for assimilation'.[13] The entire play takes place within the psychic realm of the subway car as a recurrent symbol of the failed Black American experience. There is no escape from her blackness, her Mary-ness (as the bastard-adopted daughter of the Reverend and as the retrograde Virgin), even though she sees herself as Clara, who would Pass-more (Clara's adoptive surname is Passmore). Her face is described as pale, but she repeatedly opens her dress to reveal a blacker body – that is, her essential blackness, which is also culturally determined.[14] She screams at her Dead Father and Mother, 'You must know how it is to be filled with yearning'. At which they laugh.

At another point, She Who Is says she wants 'love or something', but doesn't know where it is to come from. The Mother asks, 'Is it to come from out there?' poignantly implying that it can't; that Clara must find it within, must construct her love of self herself, handicapped by her subject position. Any physical love constitutes rape, since none of it expresses her desire to be 'loved by her father', that is, to have a heritage. She has in effect been doubly raped, by the Negro male and the White male, both of whom subjugate her desire to their own.

In Clara's case, the Oedipal narrative is absolutely oppressive, in that she is locked outside of it and within it, by virtue of her race/gender double-bind. The play's ambiguity and near incomprehensibility articulate the impossibility of identification with a narrative position, least of all one which might provide closure, or the fiction of a coherent self. Clara – who is not one character, or person, or subjectivity – instead traverses narrative, zig-zagging across various systems of signification, seeking herself in the gaps, the spaces of unnarrated silence wherein her persistently elusive subjectivity might be found.

On the Barthesian continuum, Kennedy's work is as 'plural' as it gets – and, on the basis of the narrative theories promulgated earlier, would qualify as the most political of the three texts used here for illustration, from a feminist standpoint. But the question remains whether or not such texts ultimately make the reader aware of the operations of ideology; in other words, does the text implicate classic realist structure in the workings of an oppressive culture, by frustrating the audience's expectations *vis à vis* narrative? And to the degree which it does that, is it then a political text? Or, approaching the question of political viability from another angle, is it *sufficiently* political to offer an alternative to the complicity of dominant ideology and text found in classic realism and its Oedipal narrative? Can we assume solely on the basis of an intra-textual reading that a realist text will never engender a political response on the part of some or any readers? These questions illustrate the urgent need for a feminist theory of reception; as Tania Modleski recently noted, to retain its 'political edge', feminist criticism cannot afford to lose sight of the 'important stakes of a feminist theory of the reader'.[15]

Furthermore, the search for a feminist theory of reception is arguably more complicated for drama, because of the numerous factors contributing to the 'realisation' of the text in performance, the 'collaborators' (e.g. director, designers, performers, etc.) in the performance's 'conception', and the precise socio-historical context in which any given performance takes place. Feminist critics may well deem it virtually impossible to generalise any hypothetical response to a *text* when faced with such overwhelming variations in potential and real specific performed renderings of that same text. In the search for a 'theatre-specific' feminist criticism, Elin Diamond has recently put forth an admirable theory of what she has named 'gestic criticism', through a thorough and innovative examination of possible intersections between feminist and Brechtian theories.[16] Among many strong points in the article is Diamond's useful elaboration of the Brechtian gest for the feminist performer, particularly in terms of the way that Gestus creates a specific relationship with the spectator. By retaining her own historical subject position separate from the character and using gest to 'read' the social attitudes encoded in the play text, the feminist performer enforces an awareness in the spectator of her own temporality.[17] 'Through a triangular structure of actor/subject – character – spectator', then, each position is historicised, and, in a refusal of the Oedipal construction of subjectivity, 'no one side signifies authority, knowledge, or the law'.[18] Promising as this is, Diamond's example is a textual one which assumes a certain stage realisation as a feminist gest, which in turn depends upon the (female) spectator's agreement or acknowledgement. As Diamond notes, she is interested in locating those gestic moments which allow for the female spectator's viewing position, rescuing it from the trap of male gaze and perpetual otherness; but the gest seems to depend on 'women reading as women', on a predetermined response between and among women that would either: one, address and affirm their feminist knowledge of societal inequity and oppression; or, two, suddenly in that gestic moment, rattle/disturb their sensibilities sufficiently to politicise their perception. It also depends on the female spectator's recognition of female authorship – as Diamond says, it 'would contextualise *and* reclaim the author'.[19] While hinting at a presumed connection between women as women, this perhaps is the strongest move in Diamond's paper, about which more later. But learning that female spectators are in fact in the audience, can we assume that feminism, or even a readiness for feminism, is a condition of their consciousness? And if not, what performative measures are necessary to awaken that consciousness in political terms, and how do we measure it?

Norman's text may not be feminist or political in terms of its writing strategies, or in its näive conception of the self/subjectivity – even in performance, the structure and design elements of *'night, Mother* perpetuate narrative closure, and Oedipal constructions of identity. However, as Jill Dolan describes in detail, it has proved problematic for most male critics, apparently because of its thematic focus on Mother/Daughter rather than on the traditional Father/Son.[20] Especially on the occasion of its Pulitzer award, much debate was devoted to whether or not *'night, Mother* met canonic measures of greatness, particularly that of 'universality'. Jenny Spencer, while not claiming feminism for the play, observes that women audience members apparently experience *'night, Mother* differently from men; that Norman's tragic vision of the problems of female identity proves cathartic for women, but not for men – men may sympathise, but not identify in the same way.[21] While this observation bolsters the arguments that the play does not achieve 'universality', it also hints at another level of political function. As Modleski warns, feminist critics should not underestimate 'the most crucial factor in men's traditional disregard and contempt for women's writings and women's modes of existence: the reality of male power'.[22] This 'fact of power' accounts for much of the lack of appreciation of women's texts – 'until there is an appreciable change in the power structure, it is unlikely that women's fictional accounts of their lives in the lying-in room, the parlour, the nursery, the kitchen, the laundry will have the force to induce masculine jouissance'.[23] In this regard, *'night, Mother* may be *perceived* as a feminist text, in that it challenges on some material level the reality of male power. Quite apart from its critical reception in the theatrical press, now that its Pulitzer-Prize status guarantees inclusion in classroom anthologies, the text often becomes a basic rallying point for female students who want to argue for the right to discuss women and women's experiences, presumably in a way they have not found possible or allowed elsewhere. Its readability, which thus grants it a certain provisional status within the dramatic canon, which would presumably reinscribe dominant ideology, is thus implicated in another, political operation which serves to undermine the power structure in a material way. While no gestic moments present themselves,[24] the play (and the context of its reception) functions for many women as a kind of old *Ms* 'click', an instant of immediate raised consciousness. Admittedly, not all female viewers of this play have the same response: I myself felt primarily anger at the play's limited and insular portrait of female (im)possibility, a perception shared by Dolan in her earlier, incisive review.[25] But to the extent that any women might conceive their experience of the play in political terms, and that so many men perceive it as a threat, a feminist theory of reception must re-evaluate the work's impact as a feminist text.

By comparison, *Dos Lesbos* may depend entirely upon the performance, considering its audience, place of performance, and the performers. The original production was performed by the playwrights for a predominantly lesbian, all-woman audience. The butch–femme relationship of the performers, informing the character portrayals in an inherently gestic mode, operated to parodise both heterosexual pairings of the dominant culture and lesbian stereotypes as well, becoming far less realistic than in the reading. (There is nothing in the text to suggest a butch–femme component of the performance.) When performed for a predominantly heterosexual audience with more 'straight'-forward acting, the characters tend to be perceived more within the framework of classic realism, and the performance text must rely on content rather than form to promote a politicised reception. Whether or not it functions for the heterosexual audience as a political instrument, indelibly altering their perceptions of lesbians, is un-measurable; as Dolan notes, 'selling a lesbian text to mainstream spectators seems incongruous, but in the best of all possible worlds those spectators will come away from the performance thinking differently about their sexuality and gender assumptions'.[26] In the case of *Dos Lesbos*, its incipient realism holds both promise and threat – the promise that it might indeed reach a more mainstream audience, but therein lies its threat of assimilation: Dolan says, 'perhaps the context will prevail, and ... obscure the meaning of what they see'.[27] However, this concern raises the question of the articulation of subjectivity –

is it possible, in a culture structured by compulsory heterosexuality, for the lesbian subject to be thoroughly assimilated? Dolan so eloquently argues the lesbian's special position in relation to representation, which, in terms of identity, must produce a condition of self-consciousness: it is this process by which, de Lauretis says, 'one begins to know that and how the personal is political, that and how the subject is specifically and materially en-gendered in its social conditions and possibilities of existence'.[28] The lesbian subject on stage in *Dos Lesbos* would therefore be radical in any venue – sustaining a tension between the personal and the political that refutes a coherent, unitary conception of identity and recasts it in a material, political context.

The crucial matter of authorship again presents itself – which seems regressive when trying to theorise reception, but not so ... For feminism, the author can't be dead. Nancy Miller argues that the postmodernist obituary for the author 'does not necessarily work for women and prematurely forecloses the question of identity for them'.[29] The female subject, already historically in a different relation to Self than men, 'decentred, "disoriginated", deinstitutionalised, etc.', stands in a qualitatively different relationship to authorship and questions of authority.[30] As Diamond notes, the 'erasure from history' for women dramatists 'has been so nearly complete',[31] that issues of authority in representation – who speaks about whom – may indeed figure largely in reception of a text. In the dialogue between spectator and performance text that feminism hopes to turn into a dialectic, the intensity of the relationship between writer and text – the *personal* connection, if you will – emerges as a crucial point of context. In the theatre, this would of necessity extend to the interpreters of the text, who must somehow share in the authentic exploration of female subjectivity. This is not to reinstate 'author's intent' as a guiding principle of production; rather, it connotes for feminist theatre practice what I have been discussing for feminist theatre writing – an engagement with the issues and problems inherent in the commitment to a political agenda. As Bonnie Zimmerman notes in reference to an essay on images of the lesbian, 'there is an important dialectic between how the lesbian articulates herself and how she is articulated and objectified by others'.[32] Which is to say that context, or the specific terms of a performance and its reception, is the final arbiter of meaning, and its integrity is absolute.

Which brings us, finally, to Kennedy's text, the context of which is limited, under erasure, because it is almost never produced. As an unreadable text, it is only read, usually generating mass confusion and a loss-of-narrative despair among first-time readers. In this regard, it is a perfect teaching tool for discussing the problems of articulating subjectivity in relation to race and gender, as well as introducing contemporary notions of narrative from a feminist viewpoint. The reader is forced into an experience, albeit temporary, of Clara's confusion, and must attempt to negotiate, with her, an oppressive cultural terrain – in order to 'make sense' of the play, she or he tries to construct a narrative, and the final glaring impossibility of that project foregrounds Clara's frustration – in fact, her 'non-existence'.

But if the play is never performed, because of its difficulty, is it simply due to a repressive culture, hostile to Blacks and women as well as non-realist theatre? Or does the play, in its intense anti-realism, defeat its own, apparently subversive, agenda? Actually, I believe the play would become more 'readable' in performance: Clara's embodiment and the realisation of the production elements would lend signifying power to Kennedy's thoroughly visual images. Performance, operating in more than just the linguistic signifying system, would make Clara's plight felt viscerally, but would also provide visual connections for the images in a more comprehensible pattern. Reception of the performance text thus might outstrip the political impact of the dramatic text, allowing for a higher degree of visual readability. Unfortunately, Kennedy's text, like Clara, survives only marginally, in the gaps of Western theatre's master narrative.

I am not arguing that feminist playwrights should only write realism in order to be produced; rather, that the challenge for feminist dramatic criticism is one of empowerment, for women writers, performers and reader/spectators. This process must extend to all aspects of context within a cultural specificity. If we agree that the relationship to narrative in writing is a complex one of crucial political implications, then it is equally imperative to contextualise that relationship, to understand its question for performance practice and observe its specific reception. Not an easy task, this imperative draws us again to a difficulty of long standing for feminism, that of defining (or not defining) the differentiated viewing subject, a definition whose nature, I feel, lies in the problematics of female subjectivity. Is it indeed premature (or better yet, wholly inappropriate) for feminists to assume a postmodernist version of subjectivity (and subsequently, the death of the author)? Modleski states that 'feminists at this historical moment need to insist on the importance of real women as interpreters',[33] which includes author – actor – spectator. We thus cannot rely on theories of narrative, or of literary structures such as classic realism, which are purely textual, but must comprehend subjectivity and practice (writing and performance) within material conditions of power.

From *Modern Drama*, 32 (March 1989), 115–27.

NOTES

[This piece asks if a realist play can be a feminist play. In so doing it begins a discussion, heard throughout this *New Casebook*, about the relative success of different approaches to the writing of feminist drama and the evaluation of feminist drama. Ed.]

1. Catherine Belsey, 'Constructing the Subject, Deconstructing the Text', in *Feminist Criticism & Social Change: Sex, Class and Race in Literature & Culture*, ed. Judith L. Newton and Deborah S. Rosenfelt (London, 1985).

2. Ibid., p. 53.

3. Laura Mulvey, 'Visual Pleasure and Narrative Cinema', *Screen*, 16 (1975) 6–18; 14.

4. See Teresa de Lauretis, 'Desire in Narrative', in *Alice Doesn't: Feminism, Semiotics, Cinema* (Bloomington, IN, 1984).

5. de Lauretis, *Alice Doesn't*, pp. 103–57.

6. See, for example, Trudy Scott's review in *Women & Performance*, I (1983), 78.

7. Bertolt Brecht, 'A Short Organum for the Theatre', in *Brecht on Theatre*, ed. and trans. John Willett (New York, 1964), p. 189.

8. Belsey, 'Constructing the Subject', p. 55.

9. Ibid.

10. See Herbert Blau, 'The American Dream in American Gothic: The Plays of Sam Shepard and Adrienne Kennedy', *Modern Drama*, 27 (1984), 520–39.

11. In an interesting sidenote, Lilith – the Great Mother, who was suppressed and supplanted by the Great Father of the Hebrew tribes –

was edited out of the Old Testament except for a passing reference to her as a screech owl in Isaiah (34:14). With her elimination from inscribed religion, the creative power of the Mother was effectively erased from historical memory. It is thus deeply ironic that Clara's totem is the owl – the last trace of the lost mother, the vestigial possibility of a matrilineal heritage. I am indebted to Katharine C. Gentile, graduate student at the University of Oregon, for this information.

12. For the superb discussion of the justification of patrilineal heritage within the *Oresteia*, see Sue-Ellen Case, 'Traditional History: A Feminist Deconstruction', in *Feminism and Theatre* (New York, 1988). Most pointedly, Athena exonerates Orestes from matricide with the explanation that the parent is 'he who mounts', thus relegating the mother to the position of nurse, a mere vehicle for birth. Athena is herself a motherless child, having been born from Zeus's forehead; as Case notes, how ironic indeed that she represents the birth of democracy.

13. Blau, 'The American Dream', 531–2.

14. The image of pale skin/black body also conjures the figure of the 'Buckra', typically a mixed-blood person whose mother was Black and whose father was of European heritage. Clara is in one sense the original Buckra, the indelible evidence of cultural abandonment – she is the site of unassimilated difference; too light for one culture, too dark for the other, restrained from claiming her father's European heritage while her mother (uprooted from her own African heritage, divested of her past) represents no heritage at all. Hortense Spillers elaborates the significance of the buckra figure for Black American women's writing in a recent paper, 'The Habit of Pathos', delivered May 1988, in Dubrovnik, Yugoslavia.

15. Tania Modleski, 'Feminism and the Power of Interpretation: Some Critical Readings', in *Feminist Studies/Critical Studies*, ed. Teresa de Lauretis (Bloomington, IN, 1986), p. 121.

16. Elin Diamond, 'Brechtian Theory/Feminist Theory: Toward a Gestic Feminist Criticism', *The Drama Review*, 32 (1988), 82–94.

17. Ibid., 90.

18. Ibid.

19. Ibid.

20. Jill Dolan, *The Feminist Spectator as Critic* (Ann Arbor, MI, 1988), pp. 27–34.

21. Jenny S. Spencer, 'Norman's *'night, Mother*: Psycho-drama of Female Identity', *Modern Drama*, 30 (1987), 364–75.

22. Modleski, 'Feminism', p. 123.

23. Ibid.

24. Although, arguably, the play might be rife with such moments if subjected to a 'gestic' analysis and performance.

25. See Jill Dolan, *"night, Mother*: Review', *Women & Performance*, 1 (1983), 78–9.

26. Dolan, *The Feminist Spectator as Critic*, p. 120.

27. Ibid.

28. Teresa de Lauretis, 'Feminist Studies/Critical Studies: Issues, Terms and Contexts', in *Feminist Studies/Critical Studies*, p. 9.

29. Nancy K. Miller, 'Changing the Subject: Authorship, Writing, and the Reader', in *Feminist Studies/Critical Studies*, pp. 102–20.

30. Ibid. p. 106.

31. Diamond, 'Brechtian Theory/Feminist Theory', p. 90.

32. Bonnie Zimmerman, 'What Has Never Been: An Overview of Lesbian Feminist Literary Criticism', *Feminist Studies*, 7 (1981), 459–75; 464.

33. Modleski, 'Feminism', p. 136.

2

Beyond Brecht: Britain's New Feminist Drama

JANELLE REINELT

Bertolt Brecht's theory and practice have had a strong influence on the British theatre, dating from the first visit of the Berliner Ensemble in 1956 and the English publication in 1964 of John Willett's compilation of the theoretical writings, *Brecht On Theatre*. Political theatre practice in England had benefited from the socialist movement as well as the impact of the Beveridge Report on the arts. Following Beveridge's mandated university grants, educated working-class men and women had found their theatrical voices in playwrights such as Shelagh Delaney, John Osborne, and Arnold Wesker. The continuing search for a political form and technique led to Brecht who, in shaping a dramaturgy specifically suited to social critique, provided a path beyond social realism to the epic theatre. Brechtian techniques provided a methodology for embedding a materialist critique within the theatrical medium. Political theatre requires the ability to isolate and manifest certain ideas and relationships that make ideology visible, in contrast with the styles of realism and naturalism, wherein ideology is hidden or covert. Brecht's theorisation of the social gest, epic structure, and alienation effect provides the means to reveal material relations as the basis of social reality, to foreground and examine ideologically-determined beliefs and unconscious habitual perceptions, and to make visible those signs inscribed on the body which distinguish social behaviour in relation to class, gender, and history. For feminists, Brechtian techniques offer a way to examine the material conditions of gender behaviour (how they are internalised, opposed, and changed) and their interaction with other socio-political factors such as class.

The implied interchangeability of feminist and socialist concerns within this conception of political theatre glosses over the history of the relationship between socialism and feminism. In England, as elsewhere, this relationship has been characterised by theoretical and practical struggle. Michelene Wandor, Michèle Barrett, Sheila Rowbotham, and others have written extensively about feminism in England and its relationship to the socialist movement.[1] In England, the feminist movement is at once largely working-class and heavily socialist, in contrast with America where feminism is strongly based in the middle class. The first national conference on Women's Liberation took place in 1970. During the next few years, socialist-feminist conferences were held in various locations. Several papers and journals began publication, including *Spare Rib*, *Women's Voice*, and *Red Rag*, and in 1974 women and men in the labour movement drew up the Working Women's Charter, proposing demands for material change. Contemporary with these events, the first Women's Theatre Conference encouraged the formation of a number of feminist theatre companies while also providing a new agenda for some of the socialist theatre groups which had previously ignored the 'woman question'. The attempt to develop an adequate theory of the relationship between socialism and feminism was carried on in artistic as well as political practice. Two of the central theoretical issues were and still are: the relationship of class oppression to sexual repression; and the ideological interpretation of production, reproduction, and procreation.

With regard to the first issue, socialist men criticised feminist women for being diverted from the 'true' struggle (the class struggle) to what was essentially a bourgeois movement. The feminists replied that historically, women have been subject not only to the ruling class, but also to the patriarchy. They pointed out that the advantages to men resulting from the subordination of women are not restricted along class lines, and that even existing socialist practice still reveals structures of female oppression. Shulamith Firestone's early and influential work, *The Dialectic of Sex*, claims that the relations of procreation rather than production belong to the base and that other economic factors are actually part of the superstructure. She writes, 'The sexual-reproductive organisation of society always furnishes the real basis, starting from which we can alone work out the ultimate explanation of the whole superstructure of economic, juridical and political institutions as well as of the religious, philosophical and other ideas of a given historical period.'[2]

Radical feminists had theorised a trans-historical subjection of women to men in the patriarchy as the central problem and fact of reality. This view encouraged socialist women to abandon alliances with men, even for purposes of class struggle; men were seen as the fundamental enemy, regardless of class affiliation. The socialist response was that the real oppression stems from capitalism and women must not abandon their historical place in the struggle against it through engaging in a bourgeois liberal movement. The question of men and their place in a feminist struggle caused deep disagreement among feminist groups and split the National Women's Liberation Conference in Birmingham in 1978, which was to be the last such conference. This issue continues to problematise socialist-feminism. In 'The British Women's Movement', Angela Weir and Elizabeth Wilson argued that the current political climate is fostering retreat from class politics and dilution of the socialist edge through a splintering populism, especially in feminism.[3] Anne Phillips replied in 'Class Warfare' that other oppressions such as gender and race are related to but not reducible to capitalism and that the whole concept of class must be reconstituted in more complex terms.[4]

In relation to the meaning of production, reproduction, and procreation, traditional Marxist analysis, following Engels, conceptualises production as the conditions of labour in the workplace, locating issues of production in the public sphere. The domestic sphere is engaged in procreation and the reproduction of human labour power. The domestic sphere, therefore, is outside of the economic arena where the 'real' material base lies. The home and family are part of the superstructure, determined by conditions of production in the public sphere. Socialist-feminists suggest a revaluation of domestic labour, or 'women's work', as a productive form of labour having the same status as wage labour, mutually determining, along with traditional economic factors, the course of historical change. Issues of domestic labour focus on the reproduction of the labourer both through childbirth and through the material support the home offers the labourer.

The project of reconceptualising production to include reproduction or the production of people is not without problems, and socialist-feminists do not all agree on the relation of the market to family relations, nor on all the differences between producing commodities and people. However, the exclusion of the domestic sphere from the conception of the economic base of society marginalises women and the family, leaving them in the unacceptable position of being incidental to and determined by the 'real' economic base.[5]

These two theoretical issues focus the concern for socialist-feminism on the exploration of the relationship between social, economic, and sexual conditions in society. Alternative conceptions of these two issues are demonstrated or implied in playtexts, aided in many cases by Brechtian elements which have proven integral to the dramatisation of these complex issues. The playscripts become working examples of possible ways of understanding the relationships between class, gender, labour, and capital.

Strike While the Iron is Hot affords an opportunity to perceive an evolving theoretical position actualised in theatrical practice. The Red Ladder Theatre which developed *Strike* began as an agit-prop group committed to the Labour Movement. They had looked to Brecht as a model for some time, and deliberately used *The Mother* as an early reference point for this script. In both plays, a central woman character has her consciousness raised and undertakes direct political action because of her experience of injustice. However, Brecht's play is male-biased and confirms traditional sex-role stereotyping while *Strike* challenges the distinctions between public and private spheres and the whole gender/class system.

The relationship between class and sex was actively debated in the group when the ideas for the play were forming. Some argued from the traditional Marxist position that class struggle is pre-eminent and sexual oppression subordinate to it. Others argued that sexual oppression was primary and must be dealt with independently. The play, while not resolving this issue neatly, dramatises some of its complexities. Helen goes to work, joins a union, and becomes a fighter for economic justice, but she also struggles with her husband to change the conditions of the 'labour' she performs at home. Thus the play focuses on the problem of the relationship between gender and class as well as the problem of the relationship of wage labour to household and family activity. *Strike* portrays the way in which class may sometimes subvert alliances based on sex. It also, however, shows how sexist behaviour cuts across class. The female manager at the plant where Helen works will not allow the women time off when their children are ill. She is not sympathetic because she has an *au pair* girl to care for her children; class divides the experiences of women in the play. The men, on the other hand, when bargaining to settle a union wage dispute, cross over class lines to share sexist jokes, and the union men settle for a job evaluation scheme instead of equal pay for the women because they do not work for the women's interests as they had for their own. Thus the 'old boy' network seems to transcend class, although the benefit, the play is quick to point out, falls to the management which evokes male fraternity to its own advantage. The play's final synthesis of the relationship between class struggle and feminist struggle is expressed on two banners raised at the end of the play, one saying, 'Workers will never be free while women are in chains' and the other, 'Women will never be free while workers are in chains'.

The position on modes of production, developed through the dramatic action, is that the traditional division of labour in the home duplicates the oppressive exploitation of workers in the work place. Helen struggles to get her husband to help around the house when she goes to work. The connection between wage labour and home labour is explicit when Helen sings: 'I'm not your little woman, your sweetheart, your dear. I'm a wage slave without wages. I'm a maintenance engineer.'[6]

Red Ladder was persuaded at the time that women's work at home was a hidden wage-labour cost. In addition to profiting from the benefit of men's labour, owners also profit from women's domestic labour that maintains and services the worker so that he can maximise his output. This analysis produced agitation on two fronts: at the workplace for better wages, and at home for an end to the traditional division of labour. Helen's song makes this agenda and analysis explicit. 'The truth began to dawn then / how I keep him fit and trim / so the boss can make a nice fat profit / out of me and him. And as a solid union man / he got in quite a rage / to think that we're both working hard / and getting one man's wage. / I said "And what about the part-time packing job I do? / That's three men that I work for, love, / my boss, your boss, and you" / He looked a little sheepish / and said "As from today, / the lads and me'll see what we / can do on equal pay. / Would you like a housewives' union, / do you think you should be paid / as a cook, and as a cleaner, / as a nurse and as a maid?" / I said "Don't jump the gun, love, / If you did your share at home, / then I might have some time to fight / some battles of my own".'[7] The song argues that women's work is undervalued both in the workplace and at home, and that what is needed is not just better wages, but an end to the sexual division of labour.

The play also addresses the issues of equal pay and parity. In Brecht's *The Mother*, Vlassova learns about economic exploitation through comparing a table and a factory. This scene is directly adapted by Red Ladder, becoming a pub scene entitled 'The Disputed Pint' in which Helen learns about the factory struggle for equal pay for similar work. Beer glasses provide the basic social gest of the scene. The shop foreman, impersonating Henry Ford, fills one man's pint glass half-full while he fills another's completely. Helen sees immediately that it is not fair to pay different wages for the same work, but she extends the argument to women's wages as well: 'I'm still not getting as much as Mike and I'm doing the same work.... That means I should go on strike for parity with Mike.'[8] The men had not anticipated this interpretation. Realising that all the women at the table have half-pint glasses while the men have full, Helen decides that on the next round, she will have a full pint. Richard Seyd, who collaborated on the script development, cites this scene and its gestural technique with the beer glasses as Red Ladder's typical adaptation of Brecht. 'We wouldn't talk about economic questions in the dialogue – we sought a more painterly approach where a physical element could communicate the idea. Then we wrote the scenes so that each would have a turning point, and gave them a title like *The Mother* had.'[9]

The use of Brechtian techniques to provide a physical correlative of relations between genders appears in its clearest form in the play *Trafford Tanzi*. Brecht's gestural technique, the method for creating a central gesture or 'gest', was employed by feminists to reveal the relations between the sexes. This technique is the central device in *Trafford Tanzi* where all the action takes place in a wrestling ring. Author Claire Luckham writes, 'I also read a lot of Brecht's writing about the theatre and was particularly interested in his enthusiasm for boxing and the relationship between fighters and their audience, though then I thought, "What is he on about" rather than, "I want to write a play about a lady wrestler".[10] Brecht's 1926 essay, 'Emphasis on Sport', lauds the sporting attitude which is missing in the theatre. People come to sporting events to have fun and to enjoy the skills they see presented. 'A theatre which makes no contact with the public is a nonsense.'[11]

Roland Barthes also perceived the appeal of wrestling and its fundamental possibilities for theatrical spectacle: 'Wrestling is like a diacritic writing: above the fundamental meaning of his body, the wrestler arranges comments which are episodic but always opportune, and constantly help the reading of the fight by means of gestures, attitudes and mimicry which makes the intention utterly obvious.'[12] Wrestling cannot be disinterested; watching it one takes sides. Because it provides clear distinctions between good and evil, it engages moral judgement. It is, in short, a perfect gest for feminist theatre.

Luckham wrote *Tanzi* for the Everyman Theatre Company to tour in pubs and clubs in and around Liverpool in 1978. The play was written for a working class audience and Luckham wanted something with direct appeal to active audience involvement. She decided to use wrestling to portray Tanzi's struggle to grow up, using wrestling as a metaphor for the struggle against gender-specific oppression and conditioning. The physical acting space and dominant action present a male-dominated world where the outcome is 'fixed' because the outcome of each round is a foregone conclusion. Trafford Tanzi gradually becomes a successful wrestler and triumphs over the 'beatings' given her by father, mother, and husband. Professional wrestling trainers coached the cast who actually performed the various holds and moves of wrestling. The referee comments on the action, announcing the rounds and their winners: 'In Round Four, a submission to Dad by means of a Boston Crab.' Various songs provide additional comment on the action and break up the narrative. Tanzi's mum sings, 'I wanted a boy / And look what I got / Well I got a girl / All covered in snot.'[13]

The songs, the referee, and the wrestling ring can all be perceived as Brechtian elements. The content of the play, however, seems to privilege a personal struggle for equality more than the specifically socialist issues outlined above. In fact, Michelene Wandor has argued that the play became a success in the commercial theatre because it did not pose a direct challenge to the prevailing socio-economic order. She writes, 'In the end, the dynamic of the play remains most rooted in bourgeois feminism: in its positive aspect of celebrating women's equality with men, and in the negative aspect of taking the values of men as the norm.'[14] Considering the audience for whom the play was originally conceived, Wandor's critique of the play as 'bourgeois' seems a bit ironic. The play takes certain relationships for granted – all of the characters are working class, making it an in-house discussion. Actually, the co-option of women's work for capitalist profiteering is vividly portrayed when Tanzi's father attempts to become her manager and take a 50% cut of her wrestling profits. Tanzi gets him with a backhammer, and when he tries to plead his case, 'But Tanzi ... please.... I'm your old dad. I'm family. And what about your mum? I've got to support her', Tanzi dropkicks him and says, 'Tough bananas, Dad'.[15] In addition, her arguments with husband Dean Rebel over the division of labour are framed in terms of the discussion of women's work as reproducing labour power mentioned above. 'Dean: Look, I come home after a hard day's work, do I find a hot meal waiting for me? No, there's a note on the table. Well, that's not how champions is maintained y'know. Tanzi: Oh, that's what I'm s'posed to be, is it? A serving unit?'[16]

Within the context of a working-class perspective already coloured with socialist ideology, the debate about the relationship of work in the home to work in the public sector is recognisable. But it is the wrestling match itself, that perfect Brechtian 'gest' for the struggle of women to free themselves from male oppression both economic and sexual, which is the central feature of the play. This struggle must be conducted in the open, in the public arena, where the audience can participate in it and identify its political as well as its personal character. The transformation of traditionally private experience into public spectacle helps transform conceptions of individual problems into social ones. As Barthes points out, both wrestling and theatre give 'intelligible representations of moral situations which are usually private'.[17]

Both *Strike While the Iron is Hot* and *Trafford Tanzi* deal with contemporary experience. One of Brecht's major discoveries was that by historicising the incidents of the narrative, a playwright can cause the audience to become conscious of certain habitual perceptions which have been established by the historical tradition and therefore partially determine the present. 'Historicising the incidents' may involve re-examining a concrete historical situation and its customary interpretation to see what is missing, or what new insights emerge if hidden aspects are thrown into relief. It may also involve making explicit the relationship between past and present, in order to show that human history is an open horizon, subject to constant change. Brecht writes, 'Historical incidents are unique, transitory incidents associated with particular periods. The conduct of persons involved in them is not fixed and "universally human"; it includes elements that have been or may be overtaken by the course of history, and is subject to criticism from the immediately following period's point of view.'[18] Reconceptualising women's place in history has been a fertile ground for feminist struggle. Not only have women discovered that they have systematically been excluded from the 'great man' orthodoxy of most historical interpretation, they have also discovered that many traditional attitudes toward women have historical precedents. Exposing hidden aspects of the past and exploring their consequences for contemporary experience has provided a fruitful undertaking for feminist playwrights.

Caryl Churchill's play *Vinegar Tom* incorporates a socialist-feminist analysis in order to attack the problem of the relationship between gender and class. Using the notion of historicising the narrative, it places sexuality within the history of witches and witchcraft, problematising the traditional interpretation of that history and pointing to the vestigial remainder of such thinking in contemporary life. Written for the Monstrous Regiment, a theatre company formed in 1975 and committed to both feminism and socialism, *Vinegar Tom* was commissioned as part of the company's effort to 'reclaim the history play from women's point of view'.[19] In researching the play, Churchill recognised that received notions about witchcraft mystified concrete relations between outcast or marginal women (the old, the poor, the unconventional) and the religious and economic power structure. She writes, 'One of the things that struck me in reading the detailed accounts of witch trials in Essex ... was how petty and everyday the witches' offences were, and how different the atmosphere of actual English witchhunts seemed to be from my received idea, based on slight knowledge of the European witchhunts in films and fiction, of burnings, hysteria and sexual orgies. I wanted to write a play about witches with no witches in it; a play not about evil, hysteria and possession by the devil but about poverty, humiliation and prejudice, and how the women accused of witchcraft saw themselves.'[20]

The central action of the play involves the scapegoating of poor women by the farmer Jack and his wife Margery, a couple who are at high risk because of their attempts at economic expansion (they have sublet two new fields). Margery cannot bear the pressure of feeling incompetent and undeserving: Jack needs a target for his sexual and financial frustration. Not wanting to believe that God judges them 'bad', they begin to interpret their misfortunes as acts of witchcraft committed by their poor neighbours, Joan and her daughter Alice. The Church provides the institutional mechanism for burning such witches; traditional prime targets are single women, economically marginal and sexually deviant from the puritan code. The accused include Ellen, the cunning woman or healer who earns her own living outside of the monetary system and works outside the sanctioned medical/male establishment; Alice, object of Jack's sexual desire, whom he accuses of making him impotent; and Susan, who has had an abortion for which she feels guilty. Internalising the prevailing social and religious code, Susan feels that she must have been a witch without knowing it. In her conflation of economic and moral codes, Susan shows how women can remain unconscious of their oppression and can victimise themselves and others. The only escapee from punishments of torture and death is Betty, the land owner's daughter. However, while she escapes class oppression, she pays the price of sexual submission: she agrees to marry and become the thing she dreads, 'a good wife'. The play unfolds in 21 scenes and 7 songs. No one protagonist dominates the action. Churchill keeps the community and its socio-economic-sexual systems at the centre of the play through several Brechtian devices. The songs, sung by modern women, break up the narrative and historicise the incidents, creating a critical distance from the historical events which allows comparisons to contemporary time and ruptures the flow of the narrative, emphasising the possibilities for intervention and change.

Gillian Hanna of the Monstrous Regiment defends the songs against the objections of some who felt they were unnecessary: 'We had a very real feeling that we didn't want to allow the audience to get off the hook by regarding it as a period piece, a piece of very interesting history. I believe that the simple telling of the historical story, say, is not enough.... You have to choose between what you keep in and what you leave out. It's at that point of choice where women on the whole find that they get left out. Our experience is that life is not the simple story, and that you have to find some way of recognising that in dramatic form.'[21] The songs determine a particular perception of the events of the narrative.

Churchill also employs Brecht's episodic play structure in which each scene is isolated and has a crucial turning point. Brecht writes, 'The episodes must not succeed one another indistinguishably but must give us a chance to interpose our judgement.... The parts of the story have to be carefully set off one against another by giving each its own structure as a play within a play.'[22] For example, in

Scene Six, a doctor bleeds Betty, who is refusing to get married as her wealthy parents want her to do for their own economic gain. As she is visibly drained of her lifeblood, and symbolically drained of her strength to fight, the doctor tells her, 'After bleeding you must be purged. Tonight you shall be blistered. You will soon be well enough to get married.'[23] Thus the gest of bleeding contains the central action of the scene, and the scene itself is a potentially independent vignette in which a discrete situation portrays how middle-class women are controlled and socialised. The other scenes which deal with poor women are also discrete and yet are related across class through the collusion of the patriarchal church and state. In each case, intervention could have changed the particular instance, but the isolation of the women from one another because of class made such collective action impossible. The audience, however, viewing the situation in the present, is able to perceive how gender and class interrelate and hopefully, how to organise a coalition opposition.

The dramatisation of sex and class systems is enhanced throughout the particular scenes by the Brechtian technique of finding a critical social gest which provides material focus. In Scene Four, Margery is churning butter without results throughout the scene. 'Come butter come, come butter come. Johnny's standing at the gate waiting for a butter cake. Come butter ... it's not coming, this butter. I'm sick of it.'[24] The sexual and economic frustration captured in this gest explains Margery's cruelty to Joan, who comes begging for yeast, only to be abused. Margery's husband begins and ends the scene by abusing his wife, calling her a lazy woman, a 'lazy slut' because the butter won't come.

The play specifies in concrete form the relationship between patriarchy and class society: they mutually support each other. Most oppressed are those who attempt to live outside the economic system like Ellen and Joan and the sexual system like Alice and Susan. The final song asks contemporary men if they are projecting evilness onto women in order to excuse their own inadequacies. 'Evil women. Is that what you want to see in your movie dream?'[25] The historically received notion of witches' evil power survives in contemporary mystifications of women as possessing dark, evil, secret power. The vestigial remainder of a false perception of the past, these ideas persist in determining aspects of contemporary ideology. *Vinegar Tom* dramatises the dialectical relationship between history and consciousness.

All three of the plays discussed here achieve the breakdown of traditional distinctions between public and private spheres. The personal lives of individuals are seen to derive meaning from their social and political relations and, in turn, to shape the social whole. Such a feminist perspective, that the personal is political, demands the dramatisation of personal, emotional life, drawing on, to some extent, the techniques of traditional bourgeois realism. Epic techniques, on the other hand, place the personal, individual experience of characters within their socio-political context, widening the focus to include the community and its social, economic and sexual relations. Out of the need to evolve a suitable dramatic form for socialist-feminist drama, a new theatrical style may be evolving which synthesises older techniques. Of the Red Ladder experience, Richard Seyd writes, 'As we were dealing with emotions on a personal level in the play ... this neccessitated strong, believable characters, because without that three-dimensionality the emotional content would appear shallow and false.'[26]

Acting in the new feminist drama also seems to require a synthesis of techniques. Gillian Hanna of Monstrous Regiment talks about playing emotional elements: 'My inclination and experience is all to do with a kind of Brechtian acting, which doesn't deny Stanislavsky but puts the emphasis elsewhere.... It doesn't work for me or for an audience, if I'm doing it just on the level of remembering some sort of pain that I've experienced.... Nor does it work on the level of "I'm showing the audience something here." The nights it seems to work best are when there is, and on a level that I've not experienced before, a meshing of those two.'[27] Thus the feminist critique of the division between private and public concerns leads in the direction of both a new dramaturgy and a revised acting style.

Feminist transformation of Brechtian techniques illustrates Brecht's notion of the criticism of the received past from the standpoint of a concrete present. These plays and others from the British feminist theatre afford the opportunity to see revisions of theatrical technique in the context of the evolving formulations of a socialist-feminist analysis. Current feminist theatre practice thus contains vigorous interaction with progressive aspects of theatrical traditions such as Brecht's, while simultaneously engaging in the process of discovering appropriate and effective contemporary methods.

From *Theatre Journal*, 38:2 (May 1986), 154–63

NOTES

[This essay discusses feminist transformations of Brechtian gests and uses of history as frames for feminist drama. It includes examples from Monstrous Regiment company, Red Ladder company, Luckham's *Trafford Tanzi* and Churchill's *Vinegar Tom*. Ed.]

1. See Michèle Barrett, *Woman's Oppression Today* (London, 1988); *Beyond The Fragments: Feminism and the Making of Socialism*, ed. Sheila Rowbotham, Lynne Segal and Hilary Wainwright (London, 1979); and Michelene Wandor, *Understudies: Theatre and Sexual Politics* (London, 1986).

2. Shulamith Firestone, *The Dialectic of Sex: The Case for Feminist Revolution* (New York, 1970), pp. 12–13.

3. Angela Weir and Elizabeth Wilson, 'The British Women's Movement', *New Left Review*, 148 (November–December 1984).

4. Anne Phillips, 'Class Warfare', *New Socialist*, 24 (February 1985).

5. For a full discussion of this problem, see Alison M. Jaggar, *Feminist Politics and Human Nature* (Totowa, NJ, 1983).

6. Red Ladder Theatre, 'Strike While the Iron is Hot', in *Strike While the Iron is Hot: Three Plays on Sexual Politics*, ed. Michelene Wandor (London, 1980), p. 51.

7. Ibid., pp. 52–3.

8. Ibid., p. 42.

9. Interview with Richard Seyd, San Francisco, 1 August 1984.

10. Claire Luckham, 'Warmup', in *Trafford Tanzi, her Hopes, her Fears, her Early Years* (London, 1983).

11. Bertolt Brecht, *Brecht on Theatre*, ed. and trans. John Willett (New York, 1964), p. 7.

12. Roland Barthes, 'The World of Wrestling', in *Mythologies*, trans. Annette Lavers (New York, 1972), p. 18.

13. Claire Luckham, 'Trafford Tanzi', in *Plays by Women*, vol. 2, ed. Michelene Wandor (London, 1983), p. 79.

14. Michelene Wandor, 'The Fifth Column: Feminism and Theatre', *Drama* (Summer 1984), 7.

15. Luckman, 'Trafford Tanzi', p. 90.

16. Ibid., p. 91.

17. Barthes, 'The World of Wrestling', p. 18.

18. Brecht, *Brecht on Theatre*, p. 140.

19. Gillian Hanna, 'Feminism and Theatre', *Theatre Papers*, 2nd series, No. 8 (1978), 10–11.

20. Caryl Churchill, 'Vinegar Tom', in *Plays By Women*, vol. 1, ed. Michelene Wandor (London, 1982), p. 39.

21. Hanna, 'Feminism and Theatre', 10–11.

22. Brecht, *Brecht on Theatre*, p. 201.

23. Churchill, 'Vinegar Tom', p. 24.

24. Ibid., p. 38.

25. Ibid.

26. Richard Seyd, 'The Theatre of Red Ladder', *New Edinburgh Review*, 30 (August 1975), 40–1.

27. Hanna, 'Feminism and Theatre', pp. 6–7.

3

The Dis-Play's the Thing: Gender and Public Sphere in Contemporary British Theatre

LOREN KRUGER

> As subject for history woman always occurs simultaneously in
> several places.
>
> 'The Laugh of the Medusa', Hélène Cixous (1981)

Women have always made spectacles of themselves, as the saying
goes. Only recently, and intermittently at that, have women made
spectacles themselves. On this difference turns the ambiguous identity of a feminist theatre.

Current discussion of feminism and theatre often proceeds as if
we can take for granted the reciprocal identification of 'feminist
theatre' and the 'representation of women', by way of the 'creation
of significant stage roles for women, a concern with the gender roles
in society, exploration of the texture of women's worlds and an
urge towards the politicisation of sexuality'.[1] This list of issues
seems right enough, but it obscures a characteristic tension in feminist work, between celebration and critique, between asserting as
self-evident the unity of women's practice and women's studies on
the basis of gender above all, and the acknowledgement not simply
and blandly of difference, but of differences and allegiances among
women (and men) that challenge any easy assumption of gender

49

solidarity. Recent feminist investigations into narrative fiction have moved beyond what Teresa de Lauretis calls 'mainstream feminism' – an insistent emphasis on finding women's voices for an alternative feminist canon – towards feminisms that include the critique of the gendered nature of all literary form and social relations as well as the interaction of gender with other allegiances such as class, age and race.[2]

In the light of these developments, the notion of a feminist theatre defined by the extent to which it offers new roles for women and that of a feminist theory basing its claim to be a unified and uniquely legitimate interpretation of such worlds on some essential 'female method'[3] is insufficient. By isolating gender as *the* source of oppression, such an approach calls for the advancement of individual cultural producers (writers, directors, performers) because they are female, forgetting that the theatre institution can absorb individual female successes without in any way threatening the legitimacy of the masculinist and capitalist definition of that success.[4] Adding 'significant *stage* roles' (my emphasis) for women may well reinforce existing relations of production in the theatre and thus participation in the institution, since it neither challenges the traditional roles of women in the theatre: sexually on display as actresses or serviceably out of sight as clerical workers; nor does it provide the means for women to run the show themselves.[5] A 'feminist theatre' based on the premise that a 'female method' or a 'feminine morphology'[6] can *in itself* overcome this hegemony may well reinforce this division of labour.

Furthermore, a feminist theatre based on the *idea* – in the 'concern for gender relations' or the 'urge to politicise sexuality' – expressed in dramatic texts forgets that the site on which these texts are performed and watched is a theatre institution that renews itself by turning such 'concerns' into the trademarks of a new commodity, 'plays by women', as the publisher's series title suggests. A feminist critique of the theatre institution – in Britain, as in Western Europe generally – demands more than the *accommodation* of women's plays on a stage designed ostensibly for general, but effectively, for masculine occupation. Our task is not simply to support a new 'women's theatre', but to critique those masculinist strategies of legitimation in the theatre institution,[7] which allow for the marginalisation of alternative and in particular certain kinds of feminist theatre practices by dismissing them as illegitimate and therefore im-properly 'theatre'.

Even a brief outline of these legitimating strategies instituting 'theatre' in Britain points to the interpenetration of material production and the ideological and aesthetic value of theatre as art.[8] The dramatic convention of a strong central hero, which persists in most plays written for the amateur as well as the professional market, is reinforced and encouraged in the commercial theatre by the emphasis on the star and the star vehicle. The subsidised theatre, run ostensibly on an ensemble system, is, in fact, obliged to respond to competition by paying dearly for its stars.[9] Economic factors also shape the hierarchy of personnel, from the division between 'artistic' and 'technical' labour (and the implication that women are not fit for the latter) to the power of the Director over the actors and support staff such as the set and costume designers. The (con)fusion of aesthetic and administrative authority in the single person of the Director, particularly in what the Arts Council has called the 'powerhouses of culture' in Britain – the Royal Shakespeare Company and the National Theatre – enables him to use administrative arguments to justify artistic control over associate or 'guest' directors and over other activities.[10]

The *ideological force* of this material organisation emerges in the contradiction between the economic and social constraints on women entering non-traditional roles in the theatre and the claim that, just like individual men, individual women have the opportunity to succeed.[11] As a survey conducted in England by the Conference of Women Directors and Administrators in 1984 indicates, the more conspicuous the institution, the less likely will be the presence of women in the artistic hierarchy:

> The more money, the more prestige a theatre has, the less women will be employed as directors or administrators, the less likely that a play written by a woman will be produced ... women contribute very little to the production of cultural matter ... This is in painful contrast to their majority in higher education Arts courses, in audiences and in their supporting roles in offices.[12]

Those women who do get the top job of Artistic Director (usually in the provinces or in the metropolitan periphery) do so despite the dearth of formal training for directors and in the face of the informal masculine network that stands in for such training.[13] Nowhere is this illegitimation of women's *authority* more evident than in the major institutions in London. To date, although more women are directing, no woman has been a *permanent* Artistic Director (not merely director of the occasional play) at either the National Theatre or the Royal Shakespeare Company.[14] While the rise of directors such as Deborah Warner (*Titus Andronicus*, RSC, 1988) is commendable, individual successes do not alter the structural inequities in the theatre; women on the rise (like Warner) may well adopt the aesthetic and political values of the institution rather than use their success to expand the social as well as the aesthetic range of performance in Britain beyond its habitually narrow boundaries.[15]

The marginalisation of women and the *legitimation* of that marginalisation is central to the question of subsidy. Institutions such as the National and the RSC, but also the Royal Court, are favoured according to the circular argument in which their 'stability' and hence worthiness of subsidy is allegedly demonstrated by their conspicuous buildings (themselves the *result* of selective subsidy) at the geographical and ideological centre of metropolitan culture.[16] This discrimination has historically excluded as illegitimate those groups whose performances in diverse and multi-purpose spaces are held to demonstrate their 'instability' and thus their unreliability in rising to the proper occasion of theatre. This exclusion was well apparent in the exclusion of popular entertainments in the nineteenth century from the dignifying title 'theatre',[17] and continues in present-day Britain with the underfunding of groups that perform topical, non-literary pieces in out of the way places to audiences that do not fit the hegemonic image of a general audience.[18] In other words, the *place* and *occasion* of a performance (in a national theatre or a makeshift hall, for aesthetic contemplation or for immediate recreational or educational use) contribute as much to its legitimation (addition to the repertoire of one of the subsidised theatres and publication) as its apparently autonomous literary value. The Arts Council has usually proceeded on the assumption that 'itinerant' groups provide 'dandelions for the many' and are thus *necessarily* inferior to the 'powerhouses of culture offering "roses for the few"'.[19] The material resources of the 'national' theatres, the high prices they charge, and the aura of monumental place and occasion that surrounds their metropolitan location function as an index of the aesthetic value of the plays performed there, as well as the exemplary authority of their directors, whereas the lack of resources for alternative theatres comes to represent their aesthetic inadequacy and thus the justification for withholding funding on the grounds that such activities do not rise to the *proper* occasion of theatre.[20]

Once we acknowledge the determining influence of place and occasion on the critical significance of a theatre event and on the audience's recognition in and of that event, we cannot make any obvious claims for the critical potential of drama on the sole basis of formal innovation. Such innovation may strengthen rather than challenge the theatre institution by expanding the range of 'legitimate theatre', while maintaining its boundaries with illegitimate forms of entertainment. The subsidy of individual playwrights (usually in the form of prizes for individual achievement at the expense of companies they have worked with) has the effect not only of aggravating the financial instability of such companies, but of encouraging the production of dramatic texts that lend themselves to literary legitimation. The effective function of literary legitimation does not of course entail the reductive corollary that literary drama *per se* is merely a form of some 'false consciousness', but – as the following comparative remarks on the 'acclaimed feminist playwright' Caryl Churchill and the collective Women's Theatre Group's shows for working-class teenagers suggest – it nonetheless alerts us to the ideological import of the place and occasion on which literary excellence is dis-played.

Even those innovations whose initial purpose may have been to critique the social as well as theatrical status quo can become essentially a profitable trademark. We can see this in the practice, ubiquitous in British theatre with radical claims, of adopting defamiliarisation techniques of disrupting the naturalist imitation of life and indiscriminantly calling these 'Brechtian'. Techniques such as gestic acting, direct address, songs or abrupt scene changes do not *in themselves* guarantee critical effect; on the contrary, they have become so much part of the repertoire of advertising, let alone theatre, that they no longer offer a critique of convention. Brecht himself continually qualified his formal experiments with the caveat that such experiments worked only in conjunction with a marxist analysis of the historical situation of the play and its audience, guarding against any permanent attachment to any form, epic or otherwise.[21] Identifying dramatic texts as critically feminist on the grounds that they use such techniques[22] ignores those institutional factors that determine the meaning of the event. On the one hand, the satirical tone of Caryl Churchill's *Serious Money* (1987) on the West End, applauded by those very stockbrokers the play presumes to attack, affirms the power of that audience.[23] On the other, the material of mass culture can be appropriate(d) for a specific, localised audience, as is the Women's Theatre Group's combination of popular songs with TV sitcom to reach the teenage, inner London working-class audience of *My Mother Says I Never Should*.[24] As Michèle Barrett notes, we cannot assume that an avowedly feminist work will necessarily be a feminist *event*,[25] regardless of the place and occasion of its performance.

Caryl Churchill offers us an exemplary case of the power of institutional legitimation. Although she is by no means the only female playwright to emerge in recent years, she is the most commercially successful. This renown does not necessarily make her better than other women playwrights but it does demonstrate the exemplary character of her legitimation. Unlike Sarah Daniels, whose work has also been performed at major theatres, but with a critical response divided on gender lines, Churchill has been acclaimed by mainstream and feminist press alike.[26]

Despite the range of Churchill's work, including radio drama and work written in collaboration with the socialist company Joint Stock (*Light Shining in Buckinghamshire, Fen, A Mouthful of Birds*) and her own wariness of any exclusive identification as a 'woman writer',[27] her feminist reputation is based not so much on the dense social and historical texture of class and gender *relations* in these collaborations as on the classification of a schematic and ahistorical fetishisation of gender *identity* displayed as a 'feminist' trademark (*Vinegar Tom, Cloud Nine, Top Girls*). This schematism takes extreme form in *Cloud Nine* (1979). Churchill certainly *intends* the cross-gender casting to reveal the extent to which women (and blacks) are stereotyped according to their value to white men: the Victorian *paterfamilias* is played as expected by a white man, whereas his wife is played by a man and his servant by a white. The effect of these techniques (old panto tricks and not, as fondly supposed, Brechtian innovation) is nonetheless to make the action of these characters completely predictable, and solicit the audience's assent to this spectacle, rather than criticism of gender stereotyping outside the theatre. *Cloud Nine* titillates its audience with the display of a 'concern for gender' rather than offering dramatic interaction of these concerns that might challenge us to think about them differently.

Vinegar Tom, hailed as Churchill's 'most accessible play and most straightforwardly feminist work',[28] also tends to displace critical interaction with the display of a feminist line, although in not so obvious a fashion. The play, created in collaboration with the feminist group Monstrous Regiment in 1977, asserts that all women who deviate from patriarchal norms of behaviour are subject to harassment if not terrorism; it juxtaposes the fortunes of seventeenth-century women burnt as witches for exercising sexual freedom, healing without a doctor's help, or refusing to marry, with the assertion (in interpolated songs) that women today continue to be stigmatised for being different (too intelligent or too independent of men, or merely too old for their use). Although the songs occupy relatively little dramatic space, they pull the weight of the performance away from the action. The result is not so much the desired critical distance of a Brechtian parable as the reduction of the seventeenth-century action to an allegory of present-day malaise, so that the plight of poor women or (in one case) rebellious daughters of the rich in early modern England becomes simply a foil for a denunciation of the eternal battle with patriarchy. What is lost in this reduction is not simply period detail; the historical and local specificity of the village and the differentiation of the women according to class, skills and interaction with other women as well as their struggles with men who try in various ways to subdue them gives us a sense not only of the oppression of *these* women, but of the particular social relations which maintain that oppression – not a generalised patriarchy but the social and political instability of the mid-seventeenth century, for which female witches were in large part scapegoats.[29] The songs, on the other hand, reduce this historical determination and potential for change to the claim that women are always already trapped by patriarchy. What we are left with is the static image of feminine victimisation.

In contrast, *Light Shining in Buckinghamshire* does not at first display itself as a feminist event. Nonetheless, *Light Shining* is more successful than *Vinegar Tom* in dramatising gender relations because it avoids simply targeting the fate of female victims, and instead explores gender identity within as well as against emerging class conflict. The title alludes to a Digger pamphlet published during the first English Revolution, when it seemed briefly and uniquely possible to overturn the oppressive power of religion and property along with the monarchy. The play follows several characters who have a stake in the revolution, from their anticipation of egalitarian reform to their resignation to the hierarchical social order re-established by Cromwell.

The action of *Light Shining* portrays these conflicts not in the high heroics of pitched battles, but in the struggle over the language that motivates and interprets the off-stage battles and the material sustenance that the common people fight for. We move from the Ranters' and Diggers' radical reinterpretation of the Bible and the law of the land and women's challenge to domestic hierarchy to the reinforced allegiance between the established Church and the old (feudal) and new (capitalist) landowners, reinstating the language of patrimony and inherited rule. At the centre of the play, in a long scene at the end of Act I, is a dramatisation of the historic Putney Debates on property and law, in which Cromwell and his fellow Parliamentarians usurp the rhetoric of freedom and birthright proposed by the Levellers, to reinforce the hegemony of inherited power. Their strategy makes illegitimate the very appeal to the rights of the disenfranchised and consolidates legitimate power in the hand of those who already have it, setting the precedent for conservative reaction that has dogged English reform politics to the present day.[30]

Around the legitimate authority of this event, Churchill gives us scenes in dramatic and ideological tension with the Debates, in which the common people challenge the rhetoric of inherited power. Any reading that would highlight the emancipatory potential of the characters in these scenes cannot simply extract that potential representation of social struggle, without negotiating the legitimate power of the received history against which these struggles must be defined. We ought to respect the dramaturgy of the piece that shows us disenfranchised women and men not simply as individually suffering women or men, but as gendered social agents whose concerns and affiliations may overlap as well as contradict one another. We cannot merely concentrate on those moments in which women rebel or assert themselves, without understanding what they are rebelling against and to what dramatic and historical effect.[31]

The action of the play opens within the historical constraints on women appearing in public. Before we see women who violate this norm of silent exclusion, Churchill gives us a scene in which the apparent absence of gender conflict makes it all the more palpably present. In this scene, the servant Claxton waits on the vicar, serving him food and wine, while the vicar casually offers an orange while asking after Claxton's child, who is probably dying of hunger. This scene shows us Claxton's dependence on the vicar's favours and reinforces that dependence by feminising his role; his deference prepares us for the even more cowed mien of his wife later on. Moreover, the scene establishes the image of the master eating in the servant's presence as an index of the status quo, resisting the talk of change in the dialogue. Even before we *hear* the Putney Debates put an end to real debate, we (fore)*see* the Roundheads' usurpation of the Cavaliers' hereditary power they claimed to abolish; after Lieutenant Star has recruited soldier Briggs to an army that supposedly eschews hierarchy, we watch as Briggs watches Star eating his mutton, while the latter lectures Briggs about countering the Norman antichrist with Saxon words like sheep, and, incidentally, mentioning that the army deducts soldiers' pay for food. Despite the appeal to the company of men, equal before God, in the army, Star's concluding remark that the leaders have 'God's authority' to enforce discipline reminds us of the master/servant relationship in the earlier scene and foreshadows Star's later appearance as a landowner.

These scenes point to the limits of gender (in this case masculine) solidarity across class lines, but the dramatic tension established here between the language of solidarity and the enactment of oppression echoes through the play, continually reminding us of the discrepancy between utopian democratic hopes and the real politics of authority. There are utopian moments, however, when this tension evaporates and speech and act coincide, albeit fleetingly, to enable the people to recognise themselves as agents of their own liberation. Immediately before the Putney Debates extinguish these hopes is an episode in which anonymous women challenge the authority of their absent lord and begin to recognise their potential for action. The scene shows the power and limitations of this potential:

> *First woman comes in with a broken mirror. Second woman is mending.*
> **Second Woman:** What you got there?
> **First Woman:** Look, who's that? That's you, that's you and me.
>
> (Plays, p. 207)

The shock of literal recognition moves the women not just to assert themselves, but to assert their rights against the lord's traditional means of inherited self-representation:

> **First Woman:** We're burning his papers ... That's like him burnt. There's no one over us. There's pictures of him and his grandfather and his great-great ... we pulled them down....
> There's an even bigger mirror that we didn't break. I'll show you where. You see your whole body at once. They must know what they look like all the time. And now we do.

The action progresses from a feminine stereotype – a woman admiring her spectacle in a mirror – to a growing sense of identity and empowerment. This shift is marked by the shift in pronouns in the last section from the confidential 'I/you' to the (potentially) collective 'we', but also by a tension between narcissistic self-absorption and transitive social action. The mirror displaces the aristocratic family portrait as a representation of this identity: unlike the portraits, the mirror shows the people who they really are – ordinary women – but cannot guide them from self-recognition to action.

Far from weakening the political force of this displacement, this identification of the people as *anonymous women* strengthens the resonance of the scene; by making the women anonymous, Churchill emphasises the collective nature of their action; by making them women, she asserts the legitimacy of women as the *general* subject of social change, rather than merely the subject of historical variations on the woman's question. At the same time, the scene already contains the undermining of this utopian moment in which women recognise themselves as the vanguard: these women are still in awe of the lord's presence embodied in his property. The ambiguous links between property and birthright are reinforced in the Putney Debates; even before Ireton and Cromwell condemn the Levellers' call for redistribution as incitement to loot property, the Levellers' own demands for birthright and the rights of *man* displace women once again from the (utopian) position of general political subject. By juxtaposing the dispute contained in the historical document of the Debates with the undocumented imagining of the women's initiative to burn the lord's titles of ownership, Churchill highlights the gender as well as the class inflection of the received history of this period, while entertaining no illusions about the enduring legitimacy of that history. The Putney Debates remain the gravitational centre continually pulling on attempts at resistance dramatised in the play.

While the play ultimately measures such attempts against the legitimate history, local acts of resistance fare differently depending on the characters involved. The play does not elevate any one character to the status of hero, but neither does it reduce all characters to generic speakers for an alternative history. We see the Ranter Hoskins, for example, challenging the authority of the new church that continues to forbid women to speak and we measure her challenge in relation not only to the vagrant woman Brotherton, whom Hoskins might *perhaps* (in some other drama) resemble if she didn't exercise her ability to speak, but also in relation to the slightly greater freedom available to the male servant turned Seeker Claxton as opposed to his cowed and anonymous wife, as well as – by extension – to the dominant discourse of the rulers, new and old. The affiliations and oppositions which define Hoskins's dramatic position (and that of the other characters) makes it impossible for the audience to entertain any easy schema in which a feminist or socialist or 'progressive' position can be identified and identified with. After Hoskins's challenge to the preacher: 'we are all saints ... We can all bind the king' (*Plays*, p. 200), we have the complex of allegiances in the following exchange:

> **Wife:** But what you go there for?
> **Claxton:** Just to see.
> **Wife:** Its not proper church ... Parson won't like it.
> **Claxton:** Parson needn't.
> **Wife:** I'm not going there if they beat women.
> **Claxton:** No but they let you speak.
> **Wife:** No but they beat her.
> **Claxton:** No but men.
>
> (*Plays*, p. 203)

We can see that the wife's sympathy with Hoskins as a woman is nonetheless qualified by her fear of change:

> **Wife:** What are you doing here then?
> **Hoskins:** Travelling.
> **Wife:** Are you married? Or are you on your own?
> **Claxton:** Who are you with then?
> **Hoskins:** Different men sometimes ... Who I'm with is Jesus Christ.
> **Claxton:** How do you live?
> **Hoskins:** Sometimes people give me money ... for preaching. I'm not a beggar....
> **Wife:** No one looks after you?
>
> (*Plays*, pp. 203–4)

The wife continues to speak as wife, reiterating the received Biblical justification of women punished for original sin, while Claxton and Hoskins defend their revisionist reading of Revelations which supports revolution. The scene ends with the latter two convinced of their ability to change reality through naming, while the wife reiterates her fear of speech: 'No don't speak. I can't' (p. 205).

The complex interaction of class and gender positions and their intersection in particular individuals in this scene is typical of the play as a whole. The last major scene, the Ranters' Meeting in a 'drinking place', offers an elaboration and reprise of the play's thematic focus on the relations among language, power and material sustenance (food and money). The inventive disorder and intimacy in speech and behaviour in this scene provide a sharp contrast to the Putney Debates in which the orderly return to legal terms and definitions discriminates between men on the grounds of inherited class and does not bother even to mention women. Likewise the sharing of food offers an implicit challenge to the association of food with wealth and power that the play has shown us so far. Nonetheless, the Ranters' celebration of community under a new divine and worldly dispensation occurs in the same place as a drunkard's parody of their camaraderie and the principle behind their foodsharing is muddied by echoes of the previous scene in which a butcher rails against the overconsumption of the rich in times of famine and is buried in Cobbe's celebration of cosmic defecation: 'Christ shits on the rich. Christ shits' (p. 230). The shift from a transitive attack on the rich and powerful to an intransitive discharge reverses the utopian movement in the mirror scene; the people at this meeting who were once inspired to act by words now might as well eat them, since that is all they will get.

The impacted eloquence of the Ranters in this scene is set against the weary cynicism of Briggs whose experience in 'God's army' has taught him not to expect much from prophets of the second coming. His impotence turns on himself: he ends up refusing to eat as a gesture of resistance to those who eat too much. The play ends with a return to political and religious quietism: in an odd homage to the Biblical taboo on talking women quoted by his wife, Claxton resolves: 'my greatest desire is to see and say nothing' (p. 241). The passive resistance by two men – Claxton and Briggs, speaker and soldier – conveyed in their refusal to speak or fight, reflects back at us the traditional image of women bound to silence and inaction. In this enactment, 'gender', as Joan Scott reminds us, 'is a primary way of signifying relations of power' beyond and including relationships between the sexes.[32] By ending with a sort of willed impotence, these men remind us not only of the active women in this story, but also of the degree to which empowerment for all is restricted under these conditions.

The shifting of characters' positions keeps the audience from identifying with single characters and moves us towards an understanding of the formation of character at this particular historical juncture. The juxtaposition of unnamed figures (always women), named but in fact anonymous characters (again women), with historically known men from Cromwell on the one hand, to the Levellers and Ranters on the other, works not simply to show women as the underdog and thus most worthy of our sympathy, but to dramatise the intertwining of factors that maintain as well as challenge received history. That challenge lies in the presentation of women as agents of broader social change. Instead of the comforting substitute of female (or proletarian) heroes for the members of the ruling class usually on public display, *Light Shining* offers us a history made by common people who are often out of sight.

This thematic emphasis on collective agency is sustained by the mise en scène in Joint Stock's production: even the 'major' characters were played by several actors in the course of a single performance (*Plays*, p. 184). The point of this choice is not a generalised 'struggle against male authoritarianism' in the theatre or a simple 'commonality of experience',[33] but to highlight critically the interaction of gender and class roles in social relations, first, in the play's representation of commonalities and differences of experiences of revolutionary upheaval and, second, in Joint Stock's own collaborative organisation that acknowledges the different contributions of director, writer, actor, and technical support, while involving all collaborators in workshops to thrash out the final shape of the play in performance.[34]

The power of *Light Shining in Buckinghamshire* emerges finally less in providing exemplary heroes of an alternative history that can replace the official account, than in the play's capacity to draw us in to a sustained critical engagement with the strategies – most powerfully, the creation of heroes–that legitimate the premises of that official history celebrating the visible activities of 'great men'. Joint Stock's performance sustains that engagement by challenging our customary identification with the actor as hero. What happens, however, when we locate the performance within its proper place and occasion at the Royal Court's Theatre Upstairs, venue for introducing new writers to an habitual audience for new theatre?

The Royal Court occupies an odd position in the British theatre institution. Less favoured by the Arts Council than the national 'powerhouses', it nonetheless sees its role as a 'writers' theatre', 'adding writers to the pool' from which the RSC and National choose their plays.[35] As a sort of testing ground for exemplary drama, however, the Court remains the venue for the educated metropolitan minority, which it has been since George Devine and Tony Richardson founded what they hoped would be a popular theatre.[36] More recently, the Court has certainly produced plays of a more overtly political character (than the social drama – from Osborne to Wesker – of the Devine years) and has been especially influenced by and influential in the writing and production of work by feminists, including Sarah Daniels and Louise Page as well as Caryl Churchill. As such, we might reasonably claim that the Court has provided on the *institutional* scale what *Light Shining* offers immanent to the dramatic text: a virtual or potential public sphere, within which women's talk can be legitimate speech, even though it is not (yet) honoured by institutional ratification.[37]

Nonetheless, as theatre activist and theorist John McGrath observes, the terms of legitimation – celebration of the individual talent on display for the exemplary audience – remain unchanged. McGrath, who worked as Literary Adviser at the Court during its seminal early years, recalls that its directors were interested in plays on working-class themes not because they might draw a new and radically different audience, but because they would be 'thrilling' for the habitual audience and would thus revitalise mainstream (metropolitan middle-class) theatre with new material.[38] He argues that the current practice of audience outreach (such as the Court's Young People's Theatre), however commendable, does not significantly alter the Court's institutional role of testing *works* worthy of national display, nor does its work impinge on the majority of the people [even in London] for whom 'legitimate' theatre remains foreign and who do not *automatically* have access to this occasion in this place.

The audience – the people who watch the show as well as their individual and collective reactions to it – plays a crucial role in validating certain practices as 'legitimate theatre'. More than any other activity of aesthetic reception, theatre spectatorship is inevitably *social* as well as aesthetic; the character and composition of the audience confirm or challenge the hegemony of particular forms of performance. The location of theatres in the West End or even on its periphery in Chelsea, rather than on community 'home territory' – pubs, youth clubs, women's centres – makes them more remote. On the other hand, the efforts of alternative theatres performing on this home territory may be judged by the extent to which they draw people who would normally feel out of place in a theatre.

Identifying an audience for alternative and specifically feminist theatre is a tricky business, no less than the members of that audience's own identification of themselves as audience. If feminist theatre is to be more than one more novelty option in the theatre market that usually serves the tiny educated middle-class minority,[39] it has to address the complexity of audience formation. Given the class composition of the usual theatre audience, we can solve nothing by simply repeating the isolated fact that *this* audience is more than half women. Before feminist theatre can lay claim to a critical representation of social and political relations, it has to recognise the interaction of class and gender. The simple portrayal of women on stage in roles written by a woman will not draw those women for whom theatre is the exclusive and excluding property of the minority that usually attends it.

The complexity of the social representation in theatre – on stage and in the house – resists analysis by notions of a 'female spectatorship' derived from feminist film studies.[40] Despite gestures in the direction of 'women as historical subjects', much feminist work on film tends to collapse the historical and institutional complexity of *public reception* into the more easily theorised notion of *private* spectatorship revealed in the structuring of the text itself.[41] Moreover theories of spectatorship have all too often been predicated on an inevitable separation between the female spectator and the apparently agentless 'production' of the film, in which the imperviousness of the latter becomes the justification for the theoretical location of critique solely in the former. Such theories of the spectating subject cannot conceive of critique in any terms other than the individual spectator's subversion of an already made text and provide no help in exploring the dynamic relationship between audience and performers at a theatre event whose sense exceeds any written report or pre-text, or in evaluating theatre work conceived and performed in *response* to the needs and tastes of a specific, even localised audience.

A critical exploration of the complex and sometimes contradictory affiliations and differences in an audience should lead us to examine the choices of theatrical means to address that audience. The relentless *literariness* of most subsidised, but also much alternative, theatre excludes audiences accustomed to TV, panto and (even now) music hall, rather than the faithful representation of dramatic literature.[42] Although we should not of course ignore literary dramatic texts, we would do well to look at them in the context of a whole range of performance options not directly derived from the *canon* (established or emergent). While an alternative theatre with popular aspirations might not want simply to adopt the predictable forms and situations of TV along with its familiarity and intimacy, or the parochial and sometimes racist and sexist elements in panto and music hall along with their vitality, variety and direct engagement with a popular audience, those groups succeed best that engage their audience with a combination of the new and the familiar, so as to then surprise them with critical theatre.[43]

The Women's Theatre Group, a collectively run group of women producers and performers, have taken the needs and tastes of their actual and prospective audiences as their point of reference in both form and content of their work. Instead of merely calling for more respect for women's work, the WTG's activity demonstrates the capabilities of women to run the show as well as star in it, while their portrayal of daily concerns for specific and localised audiences on their home ground avoids glamorising the theatre event while maintaining its entertainment.[44] Although, in recent years, WTG has performed commissioned literary pieces, such as Deborah Levy's allegorical peace play *Pax*, partly in response to the Thatcher government's hostility to projects that challenge too overtly the aesthetic as well as the political status quo, their most characteristic work has been on shows devoted to everyday subjects of interest to women, such as *My Mother Says I Never Should* (1974–5) (on teenagers and the double standard in sex education) and *Timepieces* (1982–3) (a montage of scenes dramatising in the history of the women in one family, the links and tensions between the suffrage movement and the struggle for socialism).

This direct and local appeal is clear in the WTG's first show for schools, *My Mother Says I Never Should*, produced part-time with only a project grant (as opposed to a full company subsidy). The play, which portrays the conflicting social pressures and inducements facing teenage girls who confront the double standard in sexual mores, was performed for teenage audiences and their parents and teachers, by informal arrangements only later ratified by the Inner London Education Authority. Since their concern is thus to *represent* the members of the audience to themselves rather than to create an independent work of art, WTG combined forms familiar to their audiences from TV (sit-com and family drama) and panto (songs to traditional tunes sung directly to the audience) with functional staging and *use* of songs to challenge the audience:

> The way in which we wrote was affected both by the content of the play and the proposed audience; there was a wariness of experimental, 'art'

> theatre and stark agitprop forms, because we felt that the most effective
> way of making sense to an audience whose principal theatrical experi-
> ence had been mediated by television was to use a conventional TV style
> with a story and lots of laughs.   (*Strike*, p. 115)[45]

At the same time, WTG recognised the ambiguity of audience
identification with characters or their actions:

> Because of the importance of this identification we paid meticulous
> attention to styles of clothing and speech... There are however contra-
> dictions in trying to engage an audience through ... identification: there
> is always a danger that attitudes which are presented in order to be criti-
> cised can actually be reinforced ... for example, the girls' tremendous
> concern with their appearance could be construed as behaviour we
> found acceptable.   (p. 116)

WTG defends this decision on the grounds that *dramatising* the
contradictions and virtues in common attitudes to and of women
and in conventional ways of portraying those attitudes on TV is
finally more effective than simply offering unequivocally positive
role models of feminists, whose very independence from a 'culture
of femininity' might simply contradict the girls' experience without
engaging critically with it.[46]

Rather than presenting each character as merely the representative of a unified position on sex (education), *My Mother Says* shows
the two teenagers in a variety of social situations that make different demands on their allegiances. After they introduce themselves
directly to the audience, we have a scene that shows their shared interests (most immediately, in an upcoming party) as well as their
differences:

> Wendy: Last week I put banana on my face ..., just like it said in
>   *Petticoat*...
> Terri: You believe everything you read... I think it's stupid, every-
>   one trying to look the same.
> Wendy: Yes, but people look at you funny if you're not wearing
>   the right thing and no fella would want to be seen with you.
> Diane: Yes, she's right, you know; look at you, love, always in
>   trousers. Men don't like that ...
>   (p. 122)

Instead of an endorsement of Wendy's desire for sex and the social
acceptance of girlfriendhood or Terri's relative indifference to this
identification, we have the dramatic rendering of their respective attitudes. While the subsequent action focuses primarily on the girls,

their lives are not isolated and glamorised, but emerge always in interaction with others: their parents, their teachers, a (woman) doctor, as well as their peers. In addition to the arguments over appropriate behaviour for girls, the play shows us the way this behaviour is influenced by class expectations as well. The dialogue, while spare and functional, is flexible enough to be matched more precisely to any particular performance occasion.

The feminism in the play lies not in any proffered solutions, but in encouraging young women to 'see themselves as agents capable of making choices about their lives' (p. 115). The ending, in particular, juxtaposes rather than resolves the divergent views of several women on the subject of women's sexual and social roles. We move directly, but not abruptly, from the discussion with the doctor to the final statements:

> Doctor: I try to help them make choices ... after all, a girl must make decisions about her own life.
> Mum: I don't know how to tell you, Terri ...
> Diane: The more you do it, the better it gets.
> Terri: Don't seem fair ... She's got all the worry, he doesn't even know ...
> Mum: He married me didn't he? ...
> Singer: We've been talking to you about choices
> 'Cause some day we'll think you'll find:
> If you don't control your body,
> Someone's gonna screw your mind.
>
> (p. 141)

While WTG clearly does take a stand, the agit-prop note of the song complements rather than supersedes the polyphony of voices.

The feminism in the *event* emerges not simply in the play, but in the way in which the performance works. While the scenes themselves were performed naturalistically, the performers sat with the spectators when not on stage. This encourages identification with the dramatised as well as the social situation, without falling for any simple 'imitation of life'. The matter-of-fact, *disposable* character of the text suits the occasion of the performance; it allows the teenage audience to recognise themselves in the action, while at the same time showing them how WTG (and they) might change the action. To call the text disposable in this context does not disparage it in any way. On the contrary, *My Mother Says* is disposable in that it makes timely issues *available* and *accessible* in performance and in that the flexible form of the play makes possible local adjustments to particular audiences and enhances rather than undermines the directness and effectiveness of its entertainment.

The significance of the larger event depends on the audience's response, in the straightforward sense of their enthusiastic (or sceptical) comments on the performance, as well as their acknowledgment of the story as their own *and* as the occasion for public representation. This articulation of local story and public sphere is both vital and contentious. We can see this articulation not only in the support of the targeted audience – working-class girls, their parents, and teachers – but also in requests for performance from boys. The ILEA Health Inspector's praise for the play: 'Excellent ... Covered all the issues. I wonder if your next play could be about teeth' (p. 117) reinforces the performance's accession to a legitimate place and occasion in the public sphere, by hailing the *normality* of its subject. Subsequent complaints that the play 'incite[d] underage *children* [emphasis added] to break the law'[47] demonstrate that legitimation even as they contest it.

The circumstances of this particular performance may well seem remote in Conservative Britain, even though the tenor of the above complaint (four years after the play's first performance) aptly heralds Margaret Thatcher's explicit endorsement of a 'return to Victorian family values'. Since the early 1980s, the Arts Council has moved away from a European model of regular subsidies for companies towards procedures more common in the US, such as grants for individual projects, each of which must solicit funds separately, or favouring more established groups who can first gain stability through private funds and commercial sponsorship.[48] This focus on the tried and tested jeopardises the production of new dramatic work of all kinds, but especially threatens the survival of theatre critical of the status quo.[49] Furthermore, the Conservatives' attacks on local government – from the abolition of the (Labour) Greater London Council (1986) to the imminent dissolution of educational authorities such as ILEA – have limited the place and occasion for a counter public sphere.

Participants at a recent 'Theatre in Crisis' conference, including playwrights such as Churchill and Deborah Levy, directors such as Pam Brighton and John McGrath, as well as the former National Theatre Director, Peter Hall, stressed the degree to which the current 'authoritarian climate' tends to favour profitable commodities in the metropolis rather than critical diversity in various communities, and pointed to the value of *informal* local support and

engagement in the absence of 'democratically organised' structures.[50] As central support for such alternative representation continues to dwindle, we should remember that *My Mother Says* was
produced part-time by a mixture of amateur and professional
women and reached a substantial audience in schools and youth
clubs even before being endorsed, filmed, and circulated by ILEA.
Their example not only shows the particular value of an informal
community of women but also reminds us that critical theatre in the
community contesting the official line can, if necessary, operate
without long-term subsidy, and remains testimony to the potential
of local initiatives.

Although, at first glance, the historical theme and literary language of *Light Shining* seems to set it apart from the everyday,
disposable, text of *My Mother Says*, the plays are alike in challenging the domestication of women's speech. At the same time,
both performances refuse an easy reversal of this marginalisation
either by introducing female protagonists in the public arena or by
celebrating domestic space as more appropriate terrain. Instead,
they delineate specific and local contexts in which women and
men conduct their lives and the ways in which affiliations to communities by gender, class, and age (among others) shape those
lives and tentatively articulate what Raymond Williams called a
'politics of place' that challenges any simple opposition of public
and private, general and special interests.[51] Without promising
women (protagonists or audience) an illusory identification with
stage personas, these theatre events offer a 'place from which to
speak' in which women can be at home in public.[52] Acknowledging the 'conceptual [and dramatic] dissonance' between traditionally silent femininity and the traditionally masculine property
of public speech,[53] they attempt to heal the breach with a performance of that dissonance, which simultaneously occupies and
creates a public sphere, a legitimate place and occasion, for
women's speech. Feminist theatre worthy of the name rearticu-
lates the feminist slogan 'the personal is the political' to avoid the
all too common corollary 'the political is [only] the personal' and
to show us that only the representation of interaction in both
spheres can engender critical theatre.

From *Theatre Journal*, 42:1 (March 1990), 27–47.

NOTES

[This piece argues for attention to the marginalisation of women in the economics and institutions of theatre, and for critical attention to the insufficiency and thinness of some feminist uses of Brechtian techniques. It includes substantial discussions of Churchill's plays, of the Women's Theatre Group and of audience in general for feminist theatre. The article has been revised by the author for this volume. Ed.]

1. Helene Keyssar, *Feminist Theatre* (London, 1982), p. xi.

2. See *Feminism, Culture, Politics,* ed. Sonia Ruehl (London, 1982); *Feminist Studies/Critical Studies,* ed. Teresa de Lauretis (Madison, 1986); Cora Kaplan, *Sea Changes: Culture and Feminism* (London, 1982); *Feminism and Social Change,* ed. Judith Newton and Deborah Rosenfelt (New York, 1985). Despite her relentless dissection of the patriarchal repertoire and performance morphology that make up the fabric of Western theatre history, in *Feminism and Theatre* (New York, 1988), Sue-Ellen Case tends to *isolate* the representation of women from the dramatic fabric of the work. Exceptions to this tendency have come from British work in dialogue (though not necessarily in agreement) with the socialist tradition: see Michelene Wandor, *Carry on Understudies* (London, 1986) and Catherine Itzin's account of alternative theatre in Britain, as yet unsurpassed for its information and critical analysis: *Stages in the Revolution* (London, 1980).

3. Mary Remnant, Editor's Introduction to the most recent (sixth) volume of *Plays by Women* (London, 1987), p. 9.

4. This discourse may well be 'radical in its discussion of gender' but it is 'implicitly conservative in its assumptions about social hierarchy and female subjectivity'. (Cora Kaplan, 'Pandora's Box: Subjectivity, Class and Sexuality', *Sea Changes: Society, Feminism, Culture* [London, 1983], p. 148.) Criticism that claims to establish an alternative feminist pantheon presumes that a sort of individualistic pluralism – the accumulation of individual female successes to match the male – is the best mode of feminist reform, and largely ignores the fact that hegemonic institutions can tolerate a fair amount of token women without undergoing fundamental structural transformation (as the current percentage of plays by women staged professionally in Britain – a mere 7% – implies).

5. As Michelene Wandor remarks in her Editor's Introduction to the first volume of *Plays by Women* (London, 1982), p. 10, these apparent polar opposite roles both turn on persistent and contradictory demands on women to make spectacles of themselves and be ashamed of that display, effectively locking women out of activities such as directing or technical management that do not depend on the economy of display and retreat.

6. Sue-Ellen Case, *Feminism and Theatre*, p. 131.

7. Legitimation is the means by which the practices or habits of an institution or (representatives of) a class become hegemonic, that is, take
on the force of *natural* law. I use the term *masculinist* rather than patriarchal to emphasise the following key point. The institution of
theatre, like other cultural, educational or commercial institutions,
depends on capitalist, heterosexist social relations but does not maintain legitimacy solely by patriarchal means. As historian Joan Scott
shows, in 'Gender: a Useful Concept for Historical Analysis',
American Historical Review, 91:5 (1986), 1053–75, analyses of
society and culture that assert patriarchy as primary oppression tend
to operate 'internally to the gender system' and thus cannot show '*how*
gender affects those areas of life apparently outside it' (1057–8).

8. See Kruger, *The National Stage: Theatre and Cultural Legitimation in
England, France and America* (Chicago, 1992), pp. 3–29, for a critical
account of the factors contributing to the legitimation of theatre practices in Western Europe.

9. Harley Granville-Barker, who, together with the dramatist and translator William Archer, drafted the celebrated *Schemes and Estimates for
a National Theatre* (London, 1908), recognised early on that a
National, i.e. subsidised theatre, would have to accommodate itself to
market pressures. See also Kruger, '"Our National House": The
Ideology of the National Theatre of Great Britain', *Theatre Journal*,
39:1 (1987), 42–5.

10. For evidence of such consequences of the Director's power in the
National Theatre, see John Elsom and Nicholas Tomalin, *A History of
the National Theatre* (London, 1978); Robert Hutchison, *The Politics
of the Arts Council* (London, 1982); Itzin, *Stages in the Revolution*.

11. The power of this masculinist order of things extends to the point
where women in clerical and service jobs become equally invisible to
women and men in management. See Liane Aukin, 'Insider', in
Women in Theatre: Calling the Shots, ed. Sue Todd (London, 1984),
pp. 108–16.

12. See Sue Dunderdale's report on the Conference of Women Directors
and Administrators in Britain, *Drama*, 152 (1984), 9–11.

13. Pam Brighton (Artistic Director for the Half Moon in the East End of
London, 1975–6), 'Directions', in *Calling the Shots*, pp. 47–61; Clare
Venables, 'The Woman Director in the Theatre', *Theatre Quarterly*,
38 (1980), 3–8; Wandor, *Carry on Understudies*, pp. 108–13.

14. The first woman to direct a major production at the National was
Nancy Meckler, who directed *Who's Afraid of Virginia Woolf?* in
1981. The 1988/89 season at the National included no women directors at all. Since Buzz Goodbody, who was on the RSC staff in the

early 1970s, no woman has been on the RSC permanent staff (a more accurate measurement of artistic control of the company than directing the occasional play).

15. See 'Life and Death are the Actors on her Stage', interview with Deborah Warner by Joan Dupont, *New York Times*, 23 April 1989, in which Warner dismisses drama on contemporary social themes for not being having the 'depth' of the classics, and evinces an interest in Brecht that is almost purely formal.

16. This discrimination in favour of the theatrical establishment on the grounds that any funds 'wasted' on lesser known groups might trigger a 'blackout' in the 'powerhouses of culture' (Arts Council, *A Brighter Prospect* [17th Annual Report of the Arts Council] 1961–2, p. 14) has persisted despite the Council's Charter to bring culture to people and places hitherto neglected. For critical views, see Hutchison, *Arts Council*, pp. 60–96; Itzin, *Stages*, pp. 244–6; Sandy Craig, 'The Bitten Hand: Patronage and the Alternative Theatre', in *Dreams and Deconstructions: Alternative Theatre in Britain*, ed. Sandy Craig (London, 1980).

17. Michael Booth, *Prefaces to Nineteenth Century Theatre* (University of Manchester Press, 1980).

18. For detailed evidence of the Arts Council's selective support for high culture for the few at the cost of outreach and community response, see Hutchison, *Politics of the Arts Council*. For critical accounts of the political, cultural, and gender economy of alternative (or what I have called 'itinerant' as opposed to fixed) theatre seeking out new audiences, see Itzin, *Stages*; Sandy Craig (ed.), *Dreams and Deconstructions*; and Wandor, *Carry on Understudies*. Also John McGrath, *A Good Night Out. Popular Theatre: Audience, Class and Form* (London, 1983); Steve Gooch, *All Together Now: An Alternative View of Theatre and the Community* (London, 1984).

19. Roy Shaw (Secretary General), Introduction to the 34th Annual Report of the Arts Council of Great Britain, 1978–9, pp. 6–7. Even after five years of Labour rule and the policy of Culture Minister Hugh Jenkins of supporting outreach and access over 'excellence', the Arts Council relied on the tastes and prejudices of its (overwhelmingly) public school appointees, not the 'advisory' Drama panel. Since the Conservatives returned to power in 1979, Arts Council power has been more concentrated than ever. See 'Theatre in Thatcher's Britain: Organising the Opposition', *New Theatre Quarterly*, 18 (1988), 113–23.

20. For a critical analysis of the ideological power of the National Theatre's monumental hegemony, see Kruger, *The National Stage*, pp. 83–131; for an indication of the consequences of this policy of 'selective excellence', see Itzin, *Stages*, pp. 156–60.

21. We can see this stress on *effectiveness* rather than mere *effect* through-
    out Brecht's work, from his early polemic on the 'Funktionswechsel
    des Theaters' (the change of theatre's function in society, *Gesammelte
    Werke*, 15, 1967, 220), to his mature reflections on a dialectical
    theatre no longer wedded to 'epic techniques' for their own sake
    (*Gesammelte Werke*, 16, 1967, 924), from his notes that explicitly
    define *Verfremdung not* as 'alienation' (*Entfremdung*) but as a critical
    return from alienation (*Gesammelte Werke*, 15, 1967, 360) to his
    gloss on the political force of critique as 'in die Krise bringen'
    (*Gesammelte Werke*, 20, 1967, 153). Post-war British theatre, relying
    on excerpted translations of the *theatre writings* (most of the aesthetic
    and political writing is still not available in English) has tended to
    adopt the techniques without regard to Brecht's caveat. For a critical
    account of his influence in Britain, see *Bertolt Brecht in Britain*, ed.
    Nicholas Jacob and Patricia Ohlsen (London, 1977); for theoretical
    reflections of the politics and problems of representation in Brecht, see
    Marc Silberman, 'The Politics of Representation: Brecht and the
    Media', *Theatre Journal*, 39, 4 (1987), 448–60.

22. See Janelle Reinelt, 'Beyond Brecht: Britain's New Feminist Drama',
    Theatre Journal, 38:2 (1986), 154–63, and Elin Diamond, '(In) Visible
    Bodies in Churchill's Theatre', *Theatre Journal*, 40:2 (1988), 188–204.
    Both Reinelt and Diamond seem oddly compelled to hang otherwise
    cogent readings of the plays on abstract and ahistorical icons such as
    'Brechtian alienation (sic)', 'Brechtian devices', etc. This formulation
    does considerable damage on two fronts: (1) it obliterates the complex
    interaction of Brecht's critical *attitude* and *intentions* with methods at-
    tributed to Brecht, but also present in popular entertainment as well as
    early political theatre in Britain before the 'official arrival' of the
    Berliner Ensemble in 1956; (2) the emphasis on extractable Brechtian
    forms short-circuits analysis of the institutional and ideological *varia-
    tion* in the 'ideology of representation' for which no definitive tech-
    niques are always already available.

23. For a particularly trenchant critique of *Serious Money* as a 'bourgeois
    comedy of manners' borrowing the 'rhetoric of political plays', see
    Pam Brighton's comments at the symposium on 'Theatre in Thatcher's
    Britain', 121.

24. We cannot dismiss techniques just because they are often accompanied
    in Brecht's work by notions of political activism defined by the image
    of masculine workers on the job and *simply* return to our 'own' terri-
    tory. In her sometimes abruptly symptomatic reading of the gender
    bias in post-war British drama, *Look Back in Gender* (London, 1987)
    Michelene Wandor claims that feminist theatre suffers from too much
    Brecht and would do better to pay attention to proper women's issues
    such as the home and childcare. Although this focus on feminist poli-
    tics in the domestic arena in explicit opposition to the dominant as-

sumption that politics is always in the streets or on the job is in part justified, it tends to reinforce the ideology that puts women back in homes where they are *not* 'on their own territory', but financially and emotionally dependent on men. (See Michèle Barrett on the ideology of the 'family', in *Women's Oppression Today* [London, 1980], pp. 187–206.) In this light, I find it difficult to reconcile Wandor's nostalgia for the private shelter of the hearth with the evidently and *necessarily* public character of the theatre event.

25. Michèle Barrett, 'Feminism and Cultural Politics', in *Feminism, Culture, Politics*, p. 57.

26. For a critical assessment of the reviews of Daniel's work, see Mary Remnant's introduction to *Plays by Women*, pp. 9–11 and Sarah Daniel's comments on the hostility of the 'fraternity of critics', in 'There are fifty-two percent of us', *Drama*, 152 (1984), 23–5. For Churchill's status, see the editorial introduction to 'The Common Imagination and the Individual Voice', Interview with Caryl Churchill by Geraldine Cousin, *New Theatre Quarterly*, 13 (1988), 3. Until 1990, Churchill was the only woman playwright to graduate from the publication of single plays to Methuen's *Plays* series (devoted to those playwrights whose 'works' as a whole are deemed worthy of publication). Only since 1990 have Sarah Daniels and Louise Page joined the ranks.

27. See Interview with Itzin in *Stages*, p. 279, and 'The Common Imagination', p. 5.

28. Keyssar, *Feminist Theatre*, p. 91.

29. Churchill, 'Vinegar Tom: Notes on the Production', *Plays One* (London, 1986), p. 130 (hereafter *Plays*). For a more complex and no less indicting treatment of similar themes, see Sarah Daniels, *Byrthrite* (London, 1986) (first performed at the Royal Court Upstairs).

30. See Perry Anderson, in 'Figures of Descent', *New Left Review*, 161 (Jan.–Feb. 1987), 20–77.

31. An exclusive focus on the women in the play (see Keyssar, *Feminist Theatre*, pp. 87–90) threatens to erase the historical *and* dramatic situations that define their options. Far from elevating the women to something like 'equal status', this approach *reduces* their struggle by isolating their 'heroic' action from the complexity of social relations. Significantly, those feminist critics looking for individual role models in Churchill's plays have little to say about this play. We have to turn to an account of alternative political theatre in Britain whose agenda is not feminist in an exclusive sense, Catherine Itzin's *Stages in the Revolution*, pp. 223–5, 283–4, to find an account of this play and its performance by Joint Stock, that enables the full evaluation of its critical (socialist and feminist) potential at *all* levels of theatre production.

32. Scott, 'Gender', 1067.

33. Keyssar, *Feminist Theatre*, p. 90.

34. For a more detailed account of Joint Stock's working methods see Itzin, *Stages*, pp. 220–7; for Caryl Churchill's retrospective comments, see 'The Common Imagination', 5–8 (note 26 above).

35. In interview, *New Theatre Quarterly*, 2 (1985), the artistic director of the Court, Max Stafford-Clark (who directed Joint Stock until 1979) notes that, while the Court does receive more than any other theatre company after the NT and the RSC from the Arts Council of Great Britain, it receives nothing from the boroughs of Chelsea and Kensington and therefore receives less total subsidy than those London theatres in more sympathetic boroughs.

36. For a detailed account of the Court as 'writers'' theatre from its inception in 1956, see Terry Browne, *Playwrights' Theatre* (London, 1975). As Browne notes, the Court operated within the terms of the West End box office. At no time did the theatre actively seek out a popular audience. 'Popularising good theatre' continues to mean 'flooding the West End' with it (p. 101). Even in the Gaskill years, this meant balancing new and risky material with revivals of early successes and Shakespeare (see Philip Roberts, *The Royal Court Theatre, 1965–72* (London, 1976). Gaskill himself grants that, even during its most risky venture, the Court remained tied to a West End economy and West End audiences. See William Gaskill, *A Sense of Direction: Life at the Royal Court* (London, 1988), esp. pp. 62, 129–34.

37. Neither the *locus classicus* of the term 'public sphere' or 'publicness', Jürgen Habermas's *Structural Transformation of the Public Sphere*, trans. Thomas Burger (Cambridge, MA, 1989) as a liberal bourgeois space of public opinion formed by private individuals, nor its extension by Oskar Negt and Alexandar Kluge in *Public Sphere and Experience*, trans. Peter Labanyi (Minneapolis, 1993), which proposes a separate proletarian public sphere, has much to say on the masculinist *engendering* of the legitimate public sphere. Nancy Fraser's critique of Habermas, 'What's Critical about Critical Theory? The Case of Habermas and Gender', *New German Critique*, 34 (1986), 97–130, demonstrates the conceptual and practical interpenetration of private and public spheres in 'feminine' activities such as childrearing, and women's uneasy occupation of citizenship, which retains a masculine inflection. Kluge's and Negt's formulation has the advantage of positing experience rather than the institutions of political representation as the condition of publicness; their argument provides a way of conceiving of the experience of apparently unrepresented people such as the women in *Light Shining*, as a potential public sphere.

38. John McGrath, *A Good Night Out*, pp. 10–15.

39. See Dunderdale and Daniels. Also Kenneth Tynan, 'Notes on the National Theatre', in his *A View of the English Stage* (London, 1975), p. 377.

40. The *locus classicus* of this concept, Laura Mulvey's 'Visual Pleasure and Narrative Cinema' (1975) in *Movies and Methods*, ed. Bill Nichols (Berkeley, CA, 1985), vol. 2, 304–15, is also the locus of its absence; Mulvey's argument turns on the definition of female spectatorship in terms of male options: vicarious identification with the male gaze or masochistic identification with the object of that gaze. Despite an afterthought on the (undefined) value of 'popular cinema's alternative story-telling', in *Framework: a Film Journal*, 15/16/ 17 (1981), 13, Mulvey's call for avant-garde subversion of this libidinal economy is based on a phenomenological conception of spectatorship constructed by the text, without recourse to the cultural, economic, institutional dimension of that construction. For a rigorous analysis of these dimensions of cinematic spectatorship, see Miriam Hansen, *Babel to Babylon: Spectatorship in American Silent Cinema* (Cambridge, MA, 1991).

41. Teresa de Lauretis, *Alice Doesn't: Feminism, Semiotics, Cinema* (Bloomington, IN, 1984), pp. 5, 39, 136, and Christine Gledhill, 'Developments in Feminist Film Criticism', in *Re-vision: Essays in Feminist Film Criticism*, American Film Institute Monograph Series, vol. III (Frederick, MD, 1984), pp. 33, 35, point out a hiatus between the feminine position constructed by language (and film) and women produced by historical and social forces, but stop short of theorising the latter. Annette Kuhn, in 'Women's Genres', *Screen*, 25:1 (1984), 25–6, offers a cogent critique of this problem: neither a notion of the spectator as a subject position, nor quantitative surveys of actual audiences can make up for an adequate theory of *audience*. Joan Scott, in 'Gender', esp. pp. 1061–75, provides a more systematic theoretical analysis of the limitations of this 'fixation on the question of the subject', that allows for the conceptualisation of history only as something outside and somehow separate from the subject. For a sense of the range of practices and concepts contained by the term 'female spectatorship', see *Camera Obscura*, 20–21 (1989) (special issue on spectatorship).

42. See Women's Theatre Group's introductory comments to *My Mother Says I Never Should*, in *Strike While the Iron is Hot*, ed. Michelene Wandor (London, 1980), pp. 115–17; McGrath, *A Good Night Out*, pp. 27–60.

43. In other words, alternative theatre must tread the line between critical response to its popular audience and what John McGrath calls 'tailism': sentimental concessions to all aspects of the tastes of working-class people, on the grounds that they are 'authentic', without regard to the sometimes uncritical mix of vernacular and mass culture

in what can be called popular. See McGrath, *A Good Night Out*, pp. 59–60; Raymond Williams, *Culture* (London, 1983), p. 228.

44. Itzin, *Stages*, p. 230.

45. Page numbers refer to *My Mother Says I Never Should*, in *Strike While the Iron is Hot*.

46. I take this phrase from Angela McRobbie, 'Working Class Girls and the Culture of Femininity', *Women Take Issue*, ed. Women's Studies Group, Birmingham Centre for Contemporary Cultural Studies (London, 1978), pp. 96–108: the girls' fierce defence of a 'feminine' space defined by their interest in fashion, 'boys', and marriage is a real, if contradictory, response to the limits of their aspirations. Attempts, such as those by feminist teachers, or by feminist performers, to present alternatives, must take account of this subculture.

47. Anonymous letter from a London teacher to the *Evening Standard*, 10 December 1978. Quoted by Itzin, *Stages*, pp. 228–9.

48. The Arts Council Annual Reports from 1979 to the present demonstrate this shift as well as a growing reliance on corporate sponsorship, which tends to go towards already conspicuous institutions rather than emerging groups. See especially the Chairman's and Secretary General's comments in the 1986/87 reports.

49. The number of new plays is down to a third of the figure of a decade ago, and the Arts Council's new 'appraisal teams' make direct political manipulation of funds much more efficient than the 'arms's length policy' of the Labour years. See 'Theatre and Thatcher's Britain', 116–17, and 'Theatre in Crisis: Conference Report', *New Theatre Quarterly*, 19 (1989), 210–16.

50. 'Theatre in Crisis', 213. Also note the remarks of Peter Holland on community sponsorship, Bev Randall and Phyllida Shaw on theatre with and for Black women in Brixton (p. 212), as well as John McGrath's comments on Scotland, where local and regional institutions offer the arts more support and less interference than in England (see 'Theatre in Thatcher's Britain', 123).

51. This concern with the theory and practice of critical community informs all of Williams's work but emerges most forcefully in his last essays, especially 'The Importance of Community', and 'Decentrism and the Politics of Place', in *Resources of Hope* (London, 1988). For an exploration of these issues and their implications for performance, see Kruger, 'Placing the Occasion: Raymond Williams and Performing Culture', in *Views Beyond the Border Country: Essays on Raymond Williams* (London and New York, 1992), pp. 55–71.

52. In their reading of Minnie Bruce Pratt's autobiographical narrative 'Identity: Blood, Skin, Heart', in 'Feminist Politics: What's home got to

do with it?' *Feminist Studies/Critical Studies*, Biddy Martin and Chandra Mohanty call 'home' 'a secure place from which to speak' (p. 206), challenging the separation of private experience and public politics that persists in feminist and socialist discourse.

53. Although Fraser does not connect her remarks in 'What's Critical about Critical Theory?' on the 'conceptual dissonance between femininity and the dialogue capacities central to [the] conception of citizenship' (p. 116) to theatre, her remarks nonetheless illuminate the way in which the institution of symbolic public speech that is the theatre makes the very thought of equal access to public speech illegitimate.

4

Frame-Up: Feminism, Psychoanalysis, Theatre

BARBARA FREEDMAN

> In the dark I orient myself in a familiar room when I can seize on a single object whose position I can remember. Here obviously nothing helps me except the capacity of determining positions by a subjective ground of distinction. For I do not see the objects whose position I should find, and if someone had played a joke on me by putting on the left what was previously on the right while still preserving their relationships to each other, I could not find my way in a room with otherwise indistinguishably equal walls. But I soon orient myself through the mere feeling of a difference between my left and right sides.
>
> (Kant, *Critique of Practical Reason*)

I

Was it always so difficult to orient oneself, to place oneself, to choose sides, to step into a frame? Consider the scene of *The Taming of the Shrew*. A woman surveys the scene. A page, dressed up as a woman, surveys the scene. A boy, dressed up as a page, dressed up as a woman, surveys the theatre of which s/he is a part. The character beside him lusts for him. It is, we are told, his part. And so, and yet, 'we' lust for the page/woman, the page of woman, the scripted woman. We entertain the sexual longing, enjoy the masquerade of femininity, deny our own construction within this carnivalesque version of aristocratic/sexist/sadistic theatre which gazes at itself and fondles its own power relations. And as we watch

78

these characters watching these plays within plays located some-
where within the always elusive boundaries of *The Taming of the
Shrew*, as we sit silently in the protective darkness and fulfil our
role as sanctioned voyeurs, our gaze always returns to that enig-
matic construction of a construction otherwise known as Sly's
'madam wife'. Is s/he not a part of the play s/he observes, since it
concludes at the same time as the spectacle in which s/he appears as
audience, in which we appear as audience, erasing distinctions
between play and reality? And yet is not this ambiguous goddess –
both audience and character, male and female, servant and mistress
– who reigns over this labyrinthine theatre the true guardian of
Shrew and its enshrined shrew, the comptroller of the cultural law
of difference and the protector of that animal within its confines
who remains unconquered?

How uncanny a figure s/he is, calling to mind both how easily we
are fooled and how quickly we deny the differences that we know.
It is certain that at some level gender uncertainty is engaged by this
figure, much as it was when we first disavowed, after having perceived, genital difference. Freud would read in this page proof of
the male subject's perception of the little girl as castrated, and so of
the woman as always already a man in drag – the little girl as a
little man.[1] We may read altogether differently, and find in this
character the character of sexual difference itself, a surplus as well
as a lack. The guardian of the 'truth' of sexuality – which is always
withheld because always an imposture – the page flirtatiously,
fraudulently suggests consummation and tantalises with the fiction
of difference. Inasmuch as we all mistake, misrecognise sexual identity, we are all, like Sly, taken in by the play. Yet the drama of the
page is the drama of language itself, which suggests not only the
masquerade that is femininity, but the inevitability of the law of
form, the mediation of sexuality by cultural representation, and the
power of language to inscribe the raw energy of the drives.

Is the relation of the sexes the quintessential *trompe l'oeil*? Most
of us are familiar with the story Lacan tells of the engendering of
the subject through language: a little boy and little girl are seated in
a train facing each other and so see opposing sides of the station
which they are approaching. '"Look", says the brother, "we're at
Ladies!"; "Idiot!" replies his sister, "Can't you see we're at
Gentlemen".' As Lacan observes: 'For these children, Ladies and
Gentlemen will be henceforth two countries towards which each of
their souls will strive on divergent wings, and between which a

truce will be the more impossible since they are actually the same country and neither can compromise on its own superiority without detracting from the glory of the other.'[2] Lacan here suggests how language and sexual difference are intertwined; perhaps less important than the misdirection of these little souls is the arbitrary identification of these bodily egos and so the misdirection of their libidinal energies, yet another form of *méconnaissance*. Lacan draws two identical doors with the words 'ladies' and 'gentlemen' written under them to remind us that the signifier does not 'stand for' the thing, but only makes sense in relationship to another signifier. Similarly, male and female, regardless of biological differences, are products of a linguistic signifying system, so that male is necessarily 'not female' and female 'not male'. As Jacqueline Rose observes: 'In Lacan's account, sexual identity operates as a law – it is something enjoined on the subject. For him, the fact that individuals must line up according to an opposition (having or not having the phallus) makes that clear.' [3]

As identity demands the fiction of closure, so sexual identity requires a fiction which, however fostered by biology or in its service, is essentially linguistic, ideological, and fetishistic. At issue is the representation of sexuality – the way in which libidinal energy is parcelled up and channelled through socially appropriate bodily zones. For Lacan, the assumption of a sexual identity is accompanied by the sacrifice of free libidinal energy necessitated by signification itself, which demands that we be one thing and not another. What Lacan refers to as 'castration' is the loss in sexuality resulting from the inevitable mediation of desire by signification. The problem, Rose observes, is that we have 'failed to see that the concept of the phallus in Freud's account of human sexuality was part of his awareness of the problematic, if not impossible, nature of sexual identity itself' as a result of which we 'lost sight of Freud's sense that sexual difference is constructed at a price and that it involves subjection to a law which exceeds any natural or biological division. The concept of the phallus stands for that subjection, and for the way in which women are very precisely implicated in its process.' [4] Yet another problem, however, is the price we pay for subjection to a discourse which enframes us; how are feminists who pass on a discourse of the phallus implicated in this process, and framed in turn?

My question regards the implacability of the law of place and frame; the potential of theatre for revisioning it and/or the complic-

ity of theatre in this frame-up. Given feminist rethinkings of narrative – particularly psychoanalytic narratives – and feminist review-
ings of cinema, especially as seen through a Lacanian lens [5] – we
come at last to the question of how theatre figures difference. At
issue is the problem of the frame and framing behaviour as intrinsic
to theatre, the extent to which theatre is always already determined
by the frames it puts onstage, and the extent to which theatre provides a means for reframing. Given the longstanding debt of psychoanalysis to classical drama and the centrality of the Oedipus to
both disciplines, is a feminist, anoedipal theatre possible, or possibly a contradiction in terms? Given the phallocentric vocabulary of
contemporary psychoanalytic theory, is feminist theory which
employs Lacan not framed in turn? In question is the potential of
feminism, psychoanalysis, and theatre to reflect and effect change –
to insert a difference in our construction of the subject and so to
make a difference.

Let us break the field with a quotation that by misunderstanding
nonetheless gets us to the root of the problem. Jane Gallop writes:
'This problem of dealing with difference without constituting an
opposition may just be what feminism is all about (might even be
what psychoanalysis is about). Difference produces great anxiety.
Polarisation, which is a *theatrical* representation of difference,
tames and binds that anxiety. The classic example is sexual difference which is represented as a polar opposition (active-passive,
energy-matter). All polar oppositions share the trait of taming the
anxiety that specific differences provoke '[6] (italics added).

Gallop succinctly assesses the shared goals of feminism, psychoanalysis, and deconstruction in the postmodernist enterprise, in so
far as all are similarly predicated upon subverting the figuration of
difference as binary opposition. Structuralism and semiotics, the
twin harbingers and now culprits of postmodernist theory, process
experiences into polar oppositions which offer an Illusion of
Alternatives – nature/culture, passive/active, male/female – rather
than a continuum of differences. The deciding gesture for the avant-
garde theorist remains Derrida's critique of the metaphysical basis
of the division of the sign into signifier and signified, form and
content, writing and speech, representation and presence, as well as
his critique of the transcendental signified or *sujet supposé savoir* –
whether Man, God, or History – who stands outside them and
guarantees their stability. The problem here is not only the pretence
that the signified is somehow immune from commutability, from

being transformed into another signifier, but the way in which such oppositions depend as well on a subject who conceives or perceives of these differences while standing somehow outside them. Further, this organisation of experience is not only ideologically coerced but coercive, in so far as it tames and binds a larger field of differences through repressive and repressing tactics, and in turn privileges and procures one term at the expense of the other, be it Male versus female or Consciousness versus the unconscious. Deconstructive techniques function to unsteady if not dismantle such oppositions, and the revival of feminist and psychoanalytic theory owes much to their success.

What surprises in Gallop's formulation is her use of the word 'theatrical'. Why is polarisation 'a *theatrical* representation of difference'? Whereas the relationship of ideology and genre is hardly Gallop's subject here, the identification of theatre with a defensive, ideologically complicit ordering of difference constitutes a serious challenge to those for whom theatre offers an epistemological model or mode of inquiry. Is theatre the guarantor of polarities – part and parcel of the 'great semiological myth of the versus' – or, as Barthes contends, designed to subvert them?[7] Is deconstruction theatre's enemy or its double? Is a feminist theatre possible, or possibly a contradiction in terms?

Those in search of the poor monster, dramatic theatre, will discover it miming the role of the scapegoat for Western humanism in a new-fangled postmodern morality play. Accused and found guilty as a machine of the state and an enemy of the people, drama is charged with the job of carrying away the fourfold sins of phallocentrism, humanism, individualism, and representation along with its demise. In this contest of the avant-garde with itself on the field of representation, theatre has indeed been hoist on its own petard.[8] Long derided as one of the last bastions of humanism in literary studies, one of the few free zones where character, plot, and even presence itself could travel undisturbed, unsuspected, and unsuspecting, theatre is only now in the process of saving itself by denying itself. Travelling incognito as Performance, denying any relation to the tradition of *dramatic* theatre upon which it preys, theatre, now *sous rature*, has become avant-garde. Aristotle is changed for Artaud, *Hamlet* for *Screens*. It would seem that such theatre, even *sous rature*, is going to have difficulty making a comeback.

Postmodernist attacks on traditional dramatic theatre are not wholly unfounded at this point in the Western cultural revolution.

As with our political party system and our gender system, tradi-tional Western theatre offers us only two stages, comic and tragic, upon which are always playing some version of *Oedipus* or its sister play, *The Taming of the Shrew*. A set-up is therefore always being staged as well – one that places its spectators in the position of Kate, Oedipus, and one Christopher Sly, all of whom 'cannot choose' but accept the interpellation or hailing that indoctrinates the subject into a confusing and limiting identity, a *méconnaissance*, a delusion.

If traditional Western theatre rests upon and remains obsessed with the Oedipus – the scene of a founding crime of sexuality and a payment which decisively orders sexuality and gender, *Shrew* rewrites that scenario for women. To participate in *Shrew* is to identify the achievement of civilisation itself with the domination of women through patriarchal exogamy rites, physical violence, and doublebinding mind games. If we conflate the complementary myths of *Oedipus* and *Shrew*, we have the tragedy of the man who discovers his sexuality and the woman who learns to disavow her own in the very apprehension of a repressive patriarchal law. One scenario identifies civilisation with male payment for his own sexu-ality, the other identifies it with male control over disordered female sexuality. Both not only record but promulgate the values of a re-pressive patriarchal culture.

Tragedy and comedy alike therefore champion what Freudians and Lacanians like to think of as civilisation-as- 'castration' – a phallo-centric concept which equates the organisation of human sexuality and gender with the birth of language and repression, and so with a psychic displacing-as-ordering which alienates the subject even as it guarantees it a place in the symbolic order. Whereas cinema is associ-ated with the pre-Oedipal look, and the desire to see oneself seeing, theatre replaces the desiring eye with the blinded eye g(l)azed over. Theatre is an Oedipal affair, the scene of the cut or wound, of the crown that burns its wearer. Theatre enacts the costs of assuming the displacing image returned back by society – the mask which alienates as it procures entry into society. In short, theatrical looking assumes a gaze which is a looking back, if not a staring down.

The Oedipal narrative – which places incestuous desire in the context of a communal law which condemns it – offered Freud a locus for his theories of childhood sexuality and male castration anxiety. In the so-called Oedipal period, the male child's fantasies of being with the mother sexually are accompanied by fears of castration for such desires. These fears signify the internalisation of social taboos, whether we term the effect superego development or the ordering and repression of sexuality. When *Twelfth Night*'s 'I would have you be', is replaced by the motto, 'that that is, is', we see how comedy as well as tragedy promotes the interpretation of identity as destiny.

As a psychoanalyst and teacher of Freudian theory, Lacan's reading of human psychic development also relies heavily upon traditional narratives of Western drama, and so is coloured by the same sense of transcendent law or necessity which limits its potential for envisioning change. Lacan's primary interest is in the splitting and so procuring of the subject in language as it impinges on human psychic functioning. This leads him to be as interested in the instability of sexual identity as ego identity, and to see both as a function as division and repression, of the ordering fictions by means of which the ego as supplement gets set into place. Lacanian theory has proven especially useful for describing how masculinity depends upon woman as both the castrated Other and as externalised lack. And this model of woman as lack constituted the basis of the early analyses by feminist theorists of traditional phallocentric narrative and cinema.

The most influential feminist analyses of cinema and narrative have been set forth by Laura Mulvey and Teresa de Lauretis, both of whom expose the way in which the pleasure of these genres depends upon and in turn develops coercive identifications with a position of male antagonism toward women. In so far as theatre incorporates many of the scopic and narrative pleasures as cinema, these formulations – however limited – also apply to theatre, and yet may also help to clarify the differences between the ways in which theatre and cinema stage difference. Since the male is traditionally envisioned as the bearer of the gaze, the woman represented as the fetishised object of the gaze (Mulvey), the gaze itself emerges as a site of sexual difference. The classic cinematic gaze splits us into male (voyeur) and female (exhibitionist). Seeing, according to this staging of the cinematic apparatus, is always already a matter of sexual difference. In so far as classic theatre incorporates not only spectacle but narrative – so that the male is represented as a mobile agent as well as a bearer of the gaze, the female as the object to be actively transformed by him – action as well as sight has implications for the study of gender ideology. Not only pleasure but plot is derived from male fantasies which depend on the scopic and narrative exploitation of woman;

she is the linchpin in the system whose losses propel the relay of looks and whose sins move the plot forward. In question, then, is the reliance of theatrical desire on the fetishised spectacle of woman and the narrative of her domination and punishment. Can we ever escape *The Taming of the Shrew*?

The join of feminism and cinema has clearly proved productive for the critique of traditional cinema and the construction of avant-grade films alike. Yet whereas cinema can challenge or deconstruct the symbolic by dissolving or dispersing the image, traditional theatre is necessarily more tied to the Symbolic – to the ego, the image, the unitary individual. Whereas theatre questions the validity of masks by virtue of their ability to be exchanged, it cannot dissolve or otherwise destroy them. As Shakespearean comedy reminds us, master and servant, husband and wife may exchange roles but never escape the tyranny of roles themselves – which is, after all, simply a function of the gaze, of being and so being seen in society. Theatrical narratives appear to promote the very ideology of difference they expose as arbitrary – in so far as their reliance on roles based on ego-identifications prevents it from moving outside of itself. If poetry exposes the limits of language, and cinema of the image, theatre exposes both along with the those of the ego at play in the gaze.

Traditional drama therefore mimes socialisation, juxtaposing the deconstruction of the gaze against the inevitability of a theatre of representation, the Imaginary as alterity against the Symbolic of Oedipally inscribed inevitability. Its narrative form denies or contains the core theatrical impulse which displaces or fragments the ego (as in the middle of most Shakespearean comedies), offering stability in the form of provisional closure. Given traditional theatre superimposition of narrative inevitability, given its scopic regime of voyeurism and exhibitionism, and given its narrative regime of domination and mastery – all of which combine to expose traditional theatre as a taming of the gaze by the symbolic order, is a feminist deconstructive theatre possible?

Gallop would seem to be right about the fact that theatre works through polarities – as long as we replace the word 'theatre' with the term 'Western narrative drama'. As Keir Elam reminds us, 'theatre' is customarily associated with the performance aspects of a work, and 'drama' with its traditional narrative form.[9] Classic drama generates identity and difference through the agon – the mirror image whereby person and persona, body and ego as supplement, confront one another and exchange places. Kate and Petruchio,

Pentheus and Dionysus may fight for the same role, but difference is generated and complementary polar oppositions are reaffirmed as examples of 'right relationship', whether of man to God (*Oedipus*), or man to woman (*Shrew*). The agon may confuse gender and social roles, or reveal their arbitrary basis, but it cannot let go of the masks – of ego, gender, or class – even as it points to the masquerade.

Given the reliance of theatrical narratives on the discovery of identity or place in relation to others, on various forms of the socialisation process, the task of rethinking theatre may indeed require an Oedipus Wrecked. Yet a feminist theatre need not deny the limits of language, the place of images, the tyranny of gazes and roles, or the misrecognitions and displacements that attend them, as it goes about the work of reviewing them. A feminist theatre may well require that feminists share in the assumption of errors and misrecognitions associated by Lacan with the phallus alone (which explains why Lacan's attempts to subvert phallocentrism by reversing terms of value have failed). A feminist theatre may require, more precisely, that we reformulate the implications of the Lacanian gaze and the disruptive maternal gaze for feminist theory and practice in theatre and film.

This frame-up, then, is a challenge which means to expose the paradox that constitutes the theoretical standstill in feminism, psychoanalysis, and theatre studies alike. It is meant to expose the use of feminism by the avant-garde to stage itself, to invigorate its age-old rethinking of representation. It is meant to expose the way in which paradoxes and *en abyme* structures contain and entrap change, whether in *The Taming of the Shrew* or the taming of the gaze that is deconstructive philosophy. It is meant to ask what it means when Derrida writes, 'it is not impossible that desire for a sexuality without number can still protect us, like a dream, from an implacable destiny which immures everything for life in the figure 2'.[10] If self-reflexivity and theatricality are intermeshed in postmodern theory, this is not, I would argue, because theatre is the place of the *abyme*, but rather of the interruption of the *abyme* by a gaze within which explodes its container.

II

Both feminism and psychoanalysis face the central question of how to intervene in the cultural reproduction of sexual difference without always already being entangled in it – a problem posed not only by a play like *The Taming of the Shrew* but repeated in the writing on *Shrew*; not only by feminist and psychoanalytic theory but within the theories themselves. What feminism and psycho-analysis share is the goal of reconstructing subjectivity from the disruptive perspective of the unconscious and sexuality, language and ideology, so that it never rests stable or secure. Each discipline acknowledges the primacy of the signifying dependence of the subject on the Other, and is committed to developing ways of re-visioning the subject in relationship to the Other's gaze. Yet that very paradigm has also stymied productive feminist reformulations of subjectivity, in so far as 'safe' descriptions of a phallocentric order have taken the place of prescriptions for change.

The play of the constitutive gaze in postmodern theory usually registers as a witty paradox rather than the trap of ideology containing and preventing change. The bind of the constitutive gaze has surfaced most notably in Julia Kristeva's descriptions of the problem of how to convey on the side of language and representation the experience outside of it.[11] Assuming that women have been excluded from the scene of representation – how to place that experience in representation? The constitutive gaze is characteristic of cinema in that it stages the desire to see oneself seeing oneself that never gets outside itself.

If psychoanalysis and feminism similarly expose the arbitrary and divisive construction of subject positions, both are similarly constrained precisely by that which they would change. Contemporary psychoanalytic theory offers an example, inasmuch as feminists who employ Lacanian methodology are in turn framed by a discourse of castration and phallic signifiers which they may well not seek to reproduce. Apropos here is Jane Gallop's assertion that if 'the penis is what men have and women do not; the phallus is the attribute of power which neither men nor women have. But as long as the attribute of power is a phallus which refers to and can be confused . . .with a penis, this confusion will support a structure in which it seems reasonable that men have power and women do not. And as long as psychoanalysts maintain the separability of "phallus" from "penis", they can hold on to their "phallus" in the belief that their discourse has no relation to sexual inequality, no relation to politics.'[12]

Those who read Lacan closely answer that his phallocentric discourse is intentionally reflective of the problems he sought to portray. Moreover, they remind us that the specific configurations of the Symbolic are indeed open to change in the Lacanian schema. As Ellie Ragland-Sullivan observes: 'We must remember that the Symbolic here does not mean anything representative of a second hidden thing or essence. Rather it refers to that order whose principal function is to mediate between the Imaginary order and the Real. The Symbolic order interprets, symbolises, articulates, and universalises both the experiential and the concrete which, paradoxically, it has already shaped contextually.'[13] Yet Lacan's Symbolic was developed in the context of a specific historical period of intellectual thought, one heavily influenced by structural anthropology. As Louis Althusser protests, 'It is not enough to know that the Western family is patriarchic and exogamic ... we must also work out the ideological formations that govern paternity, maternity, conjugality, and child-hood.'[14] In so far as Lacan's writings ignore the material and his-torical nature of social organisation and social change, they betray a disturbing complacency toward structuralist and phallocentric ver-sions of a transcendent law, whether in the form of the phallic signifier, the law of the father, or the law of the symbolic order.

Lacan's Symbolic is heavily dependent upon Lévi-Strauss's account of the origin of our myth of difference in incest taboos, taboos which function to transform a state of 'nature' into one of 'culture': 'The prime role of culture is to ensure the group's existence as a group, and consequently, in this domain as in all others, to replace chance by organisation. The prohibition of incest is a certain form, and even highly varied forms, of intervention. But it is intervention over and above anything else; even more exactly it is *the* intervention.'[15] As an exogamy rule, the incest taboo functions to establish a system of social relationships. It replaces the taboo of intrafamilial marriage with interfamilial marriage, and so sets up social roles and values. Of crucial interest here are the mythic and ideological aspects of Lacan's Symbolic Order, since it fails to explain the practice it de-scribes, repeating the very difference it purports to explain. Observes Jacqueline Rose: 'Lacan's use of the symbolic ... is open to the same objections as Lévi-Strauss' account in that it presupposes the subordi-nation which it is intended to explain. Thus while at first glance these remarks ... seem most critical of the order described, they are in another sense complicit with that order.'[16]

Lacan's symbolic must be understood both in the context of the structural anthropology upon which it drew and the object relations theory against which it defined itself. 'Taking the experience of psychoanalysis in its development over sixty years', observes Lacan expansively, 'it comes as no surprise to note that whereas the first outcome of its origins was a conception of the castration complex based on paternal repression, it has progressively directed its interests towards the frustrations coming from the mother, not that such a distortion has shed any light on the complex.'[17] Lacan perceived the direction of object relations theory at the time as involved in a domestication of Freud's insights, in particular as involved in replacing the fundamental role of the unconscious, sexuality, and representation in psychoanalysis with the study of the quality of actual maternal care. To stress the importance of his intervention, Lacan introduced a third term, the name of the father, as an interruption of the asocial mother–infant dyad that brings to bear upon it the law of language and symbolic positions.

The context of Lacan's social role in this drama of psychoanalysis cannot be erased from the theory. Since the popularity of the project of rereading Freud is as much due to the Derridean reading of a Freud implicated in his own readings as to a Lacanian rereading of Freud's works, the reading of a Lacan implicated in his own theory of the gaze should not be surprising. We now acknowledge, for example, a Freud who represses the idea of repression, who wishes away threats to his theory of wish fulfilment, who refuses to give up the search for primal scenes which he elsewhere acknowledges exist only at the level of fantasied reconstruction, and who denies the bisexuality and gender instability he elsewhere theorises with conviction. That Lacan could recognise gender ideology at work in his portrayal of the mothering function as asocial – whether in his narrative of maturation as dependent upon the Freudian male's resolution of the castration complex in the Oedipal phase, or in his equation of the (symbolic) phallus with that which alone ensures civilisation – does not make his manipulation of that ideology more palatable. If the law of the father and the phallus is designed to expose place and position as fraudulent, rather than referring to any actual or fantasied father or phallus, the problem is that Lacan is in fact championing an equally irreversible place for his theory of displacement couched in the terms of a phallocentric discourse. And that very discourse reframes mother–infant relations as somehow always already outside language and representation. Lacan's dramatisation of psychoanalytic history, in which the son figure (Lacan) rescues the dead father's authority (Freud) to intervene and save him from the mother's tyranny (object relations theory) is nonetheless open to reframing. Can we similarly reappropriate the gaze to take into account the way in which the mother's 'no' functions as a displacing gaze and so displaces in advance the father as the privileged level of representation?

Like Petruchio, and like Freud, Lacan's work on gender is self-consciously paradoxical. At one level, he acknowledges the imposture of any cultural configuration of sexual difference posing as either natural or divine. At the same time, he regards such imposture as inevitable, as the comic theatre of misrecognitions in which we necessarily exist. Like Petruchio, Lacan articulates the feminist dilemma in terms of the impossibility of breaking the mirror of ideology, yet exemplifies in his 'corrected' misogyny the problem of being a part of the problem he would describe. He argues that woman does not exist except as a fantasy or theatrical construct, yet reifies a cultural myth of the exchange of women as the basis of civilisation. Lacan equates a particular configuration of social power with the symbolic order, universalises the Oedipal law, and identifies the paternal metaphor as the privileged level of representation itself, the inevitable third term that must intervene between mother and child, Oberon-like, to bring 'nature' to a state of 'culture'.

Following Roy Schafer's analysis of psychoanalytic narratives, Teresa de Lauretis identifies the frame here: 'while psychoanalysis recognises the inherent bisexuality of the subject, for whom femininity and masculinity are not qualities or attributes but positions in the symbolic processes of (self)-representation, psychoanalysis is itself caught up in "the ideological assignations of discourse", the structures of representation, narrative, vision, and meaning it seeks to analyse, reveal, or bring to light.'[18] If Lacan was the analyst most aware of this problem, by necessity he was also implicated by it. Juliet Flower MacCannell rightly warns us of 'the tendency . . . to over-identify Lacan's analysis of the culture of the signifier . . . with his own stance *on* that culture', noting that 'just as the physician may be said to be apart from the disease s/he discovers, even if s/he has been constrained by it, Lacan's analysis of the systems formed by the signifier, metaphor, the phallus, stand apart from his own "system"'.[19] The paradox in reading Lacan derives from the play of playfulness in his style – for he as well as his most ardent supporters acknowledge his partiality and biases, but none can decisively fix the level at which they operate. Even Jacqueline Rose admits: 'There is, therefore, no question of denying here that Lacan was implicated in the phallocentrism he described, just as his own utterance constantly rejoins the mastery which he sought to under-mine.'[20] We need to acknowledge both how Lacan played upon and with his own phallocentrism, and how that pleasure has its costs in a discourse which cannot be reproduced.

'In the psyche, there is nothing by which the subject may situate himself as a male or female being', asserts Lacan valiantly.[21] The very sentence is a marvellous example of what Lacan is talking about – how language directs biology, subverting the sexual drive into an identificatory one precisely by such manoeuvres as interpel-lating the female reader as 'he', 'him', and 'man'. Yet in so far as we are not newly enlightened sexist males of the 1930s coyly pointing to the way in which our discourse places and displaces the subject, how can feminist theory support a vocabulary of phallic signifiers?

Teresa de Lauretis rightly critiques Lacanian theory for the way in which its descriptive features all too easily become prescriptive: 'in opposing the truth of the unconscious to the illusion of an always already false consciousness, the general critical discourse based on Lacanian psychoanalysis subscribes too easily ... to the territorial distinction between subjective and social modes of pro-duction and the cold war that is its issue.'[22] More concerned with misrecognition as sites for change, de Lauretis suggests we redirect attention to the dialectical relationship between the means by which signs are produced and the codes themselves, so that we see meaning as a cultural production 'not only susceptible of ideologi-cal transformation, but materially based in historical change'.[23]

Feminist theory has itself been caught up in the double bind of the constitutive gaze. Given the increasing centralisation of a group previously defined by exclusion from and oppression by the sym-bolic order, how is that group to redefine itself without destroying itself? Should it celebrate the scorned values with which it has been identified, abandon those values for those of the ruling class, or challenge the entire structure by which it has been defined, replac-ing it with a more inclusive sense of difference? As Ann Rosalind Jones reminds us, any celebration of the feminine is problematic in that it assumes an essential feminine to be celebrated, so that 'theor-ies of féminité remain fixated within the metaphysical and psycho-analytic frameworks they attempt to dislodge'.[24] Luce Irigaray and Hélène Cixous would have us reverse the negative value assigned to woman, locating her specificity in multilevelled libidinal energy, in a feminine unconscious shaped by female bodily drives which make their way in the style of feminist writings.[25] Yet Monique Wittig blames néoféminité's universalising tendencies for making a fetish of the bar of difference, and so keeping us locked in an oppositional gender structure. Wittig demands that we 'dissociate "women" (the class within which we fight) and "woman", the myth. For "woman" . . . is only an imaginary formation, while "women" is the product of a social relationship,'[26] a group identity capable of effecting change. Yet even Wittig's political theatre, like much political theatre, is accused of various sins, among them denying a gaze that would disrupt its own. Can feminism be associated with action which effects change, assumes the image of woman and yet simultaneously disrupts any fixed image? The paradoxes of Kristeva's system, from which feminism cannot seem to escape, are very much at issue.

Could it be that feminism has (mis)appropriated the Lacanian gaze, offering readings of traditional drama and film that are incapable of interrogating their Oedipal basis, and the Oedipal basis of the symbolic? Could it be that feminism and psychoanalysis have been trapped by a constitutive gaze, by a paradox of the frame and the gaze which binds change in repetition and repression, in theories of *trompe l'oeil* and *dompte regarde*, in *mise en abyme* structures which ring hollow? Could it be that there is a radical aspect of theatre, what we might refer to as 'theatricality' or 'performance', as opposed to narrative drama, that is characterised by a disruptive gaze that never rests secure?

Against the *en abyme* paradoxes of cinema and deconstructive philosophy we may place the disruptive potential of the theatrical gaze, which is always ambivalent, always displacing one view and threatened by another in turn. The gaze disrupts *not* from the point of view of the paternal as representation, but from the point of view of a prior maternal gaze. The maternal gaze introduces the infant into the social order since it does not simply offer the infant a stable, cohesive image, but one that changes, that is not always as the infant would have it be, that reacts to the infant's gaze and reflects it differently. Like the mirror stage, the maternal gaze cannot logically be ascribed to a period prior to or outside of representation and the symbolic order. The idea of the contained breaking out of its container, of a deferred disruption always already contained within the mother–infant dyad, yields a maternal disruptive gaze characteristic of theatre, a gaze capable not only of staging theory, but of shifting and displacing its sites of inquiry, its places of desire. Theatre provides a way of interrupting this self-contained and containing gaze from a point of view both within and outside it, much as the unconscious is the blind spot of our vision which in turn is constructed through and reflected by the gaze of the Other. In so far as recent feminist performance art poses a challenge to traditional dramatic theatre by foregrounding a subversive force always already within it, and in so far as drama is itself always replaying the battle of presence and representation which occasions it, we must return theatre to its function as a disruptive and displacing gaze.

III

All of which returns us to the question with which we began: Is traditional theatre bound to certain representational models which prevent revisioning its construction of the subject? Since film theory has long ago addressed the limits of the avant-garde exploitation of feminism, a rehearsal of its debates may prove useful here. The problem of a feminist refiguring of representation has been nicely staged in the interaction between Constance Penley and Peter Gidal on feminism and the avant-garde as framed by Stephen Heath. First Penley: 'If filmic practice, like the fetishistic ritual, is an inscription of the look on the body of the mother, we must now begin to consider the possibilities and consequences of the mother returning the look.' Gidal replies: 'The last words of your piece say it all. You search for the simple inversion, the *mother looking back*. I consider the possibilities of the not-mother, not-father (looking or not).' Heath joins Gidal: 'To invert, the mother returning the look, is not radically to transform, is to return to the same economy (and cinema in the fiction film has always to transform, is to return to the same economy (and cinema in the fiction film has always and exactly been concerned to consider the possibilities and consequences within the fetishistic ritual, including the *constitutive* threat of its endangerment, the play of eye and look, vision and lack): the difference inverted is also the difference maintained.'[27]

The subtext in this game of two against one is a doubling of its content – the problem of woman. Since the cinematic look is read by these male theorists as constituted by a threat of the lack in woman (i.e. her castration), she had better not look back, nor, by implication, should Penley. Gidal's impulse is cinematic; he wants to dissolve, destroy images of women. (Is it not more avant-garde simply to delete women from films rather than to present her response to her reflection?) Penley's response is a looking back that looks forward. Her impulse is theatrical – she wants to reverse the look, which entails a rethinking of the limits of the cinematic apparatus, in so far as cinema posits the Absent One – the place of the camera – in the place of the Other as returned gaze in theatre.

Especially disturbing here is the argument that the cinematic look is constituted by a threat of its endangerment which is specifically associated with women's castration – a move which indicates how the Lacanian gaze has been reread through Freudian castration schemas to figure difference in film theory. The Freudian theory of castration explains how the human animal assumes its sexuality in a given social order: in a deferred reading of his (first?) sight of his mother's genitalia, the subject-as-little-boy interprets her 'lack' in terms of the threat of the father's punitive, castrating 'no' made good. In other words, he associates his mother's 'actual' castration with his potential castration. That Lacan rereads this scenario symbolically does not, finally, save it for feminist theory. It harms in that it keeps this sexist construction alive and maintains an association of the look with a negative view of woman and her sexuality. The theory is made no more palatable by the argument that, in so far as we are all lacking, woman is even more aware of her incomplete status.

In its stead we might consider the development of gender as identificatory and rooted in the problem of the gaze. The disruptive gaze would derive gender from an interruption of the male's primary feminism, developed in identification with the female as mothering person. Whereas the female subject resolves the mother's 'no' by moving from *being* the mother's desire to *imitating* the mother's desire, the male in our society is not free to resolve the maternal 'no' in this way. Given that the infant cannot always be what the mother wants, nor the mother what the infant wants, given that mothering involves helping the child come to trust in the return of a nurturing other who can leave and disappoint, the development of a way of coping with the mother's 'no' is especially pressing for the male. Deprived of the shift toward mimetic desire left open to the female, the male's route can only be a rapid disidentification, resulting in ambivalence toward the nurturing object.

This stance has its precursors in feminist applications of object relations theory. Feminist psychoanalytic theory, in particular the work of Nancy Chodorow, interprets some male behaviour as resulting from denied identification with the nurturing or mothering figure.[28] Object relations theory has long suggested that the mothering function is not accomplished by simply drawing the child into an illusion of magical omnipotence but in helping the child accept separateness and disillusion through various 'no's'.[29] The disruptive maternal gaze is a gaze which reflects back to the child something other than what it wants to see, but which alone makes identity possible. This in turn suggests an interesting reversal; the greater repression is not of the mother's castration (what the child doesn't want to see), but of the subject's loss of face (what the mother doesn't want to see or can't see in the child). The reading which denies this argues that the father's intervention (and not the mother's 'no') alone ensures the masculinity that the subject desired all along. The repression of the mother's crucial role in the social-isation process is denied.

A more theatrical paradigm would enable women not only to reflect how they perceive they have been perceived, but to look back and forward, to see how their looking back is interpreted and dis-rupted by another gaze in a continuing theatre of interactive reflec-tions. Lacanian theory has decisively and intentionally limited the potential of the mother's 'no' in a variety of ways, then, and cine-matic theory's use of the gaze has in turn been reduced to nothing short of male castration anxiety. However successful the applica-tion of a phallocentric theory for a reading of phallocentric films, such a model stymies the development of film theory and practice in new directions, resulting in such peculiar avant-garde stances as Gidal's refusal to portray woman in his films *since* she is always already the castrated fetishised object.

The difference inverted is not always the difference maintained. To reframe Heath and Gidal via Penley is to point to her place and the mother's place both within and outside the system, and to observe that neither can be so neatly circumscribed. Since neither Heath nor Gidal proves capable of considering the 'possibilities and consequences' of the mother returning the look, except as a reversal of the terms of the male look, which in itself is castrating, they project that threat onto Penley. Asks Heath: 'What then of the look for the woman, of woman subjects in seeing? The reply given by psychoanalysis is from the phallus. If the woman looks, the specta-cle provokes, castration is in the air, the Medusa's head is not far off; thus, she must not look, is absorbed herself on the side of the seen, seeing herself seeing herself, Lacan's femininity.'[30] If Heath would distance himself here, his framing of Penley implies that cas-tration is indeed in the air – that male fears of a reversal of their own system are being projected onto a rethinking of representation which begins on the other side of the screen.

The difference inverted is not always the difference maintained. The reply given by psychoanalysis is not always from the phallus. Penley asks about the possibilities of returning the look because she realises that no reversal of the look in the same terms is possible – except when the Woman as a construct of the male Imaginary is doing the looking, in which case she does not look from the point of view of *women*. Since Penley, following Laura Mulvey, is critiquing film practice as voyeuristic and fetishistic, her question asks for the development of new ways of looking – in essence the reconstruction of the woman's gaze. The mother's body is not simply a character in a film returning a look, but at once the material out of which a spectacle is constructed, the spectacle itself, and the means by which a spectator is constructed. To return the look in this context is to break up performance space, deconstruct the gaze, subvert the classical organisation of showing and seeing, revision spectatorship, and restructure traditional canons, genres, and personal-political identities.

One argument that stalls this movement is summarised by Stephen Heath when he asks whether it is 'possible for a woman to take place in a film without representing a male desire', since 'any image of a woman in a film, by the fact of its engagement in a process of representation ... inevitably re-encloses women in a structure of cultural oppression that functions precisely by the currency of "images of woman".'[31] He quotes Cixous, who observed: 'One is always in representation, and when a woman is asked to take place in this representation, she is, of course, asked to represent man's desire.' Yet Heath ignores the key word 'asked'; when women are not asked by men to take place in a representation created by and for men, but occupy and share the sites of production and consumption, a different economy obtains. Women take place, and refigure that taking place, in ways that challenge traditional forms of representation and gratify, as they displace, the spectatorial gaze.

Penley cites the films of Yvonne Rainer, Chantal Ackerman, and Marguerite Duras, which 'run counter to the Oedipal structuring of Western narrative form and the imaginary and fetishistic imperatives of the cinematic apparatus', effecting changes in 'narrative organisation, point of view and identification' which resituate 'both the spectator and the narrator as "outside" the scene ... not caught up in or radically circumscribed by a masculine gaze or logic of desire.'[32] Yet to what extent does this approach lead to a feminism that has so succumbed to its manipulation by an avant-garde as to be virtually indistinguishable from it, more concerned with revisioning representation than with exploring contemporary women's experiences?

One of the more challenging directions of avant-garde film has been its interest in fragmenting its representational space in the name of a feminist critique. As Jacqueline Rose observes:

> the impetus is clear: the attempt to place woman somewhere *else*, outside the forms of representation through which she is endlessly constituted as image. The problem is that this sets up notions of drive, rhythmic pulsing, eroticisation of energy pre-representation, a space of 'open viewing', which then makes film process itself socially – and sexually – innocent. Film process is then conceived as something archaic, a lost or repressed content ('continent'), terms to which the feminine can so easily be assimilated, as it has been in classical forms of discourse on the feminine as outside language, rationality, and so on; arguments which are now being revived as part of the discussion of psychoanalysis and feminism, the search for a feminine discourse, specific, outside. The dangers are obvious. That such arguments overlook the archaic connotations of these notions of energy and rhythm for women, at the same time that they render innocent the objects and processes of representation which they introject onto the screen, seems again to be not by chance.[33]

In a critique of Lyotard's exploration of a non-theatrical representational space, Rose pointedly remarks: 'We have to ask what, if the object itself is removed (the body or victim), is or could be such a space of open viewing (fetishisation of the look itself or of its panic and confusion)? And what does this do for feminism? Other than strictly nothing, dropping all images of women; or else an archaising of the feminine as panic and confusion, which is equally problematic, simply a re-introjection as feminine – the pre-mirror girl – of the visual disturbance against which the image of woman classically acts as a guarantee.'[34] It would seem that theatre, via performance, is facing many of the same problems.

IV

Is it a coincidence that definitions of feminism, theatre, Lacanian psychoanalysis, and deconstruction are becoming practically indistinguishable? All define themselves as displacing activities designed to resist the suturing coherence of any fixed place. Julia Kristeva argues that 'the very dichotomy man/woman as an opposition between two rival entities may be understood as belonging to metaphysics'[35] and offers instead a pulsion between the semiotic (pre-oedipal, pre-linguistic energy and desire) and the symbolic (made possible by the semiotic which in turn is repressed for its establishment). To work from the semiotic is to to adopt 'a negative function; reject everything finite, definite, structured, loaded with meaning, in the existing state of society'. It is to work 'on the side of the explosion of social codes, with revolutionary movements'.[36] Like Kristeva, Shoshana Felman defines femininity as a 'real otherness ... [which] is uncanny in that it is not the opposite of masculinity but that which subverts the very opposition of masculinity and feminity'.[37] Avant-garde feminism's answer, then, is that woman, like theatre, does not take (a) place (Kristeva), but rather, revisions positionality itself.[38] In what sense does a feminism so defined differ from deconstruction? Or from theatre, which manages both to acknowledge the symbolic and disrupt it from within, to acknowledge and subvert positionality on a continuous basis?

Josette Féral, one of the few theoreticians to explore feminist deconstructive theatre, assumes both are possible – but only when theatre is not theatre *per se*.[39] For Féral, theatre is on the side of inscription in the symbolic, whereas performance is on the side of deconstruction in the semiotic (thus Féral's 'theatre' corresponds to Elam's 'drama', and her 'performance' corresponds to Elam's 'theatre').[40] Féral finds theatre and performance 'mutually exclusive' 'when it comes to the problem of the subject', since 'in contrast to performance, theatre cannot keep from setting up, stating, constructing points of view' and depends on a unified subject which performance deconstructs into drives and energies, since theatre assumes and depends on the narrativity and models of representation which performance rejects in favour of discontinuity and spillage.[41] If performance highlights the 'realities of the imaginary', 'originates within the subject and allows his flow of desire to speak', the theatrical 'inscribes the subject in the law and in theatrical codes, which is to say, in the symbolic'.[42]

Yet finally Féral is describing a dialectic essential to theatre, not apart from it, which she herself acknowledges by arguing that 'theatricality arises from the play between these two realities', and by describing performance as that within theatre which deconstructs it.[43] Féral observes that 'in its stripped-down workings, its exploration of the body, and its joining of time and space, performance gives us a kind of theatricality in slow motion, the kind we find at work in today's theatre. Performance explores the under-side of that theatre.'[44]

The relationship between performance art and traditional theatre is less a polar opposition than a continuum. We seek in theatre that moment when our looking is no longer a looking (as in film), but a being seen, a return of the look by the mirror image which denies the process. Whereas traditional drama achieves this by setting into motion a series of displacing gazes which succeeds when it disrupts our own gaze without showing us how, performance art puts theatrical construction itself onstage. In *Swan Lake, Minnesota* a stripper performs to a fascinated crowd of men by throwing down cardboard cutouts of her body in various states of undress; the last cutout is a mirror which reflects their gaze. In the performance piece *Waiting*, the author holds up sheets upon which are projected images of waitresses, and then inserts her body and voice in filmed images and narratives of restaurant life, simultaneously positioning herself as author, actor, screen, and the source of their mutual confusion and deconstruction.

Like much theatre theory and practice, Féral's thesis is itself symptomatic of the battle within theatre to differentiate presence from representation, reminding us that in so far as theatre stages presence it enacts the agon between being and representation implied in the concept of enactment, and so gives birth to itself by continually reposing that relationship. Féral highlights this fact by using 'theatricality' to designate a class which encompasses both theatricality and performance, and by this doubling rightly tags theatre as a Strange or Tangled Loop. Criticised for assuming that performance reaches a presence outside of representation, she in fact merely observes that 'performance seems to be attempting to reveal and to stage something that took place before the representation of the subject even if it does so by using an already constituted subject'.[45] This is not, finally, at odds with, but rather an opposing approach to, Derrida's argument that: 'Presence, in order to be presence and self-presence, has always already begun to represent itself, has always already been penetrated.'[46] Thus the paradox of avant-garde theatre: in seeking to stage a moment outside of representation one cannot evade the play of gazes that constitutes representation.

Following Derrida, Herb Blau reminds us that theatre reveals 'no *first* time, no origin, but only recurrence and reproduction'.[47]

Traditional mime has long exposed theatre as a machine of Difference which enacts the coding and decoding of the body, the place and displacement of presence, the construction and deconstruction of the gaze, the carving up and branding of presence (thus the ease with which tattoo art and various forms of bodily mutilation make their way into performance art). Theatre has always suggested a funhouse of mirrors we never escape, a precession of simulacra which remind us we can never reach a body outside of representation. Observes Baudrillard, 'simulation is no longer that of a territory, a referential being or a substance. It is the generation by models of a real without origin or reality: a hyperreal.'[48] Theatre doesn't hold the mirror up to nature, but is the quintessential simulation of simulations, a hyperreality.

Hélène Cixous offers, inadvertently, one of the best definitions of theatre: 'men and women are caught up in a network of millenial cultural determinations of a complexity that is practically unanalysable: we can no more talk about "women" than about "man" without getting caught up in an ideological theatre where the multiplication of representations, images, reflections, myths, identifications constantly transforms, deforms, alters each person's imaginary order and in advance, renders all conceptualisation null and void.'[49] Peggy Kamuf's 'a woman writing like a woman writing like a woman'[50] is quintessentially theatrical, feminist, and deconstructive at once.

The performative side of theatre emerges here as a process of staging the disturbance and reversal of the gaze. Theatre is by definition not amenable to narratives imported to contain its bent toward subversion. The multiple stages and plots of Renaissance and postmodern theatre alike better convey its function as a philosophical model, in so far as simultaneity of space and action is best suited to its ability to interrupt and stage itself. Observes Mària Minich Brewer: 'Theatre allows a philosophical discourse to shift from thought as seeing and originating in the subject alone, to the many decentred processes of framing and staging that representation requires but dissimulates.'[51] Theatre provides a theoretical model for postmodernism in so far as it is always setting into play the subversion of its insights.

A theatrical model is thus ideally suited to the project of decentring and subverting fields of representation that face postmodern theory. This explains why theatre is the source not only of much of the vocabulary of postmodern theory (framing, staging, mise en scène, rehearsal and repetition, re-enactment), but also of many of its key strategies. A refusal of the observer's stable position, a fascination with re-presenting presence, an ability to stage its own staging, to rethink, reframe, switch identifications, undo frames, see freshly, and yet at the same time see how one's look is always already purloined – these are the benefits of theatre for theory.

Why is that theatre alone has always staged identity as unstable, exposing gender and class as a masquerade? Why is it that theatre – so associated with self-reflexivity as to become a means of describing it – manages to avoid the *en abyme* structure, evade its own closure, and refuse its own frames? Could it be that, in so far as theatre cannot rest in the *abyme*, but stages the displacing gaze, the bursting of the container by its contents, theatre offers a way of dislodging the current critical standstill whereby we must use language to describe a place outside it?

The question of whether theatre can stage through representation a presence prior to it must be answered through the gaze, which is no less than a discovery of the splitting of subjectivity in its procuring. The gaze is a discovery that one is seen – that one's look is always already purloined by the Other. 'It is not true that, when I am under the gaze, when I solicit a gaze, when I obtain it, I do not see it as a gaze. ... Painters, above all, have grasped this gaze in the mask ... . The gaze I encounter ... is not a seen gaze, but a gaze imagined by me in the field of the Other' writes Lacan.[52] Theatre's disrupting gaze reflects any look as already taken; it stages presence as always already represented, and trapped by another's look.

Like the shield held up to view Medusa, theatre offers a perspective glass by means of which we see the object of our gaze as always already reflected. Whether in Sophocles' *Oedipus* or Duras's *India Song*, whether through the displacing gaze of the Medusoid Sphinx or the displaced or out of synch voices of staged characters in avant-garde feminist drama, theatre is always staging the desire to own the purloined place of one's look. Theatre tells the story of a rape which has always already occurred, thereby involving us in a series of gazes which splits and displaces our own. Whereas film is obsessed with seeing one's look, as in Hitchcock films which repeatedly distend and peer within the space of their own voyeurism, theatre is fascinated by the return of one's look as a displacing gaze that redefines as it undermines identity. Theatre calls the spectatorial gaze into play by exhibiting a purloined gaze, a gaze that announces it has always been presented to our eyes; is designed only to be taken up by them. The spectatorial gaze takes the bait and stakes its claim to a resting place in the field of vision which beckons it – only to have its gaze fractured, its look stared down by a series of gazes which challenge the place of its look and expose it as in turn defined by the other. The *larvatus prodeo*, or mask which points to itself, is the lure of theatre, a gaze which admits it belongs to the Other, only to become the Other of the spectator in turn.

If cinema appeals to the desire to see oneself seeing, theatre appeals to the desire to expose and displace the displaced gaze – that is, to entangle the other's gaze with one's always already purloined image, to reveal the play of one's look as inevitably, incessantly in motion – displaced and displacing in turn. The striptease is quintessential theatre, its stage the battle of the place of one's look. Will the stripper maintain the place of his look as always already purloined, so as to preserve the female spectator's look, or will he look back in a way that displaces her gaze? Theatre's masks announce that the 'I' is always already another; its characters assure us of their displacement, announcing, 'I am already taken', as in 'this seat is taken', or as in, 'That was no lady, that was my wife (mother).' Theatre is the place where a male ruling class has been able to play at being the excluded other, to reveal the sense that 'I' is an other. If theatre has offered men a chance to identify with the place of a mother's look, to imitate the mother's desire, and to control the woman's looking back, theatre also offers the opportunity to reframe that moment from a point of view alien to it.

The paradox of the frame and the gaze, the problem of the constitutive gaze in relationship to key problems of change, needs to be worked out more fully both within the discourses of feminism, psychoanalysis, and theatre theory, and in the arguments with which they are involved. Feminism faces this problem in the Kristevan paradox of the semiotic and the symbolic; psychoanalysis faces this problem in the relationship of the Imaginary and the Symbolic; but theatre alone is capable of staging the paradox of the frame in a way that subverts it. Unlike feminism and psychoanalysis, theatre has no allegiance but to ambivalence, to a compulsion to subvert its own gaze, to split itself through a reflected image.

Theatre comfortably allies with feminism against psychoanalysis, with psychoanalysis against cinema, and with cinema against itself, without ever finding a resting point except as provisional and always already undermined. Whereas feminism and psychoanalysis seek to reflect the subject from a place where it can never see itself, be it gender, ideology, or the unconscious, theatre provides the tools – the stages, the mirrors, or reflecting gazes – through which perspectives are fragmented, shattered, and set into play against one another. A methodology necessarily tied to no master, theatre is quintessentially deconstructive, poses a methodological challenge to feminism and psychoanalysis to escape its terms, its goals, its identity.

We close here with an open question, one posed at the end of Lacan's seminar, 'The Split Between the Eye and the Gaze'. 'To what extent', asks X. Audouard, 'is it necessary, in analysis, to let the subject know that one is looking at him, that is to say, that one is situated as the person who is observing in the subject the process of looking at oneself?'[53] Freud prided himself on his particular positioning in the analytic setting – 'seeing ... but not seen myself'.[54] But of course Freud was fooling himself here, and it is this delusion that Lacan would seem to have discovered. Yet Lacan answers defensively, belittling Audouard and almost purposefully misunderstanding him: 'We do not say to the patient, at every end and turn, "Now now! What a face you're making!", or, "The top button of your waistcoat is undone". It is not, after all, for nothing that analysis is not carried out face to face.'[55] Yet it is in the gaze that psychoanalysis, feminism, and theatre meet and revision one another. The mere presence of the analyst sets up the gaze; the patient knows she is being heard and watched, and so hears and watches herself differently; the second mirror is in play, mirroring the first, displacing and placing body, voice, and gaze.

The associations I have drawn here suggest that theatre opens up a constructive path for psychoanalytic theory and feminist theory to follow – if they are willing to fully accept the implications of their own displacing gazes. We need, that is, to reread Lacan against himself, to accept how feminism's gaze has been purloined, to interrogate the political implications of psychoanalysis. Theatrical reading is ambivalent reading, dedicated *not* to varying the look (which simply amounts to critical pluralism) but to disrupting it, (up)staging theories through one another. It requires that psychoanalysis read cinema and theatre read psychoanalysis, and – following the motto each would prescribe for the subject – that none of these disciplines ever rests secure in itself.

The question is not, therefore, whether a feminist or a deconstructive theatre is possible, but how separate, and how theatrical, these strategies really are. Can deconstruction stand outside of theatre as a technique to be used upon it, or is it always already within it? To theatricalise one must deconstruct, insert a difference in a term which splits it, mimics it, then displaces or usurps it. 'A woman writing like a woman writing like a woman' is never the same woman. If neither feminism nor psychoanalysis can frame theatre, but only mine or mime it, the reason may be because their techniques have long been trapped inside it. The cost of exit is denial or repression – or perhaps another frame-up.

Can the contents explode the container? *Shrew* puns on the paradox of the enclosed enclosing and so nullifying its frame. Grumio jests that 'the oats have eaten the horses' (III. ii. 201–3), and Tranio plots so that 'A child shall get a sire' (III. i. 413). But can we reframe *The Taming of the Shrew*, and can we reframe its counterpart, *Oedipus*? The work has already begun. Listen – or rather, listen again: 'Long afterward, Oedipus, old and blinded, walked the roads. He smelled a familiar smell. It was the Sphinx. Oedipus said, "I want to ask one question. Why didn't I recognise my mother?" "You gave the wrong answer", said the Sphinx. "But that was what made everything possible", said Oedipus. "No", she said. "When I asked, What walks on four legs in the morning, two at noon, and three in the evening, you answered, Man. You didn't say anything about woman." "When you say Man", said Oedipus, "you include women too. Everyone knows that." She said, "That's what you think".'[56]

From *Theatre Journal*, 40:3 (October 1989), 375–97.

NOTES

[Freedman argues for the potential of theatre for revisioning representations of gender difference on the stage. Using the work of Julia Kristeva and Lacanian psychoanalysis to claim commonnesses of deconstruction, feminism and theatre, she presents yet a third possible approach to feminist theatre, one drawn from philosophical French feminism and feminist film criticism in potential dialogue with theatre. Ed.]

1. See Freud's *The Ego and the Id, the Standard Edition of the Complete Psychological Works of Sigmund Freud*, vol. 19, trans. James Strachey (London, 1923), p. 245, in which, after the little girl sees 'her lack of a penis as being a punishment personal to herself and has realised that the sexual character is a universal one, she begins to share the contempt felt by men for a sex which is the lesser in so important a

respect, and, at least in holding that opinion, insists on being like a man.'

2. Jacques Lacan, 'Agency of the letter in the unconscious', *Ecrits*, trans. Alan Sheridan (New York, 1977), p. 152.

3. Jacqueline Rose, 'Introduction-II', in *Feminine Sexuality: Jacques Lacan and the Ecole Freudienne*, trans. Jacqueline Rose, ed. Juliet Mitchell and Jacqueline Rose (New York, 1985), p. 29.

4. Ibid., p. 28.

5. See Laura Mulvey, 'Visual Pleasure and Narrative Cinema', *Screen* 16:3 (1975), 6–18; Kaja Silverman, *The Subject of Semiotics* (Oxford, 1983); E. Ann Kaplan, *Women and Film: Both Sides of the Camera* (New York, 1983); Teresa de Lauretis, *Alice Doesn't: Feminism, Semiotics, Cinema* (Bloomington, IN, 1984); and Jacqueline Rose, *Sexuality and the Field of Vision* (London, 1986).

6. Jane Gallop, *The Daughter's Seduction, Feminism and Psychoanalysis* (Ithaca, NY, 1982), p. 93.

7. Roland Barthes, *Roland Barthes by Roland Barthes*, trans. Richard Howard (London, 1977), pp. 69, 177.

8. Julia Kristeva, 'Modern Theatre Does Not Take (a) Place', trans. Alice Jardine and Thomas Gora, *Sub-Stance*, 18/19 (1977), 131–4.

9. Keir Elam, *The Semiotics of Drama and Theatre* (London, 1980).

10. Jacques Derrida, 'Choreographies', *Diacritics* (Summer 1982), 76, from an interview with Christie V. McDonald.

11. See Julia Kristeva, *Revolution in Poetic Language*, trans. Margaret Waller (New York, 1984).

12. Gallop, *The Daughter's Seduction*, p. 97.

13. Ellie Ragland-Sullivan, *Jacques Lacan and the Philosophy of Psychoanalysis* (Chicago, 1984), p. 268.

14. Louis Althusser, *Lenin and Philosophy*, trans. Ben Brewster (London, 1971), p. 211.

15. Claude Lévi-Strauss, *The Elementary Structures of Kinship*, trans. James Harle Bell, John Richard von Sturmer and Rodney Needham (Boston, MA, 1969), p. 32.

16. Rose, 'Introduction', p. 45.

17. Jacques Lacan, 'Guiding Remarks for a Congress on Feminine Sexuality', in *Feminine Sexuality*, p. 86.

18. Teresa de Lauretis, *Alice Doesn't: Feminism, Semiotics, Cinema* (Bloomington, IN, 1984), p. 164; her quotation is from Ben Brewster,

Stephen Heath and Colin MacCabe, 'Comment', *Screen*, 16 (1975), 83–90.

19. Juliet Flower MacCannell, *Figuring Lacan: Criticism and the Cultural Unconscious* (Lincoln, NE, 1986), p. 19.

20. Rose, 'Introduction', p. 56.

21. Jacques Lacan, 'Alienation', in *Four Fundamental Concepts of Psycho-Analysis* (New York, 1981), p. 204.

22. de Lauretis, *Alice Doesn't*, pp. 180–1.

23. Ibid., p. 172.

24. Ann Rosalind Jones, 'Inscribing Femininity: French Theories of the Feminine', in *Making a Difference; Feminine Literary Criticism*, ed. Gayle Green and Coppélia Kahn (New York, 1985), p. 106.

25. See for example, Luce Irigaray, *Speculum of the Other Woman* (Ithaca, NY, 1985); *This Sex Which Is Not One* (Ithaca, NY, 1985); and Hélène Cixous, 'The Laugh of the Medusa', trans. Keith Cohen and Paula Cohen, in *New French Feminisms*, ed. Elaine Marks and Isabelle de Courtivron (Amherst, NA, 1980), pp. 245–64.

26. Monique Wittig, 'One Is Not Born a Woman', *Feminist Issues*, 1:2 (1981), 50–1.

27. Constance Penley's comment and Peter Gidal's reaction are taken from Stephen Heath's essay, 'Difference', *Screen*, 19 (1978), 97; Heath's comment is from the same essay, 97–8.

28. Nancy Chodorow, *The Reproduction of Mothering: Psychoanalysis and the Sociology of Gender* (Berkeley, CA, 1978).

29. See the survey by Jay R. Greenberg and Stephen A. Mitchell, *Object Relations in Psychoanalytic Theory* (Cambridge, 1983), as well as the work of Margaret Mahler, *On Human Symbiosis and the Vicissitudes of Individuation* (London, 1969), and D.W. Winnicott, *Playing and Reality* (London, 1971).

30. Heath, 'Difference', p. 92.

31. Ibid., pp. 96–7.

32. Constance Penley, "A Certain Refusal of Difference". Feminism and Film Theory', in *Art After Modernism: Rethinking Representation*, ed. Brian Wallis (New York, 1984), p. 387.

33. Jacqueline Rose, *Sexuality and the Field of Vision*, p. 209.

34. Ibid, p. 210.

35. Julia Kristeva, 'Women's Time', trans. Alice Jardine and Harry Blake, *Signs* 7 (1981), 33.

36. Julia Kristeva, 'Interview with Xavière Gauthier', *Tel Quel*, 58 (1974), 98–102; reprinted in *New French Feminisms*, ed. Elaine Marks and Isabelle de Courtivron (Amherst, MA, 1980), p. 166.

37. Soshana Felman, 'Rereading Femininity', *Yale French Studies*, 62 (1981), 42.

38. See Kristeva's 'Modern Theatre Does Not Take (a) Place', cited in note 8 above, as well as her interview with Gauthier, cited above in note 36, where (p. 167) she identifies 'the moment of rupture and negativity which conditions and underlies the novelty of any praxis "feminine"', and adds, 'No "I" is there to assume this "femininity", but it is no less operative, rejecting all that is finite and assuring in (*sexual*) *pleasure* the life of the concept.'

39. Josette Féral, 'Performance and Theatricality', trans. Terese Lyons, *Modern Drama*, 25 (1982), 170–84.

40. See Keir Elam, *The Semiotics of Theatre and Drama*, p. 2.

41. Féral, 'Performance and Theatricality', 177–8.

42. Ibid., 178.

43. Ibid.

44. Ibid., 176.

45. Ibid., 178.

46. Jacques Derrida, 'The Theatre of Cruelty and the Closure of Representation', in *Writing and Difference*, trans. Alan Bass (Chicago, 1978), p. 249.

47. Herbert Blau, 'Universals of Performance; or Amortising Play', *SubStance*, 37–8 (1983), 148.

48. Jean Baudrillard, 'The Precession of Simulacra', in *Art After Modernism: Rethinking Representation*, ed. Brian Wallis (New York, 1984), p. 253.

49. Hélène Cixous, 'Sorties', in *New French Feminisms*, p. 96.

50. Peggy Kamuf, 'Writing like a Woman', in *Women and Language in Literature and Society*, ed. S. McConnell-Ginet et al. (New York, 1980), p. 298.

51. Mària Minich Brewer, 'Performing Theory', *Theatre Journal*, 37 (1985), 16.

52. Jacques Lacan, 'Anamorphosis', in *The Four Fundamental Concepts of Psycho-Analysis*, trans. Alan Sheridan (New York, 1981), p. 84.

53. X. Audouard, 'Questions and Answers', following Lacan's 'The Split Between the Eye and the Gaze', in *Four Fundamental Concepts*, p. 77.

54. Sigmund Freud, *Autobiography*, trans. James Strachey (New York, 1935), p. 47. (First published as 'An Autobiographical Study' in 1927.)

55. Lacan, 'The Split Between the Eye and the Gaze', p. 78.

56. Muriel Rukeyser, 'Myth', in *The Collected Poems* (New York, 1978), p. 498.

5

Drama and the Dialogic Imagination: *The Heidi Chronicles* and *Fefu and her Friends*

HELENE KEYSSAR

I first came to know the writings of Mikhail Bakhtin in the mid-seventies.[1] Increasingly hailed as one of the most daring and profound philosopher-critics of the twentieth century, Bakhtin was difficult to read but easy to admire.[2] Indeed, as striking as the growing interest in Bakhtin's ideas has been the range of people whose interest he has aroused – feminists and non-feminists, Marxists and anti-Marxists, modernists and postmodernists, social scientists, linguists, psychologists, literary critics and philosophers. Few seemed to notice that they were in strange company. The only people blatantly missing in the crowd were others like me – drama critics and practitioners of theatre.

From the start, however, my interest in Bakhtin's ideas was troubled or, in Bakhtin's own terms, multivoiced. Like several other contemporary critics, most notably Wayne Booth,[3] I had found both a confluence and an antagonsim between some key aspects of feminist thought and some key elements of Bakhtin's ideas. At the same time, and in part because of the commonalities with contemporary feminist approaches, almost everything Bakhtin had to say about language and representations sharply illuminated my ways of thinking about drama, the cultural realm to which I was and remain particularly attached as both a critic and a director; indeed, even the odd names of Bakhtin's key concepts – dialogism, polyphony, heteroglossia, carnivalisation, hybridisation – seemed to me not just applicable to drama but centred in the most elemental attributes of dramatic forms.

As I have previously argued, following J. L. Styan's lead,[4] meaning is made in the theatre by the interaction and, to use Bakhtin's term, the interanimation of two or more forms of communication (or semiotic systems). The performed drama is understood as simultaneously entire unto itself and part of the whole culture; the cultural material from which the drama is created is repeatedly mediated and revised as it interacts with the playwright, the performers, and, finally, the audience. The continuous recreation of meaning, what Bakhtin calls the heteroglossia of communication, is the basic condition and phenomenon of theatre. This condition is not only inherently present in any dramatic performance but is represented in the interaction of human voices or consciousnesses on stage. The natural condition of drama is thus that of dialogism, the quality that Bakhtin argued throughout his life was key to the de-privileging of absolute, authoritarian discourses.[5]

Yet, Bakhtin not only ignored drama in most of his writings, in explicit favour of the dialogic or polyphonous novel, but in one of his most important works, *Problems of Dostoevsky's Poetics*, he explicitly denounced dramatic literature, assaulting it with his unique curse: drama was monologic. The passage in which Bakhtin pronounces this malediction is uncharacteristically straightforward, and, because it sets the ground for what I have come to think of as the central issues relevant to the roles of drama in society, it merits quoting in full:

> Literature of recent times knows only the dramatic dialogue and to some extent the philosophical dialogue, weakened into a mere form of exposition, a pedagogical device. And, in any case, the dramatic dialogue in drama and the dramatised dialogue in the narrative forms are always encased in a firm and stable monologic framework. In drama, of course, this monologic framework does not find direct verbal expression, but precisely in drama is it especially monolithic. The rejoinders in drama do not rip apart the represented world, do not make it multilevelled; on the contrary if they are to be authentically dramatic, these rejoinders necessitate the utmost monolithic unity of that world. In drama the world must be made from a single piece. Any weakening of this monolithic quality leads to a weakening of dramatic effect. The characters come together dialogically in the

unified field of vision of author, director, and audience, against the clearly defined background of a single-tiered world. The whole concept of a dramatic action as that which resolves all dialogic oppositions, is purely monologic. A true multiplicity of levels would destroy drama, because dramatic action, relying as it does upon the unity of the world, could not link those levels together or resolve them. In drama, it is impossible to combine several integral fields of vision in a unity that encompasses and stands above them all, because the structure of drama offers no support for such a unity.[6]

For all of us who have seen drama in performance, and certainly for anyone who has ever participated in the making of a dramatic production, several of these claims seem immediately counter-intuitive: after all, the dialogue *is* the action in theatre, and any action on stage is refracted (to use another Bakhtinian term) through the diverse points of view of writers, actors, designers and spectators. Nonetheless, while there are several immediately available points of contestation in Bakhtin's argument, this is serious stuff, too informed by widely held convictions about drama to be easily dismissed as the ramblings of an eccentric Russian who might, perhaps, be overly taken with the novel because of the glories of its Russian instances. What Bakhtin demands is no less than that we rethink what it means to accept a still-prevalent Aristotelian understanding of drama, and then, to query both the accuracy and the virtues – politically, socially, aesthetically – of the Aristotelian model.

To respond to this challenge, we must return first to those Aristotelian premises to which Bakhtin points. The most obvious of these come under the rubric of the famous unities, usually taught as those of action, place and time, but in *The Poetics*, subsumed within the more basic concept of the Unity of Plot.[7] Aristotle's emphasis is on the avoidance of the episodic – of that which is neither probable nor necessary to the essential structural elements of peripeteia and anagnorisis (reversal of fortune and discovery) – and on the importance of 'an action that is complete in itself'. Bakhtin does not contest these attributes; he reaffirms them throughout the passage cited above, most notably in the assertion that 'in drama the world must be made from a single piece'. In Aristotle's elaboration of his concept of Unity of Plot, he notes that it is a mistake to equate Unity of Plot with focus on one character; that would not suffice to create strong dramatic effect: 'An affinity of things befall that one man, some of which it is impossible to reduce to unity'.[8]

Aristotle's advice to the playwright it therefore to eliminate all incidents, and, by implication, all thoughts, experiences, actions of a
character, that might 'disjoin and dislocate the whole'.[9] Bakhtin
echoes this claim, too, in his assertion that 'the rejoinders in a dramatic dialogue do not rip apart the represented world'; at least that
is a requirement for Bakhtin of that which is 'authentically dramatic'.

Bakhtin's argument, then, is not with the traditional prescription
or modelling of drama, it is with what he takes to be necessary and
essential to the medium itself. Drama can only be fully itself, as
Bakhtin understands its parameters, if it 'resolves all dialogic oppositions', if it avoids 'a true multiplicity of levels'. Further, as
Aristotle argues, drama must have a clear beginning, middle and
end. The various qualities of the polyphonic novel Bakhtin celebrates throughout his writings – dialogism, unfinalisability, linguistic diversity, the persistence of 'loopholes' of meaning – are all,
from both Bakhtin and Aristotle's perspectives, inimicable to drama
as a cultural form.

This leads me to two clusters of questions. First, is this depiction
and definition of drama, now two thousand years old, accurate,
sufficient and necessary? And, second, what are the social and political implications of the monologic attributes of drama? Put in the
most extreme terms, if drama is monologic is it a hazard to the
complexities necessary for decent human life? Furthermore, as
Bahktin implies, if drama is, in an essential way, monologic, but
deceives us by an appearance of dialogism, is it especially dangerous
to human society because it catches us unawares and deceives us?

No definitive answer to my first question is possible within the
confines of an essay; nonetheless, the only way to begin to address
this question is to call before us an array of dramatic texts. I do so
with the intent both to provoke others to argument and to delineate
the kind of ground and thinking to which this question points. That
I begin with classical texts is a reflection on my conviction that
many of the limits as well as the possibilities of modern drama are
rooted in ancient conceptions of drama and theatre.

Sophocles' *Oedipus* is the most obvious text with which to begin,
both because it is to that drama that Aristotle turns when he wishes
to provide a model of excellence in drama and because it continues
to be regarded as the paradigmatic Greek tragedy.[10] Not only is the
Oedipus structured on the perfect instantiations of Peripeteia and
Anagnorisis, but the change from one state of things to its opposite

and the 'discovery' or change from ignorance to knowledge, are themselves conjoined to effect the ideal Unity of Plot for which, according to Aristotle, all playwrights should aspire. In addition, 'improbabilities' are kept outside the tragedy in *Oedipus*, the chorus functions 'as one of the actors', thus as 'an integral part of the whole', and the diction of the dialogue exemplifies a mastery of metaphor that 'implies an intuitive perception of the similarity in dissimilars'.[11]

I have no difficulty imagining Bakhtin taking each of these attributes, with their emphases on integration and unity, including and perhaps especially the understanding of metaphor as a perception of similarity in dissimilarities, as evidence for the monoligic framework of *Oedipus*. Nor can I find solid grounds on which to contest this position. Peter Euben's discussion of *Oedipus* in his *The Tragedy of Political Theory* complicates our understanding of the monology of *Oedipus*, arguing that the play 'indicates the limits of one-sidedness'; that it '"speaks" in the "voice" of Oedipus and of Teiresias'.[12] Euben contrasts his reading of *Oedipus* to that of René Girard in *Violence and the Sacred*: 'Girard writes about "the violent elimination of differences between the antagonists, their total identity" (p. 72), whereas I want to maintain the distinctiveness within the identity'.[13] But while Euben presents a convincing case for the doubleness of meanings as well as of character voices in *Oedipus*, he also concludes that in the end, 'the self-blinding [of Oedipus] not only unites Oedipus with Teiresias, it also unites him with the god whom he recognises has been his unseen companion throughout his life'.[14] I would add that while I concur with Euben that the key agons of *Oedipus* 'deepen' rather than solve the problems of the play, there is not only in the plot the solution of Thebes' problem with the plague, but there is also resolution for the spectator in the blinding light of knowledge at which both Oedipus and the Chorus arrive. The agons or what Bakhtin calls the 'rejoinders' in the dramatic dialogue of *Oedipus* threaten to rip apart the represented world, but in the end, what this play is about, is that they do *not* rip the world apart: Oedipus is exiled from Thebes; neither the city nor the play can hold within it the difference that Oedipus represents.

Asechylus' trilogy, the *Oresteia*, presents a different model of classical dramatic structure, one that superficially appears not just to exemplify monology but to urge it as a political position. Among the various transformations of culture enacted in the *Oresteia*, few are as blatant as the privileging of the authoritative discourse of the male citizen and the silencing of counter-voices, associated throughout every situation. One of the key paradoxes of the trilogy, and a source of its resolute tension, is located in the contradiction between the dramatic efficacy of polyphony and the political efficacy of law, compromise and consensus, of community as unity.

By the end of the *Eumenides*, limits have been placed on the multi-voicedness of the polis. The 'lethal spell' cast by the voices of the female furies and their 'salt black wave of anger' are excluded from the land and hence from the discourse that shapes the city, much as Oedipus is finally banished from Thebes. Athena's last act in the drama is to call forth all of the women of the city to dress and praise the furies; as if to ensure that no female escapes, Athena specifies that girls, mothers and aged women sing the final chorus of the play. In so doing, the women of the city acknowledge and take on themselves the agreement to repress their most threatening voices and to relegate themselves to a fixed and constrained domain focused on reproduction and nurturance.

This, however, is an uneasy agreement, notably confirmed in dance more than in words. Within the social and political world projected in the drama, the women have nothing to say, and their song dutifully mimics Athena's blessings and the language of the furies. But the final theatrical gestures are neither so simple nor so definitive. The appearance of a new chorus at the end of the performance must have been disconcerting to the audience. And Athena's speech makes it difficult to ignore the ironic redundancy in the representation by men of this chorus of women of the city who are brought forward explicitly to confirm their submission to the new laws and practices of men. The medium of the male chorus that speaks as and for women is the message, but to call attention to this medium, as Aeschylus does, is also to call it into question. The talk in the *Oresteia* may resolve by debate the problem of justice, but, deeply ironically, by confirming the establishment of democratic processes, processes that should by definition be polyphonic, the verbal representations of the drama assert and demand a unified understanding of the polis.

This is the strongest impression we are left with, but it is not, however, the only meaning of the last moments of the *Eumenides*. In the end, as J.-P. Vernant contends, 'an equilibrium is established, but it is based on tensions. In the background, the conflict between opposing forces continues.'[15] At the least, the *Oresteia* reminds us that women and theatre have other languages than the verbal. As women, the men in the chorus can, as Aeschylus writes, 'carry on the dancing on and on'. Mediated by men-playing-women, the Dionysian elements of the theatre are reasserted. Women may be excluded from the polis and the theatre, but as long as theatre requires Dionysian elements, the idea of women must be present in drama, and the threat of polyphony remains.

If we doubt either the continuing temptation towards polyphony in theatre or the resistance to it, we need only turn to one more Greek drama, Euripides' *The Bacchae*. This is a play in which the fabric of the presented world, both as a whole and as embodied in the character of Pentheus, is literally ripped apart. And this is accomplished by an 'outsider', the god of theatre himself, Dionysius. But as Euben maintains, 'from one point of view the *Bacchae* presents itself as resolving the contradictions it dramatises'.[16] Euben goes on to argue that, 'still from this point of view one can say that the very existence of the play as a work of art provides a sense of healing integration in tension with the dismemberment that occurs as part of the play'.[17] I, however, find the sweet, rich poetry to which Euben points to be not so much in tension with the literal presentation of dismemberment as it is yet another attempt to obliterate that tension, to reconceal, indeed to reconcile, the heteroglossia of the world on stage behind a shimmering veil of verses.

When we turn forward in time to other key moments in the history of Western drama, we find persistent recurrences both of the threat of polyphony in drama and of resistance to it. Bakhtin himself admits that 'the mystery play is truly multilevelled, and, to a certain extent, polyphonic'.[18] For him, however, the limits to the polyphony of the mystery plays are clear:

> But the multilevelled and polyphonic quality of the mystery play is purely formal, and in fact the very construction of a mystery play, the nature of its content, does not permit the development of a plurality of consciousness and their worlds. From the very beginning, everything is predetermined, closed-off and finalised – although not, it is true, finalised on a single plane.[19]

Although he does not say so explicitly, it is likely that Bakhtin's partial attraction to mystery plays is grounded in what he came to call the carnival spirit. Bakhtin mentions carnival and carnivalisation of culture early on in his writings, but this concept is most fully developed in his work on Rabelais, submitted as a thesis in 1940 to the Gorky Institute of World Literature in Moscow and finally published in the Soviet Union in 1965. The carnivalesque has its roots in the pageants, comic shows of the marketplace, parodies, curses and oaths of folk culture. In its purest forms, it is clearly distinguished by Bakhtin from traditional drama: 'Carnival does not know footlights, in the sense that it does not acknowledge any distinction between actors and spectators. Footlights would destroy a carnival as the absence of footlights would destroy a theatrical performance. Carnival is not a spectacle seen by the people; they live in it, and everyone participates because its very idea embraces all the people.'[20]

These distinctions are important, and I want to return to them later in this essay, but equally striking – and somewhat puzzling – is Bakhtin's next move, which is not to discard but to embrace the formalisation of the spirit of carnival in works that include *commedia dell'arte* performances, Molière's comedies, and Shakespeare's plays,[21] as well as in Rabelais and the particular prose works that Bakhtin calls polyphonic novels. The attributes of carnival that he finds in such works are clearly delineated:

> In all these writings, in spite of their differences in character and tendency, the carnival-grotesque form exercises the same function: to consecrate inventive freedom, to permit the combination of a variety of different elements and their rapprochement, to liberate from the prevailing point of view of the world, from conventions and established truths, from clichés, from all that is humdrum and universally accepted. This carnival spirit offers the chance to have a new outlook on the world, to realise the relative nature of all that exists, and to enter a completely new order of things.[22]

The carnival spirit, even when removed from the marketplace to a deliberately constructed cultural form, is revolutionary.[23] Like carnival itself, carnivalisation in texts turns established hierarchies upside-down, casts aside conventional rules of dominant discourses and calls traditional values into question. It most often appears at a historical moment when a society is in the process of transforming itself, when human beings are caught between two or more different ways of seeing the world. The historical moment to which the *Oresteia* points, when ancient Greece was in transition from a familial-tribal social organisation to the creation of the polis and the articulation of a (limited) form of democracy, was just such a period. In the Western world, there may well have been a comparable historical moment in the late sixteenth and early seventeenth centuries, when understandings of what and where the world is and what it means to be a person were diverse and dynamic. The century in which we dwell may also well be such a historical moment.

As a medium that not only is public but that requires a public, we might well imagine that at such times drama would be the key cultural form for the representation of the carnival spirit and dialogism of society. But, despite repeated assaults on drama on just such grounds (Plato, Rousseau and our own contemporary theatre, film and TV critics come to mind), textual evidence and dramaturgical theory both suggest the contrary. Take, for example, *The Tempest*. Of all of Shakespeare's plays, it is here that we find the most sustained representation of multiple *types* of consciousness, diverse voices, various planes of play and action. It is also here, in *The Tempest*, that Shakespeare most thoroughly addresses the phenomenon of theatre as theatre, with its various components of spectacle, conversation and creation all at issue. It is here, too, that Shakespeare most explicitly instantiates the authorial voice in a single character, that of Prospero. As much as we may find *The Tempest* endlessly intriguing precisely because of the several planes and points of view it contains within its island world, the play itself also persistently reminds us that one character and one unified consciousness, Prospero, is in control.

The structure and authorial position of Prospero are strikingly similar to the structure and authorial position that Bakhtin discloses in Leo Tolstoy's short story, 'The Three Deaths', a text that Bakhtin analyses to exemplify the attributes of the monologic position. In Tolstoy's story, Bakhtin argues, 'all three lives and the levels defined by them are *internally self-enclosed and do not know one another*'.[24] This description could be applied equally well to Ariel, Caliban, and any of the Milan group in *The Tempest*. For Bakhtin, for *The Tempest* to be authentically dialogic, each of the distinct consciousnesses of the play, including that of Prospero, would have to argue, intersect and animate the others. Most important from Bakhtin's perspective, for *The Tempest* to be authentically polyphonic and dialogic, Prospero's voice and vision, and, ultimately, Shakespeare's, would have to have no more authority than that of any character within the play. In the monologic work, 'everything within it is seen and portrayed in the author's all-encompassing and omniscient field of vision'. This is exactly what we find to be true of

Prospero. Now we might argue that this is precisely the position that Prospero refuses when he buries his book and abjures his 'magic', and we might further argue that it is a mistake to equate Prospero with Shakespeare. But if we moved in this direction, we would also come full circle back to Bakhtin: for Prospero to discard his position of authority, for him to return to Milan where his field of vision will no longer be omniscient, requires that Prospero remove himself from the world of theatre.[25]

The Greek dramas to which I have referred and *The Tempest* lead me to make a distinction between texts that are, in themselves, dialogic and revolutionary and those that emerge during, and reflect, a transformational moment in history. In at least several of the ancient Greek tragedies, the world on stage is never fully unified within one omnisicent field of vision, and drama appears to function precisely, as Vernant argues, by presenting 'a dichtomy [dedoublement] of the chorus and the protagonists, the two types of language, the play between the community which officially represents the City as a magistracy, and a professional actor who is an incarnation of a hero from another age'.[26] It does so, Vernant continues, in order 'both to call the City into question within a well-defined context, and also ... to call into question a certain image of man, and I would even say to indicate a change in man'.[27]

This seems to me mostly accurate, and, therefore, an important challenge to Bakhtin's position on drama, but Vernant's claims in the end undermine their own position by blurring or refusing a distinction between 'calling into question a certain image of man' and 'indicating a change in man'. As I have suggested earlier, I read the *Oresteia* and the *Bacchae* (and I could add several other Greek texts to these) as performing both these functions, but this does not mean that these gestures are necessarily similar or even compatible. I have argued in several previous writings[28] that most Western dramas, pivoted on the recognition scene, are formally and ideologically conservative: they re-present as heroic a process by which a character (or characters) comes to know himself (and, occasionally, herself) by unravelling and confronting his own history. In the moment of recognition, both the character on stage and the spectator acknowledge the 'truth', a stable, fixed form of meaning whose unveiling is the primary act of traditional theatre. This type of discovery, of who a person 'really' is, dominates Western dramaturgical strategies from the Greeks to the present: think not only of *Oedipus*, but of *King Lear*, of Ibsen's *Rosmersholm*, Pirandello's

Henry IV, Hellman's *The Little Foxes*, Williams's *Cat on a Hot Tin Roof*, and Miller's *Death of a Salesman*. In each of these instances, and innumerable others, a change in a character is *indicated*, and it is the specific change that Aristotle had called for – from ignorance to knowledge. This kind of change may, for both the characters on stage and the spectator, call into question the particular image of this particular character, but it does not necessarily call into question 'a certain image of man'.

Some years ago, in my own early work, I contended (unknowingly concurring with Bakhtin's position) that the kind of change represented in recognition scenes was not only sufficient but definitive of drama; subsequently, however, informed especially by Afro-American drama and by feminist drama, I have moved to an increasingly strong conviction that drama offers another possibility, that of presenting and urging the transformation of persons and our images of each other. This latter form of change requires not that we remove or have removed disguises that conceal us from our 'true' selves, but that we imagine men and women in a continual process of becoming other. In this form of drama, recognition scenes are either subordinate to transformation scenes or are counter-productive: it is *becoming* other, not finding oneself, that is the crux of the drama; the performance of transformation of persons, not the revelation of a core identity, focuses the drama.

Earlier in this piece I indicated my agreement with Bakhtin that drama has tended to embrace monology, but qualified Bakhtin's essentialist argument by suggesting that there are significant instances in which variant voices threaten to animate the text and performance of particular plays. I would make the same argument about transformational elements in traditional drama, and want, further, to suggest that often, and perhaps, inevitably, transformational strategies go hand in hand with the dialogic imagination. I now want to pursue this further with the claim that the most distinctive quality of one type, call it a genre, of modern drama is its rejection of monologism and the patriarchical authority of the drama in performance. This genre of modern drama attempts to create a dramatic discourse that celebrates rather than annihilates or exiles difference.

Bakhtin does not have much more to say about dramatic literature written since the mid-nineteenth century (the approximate point at which I would mark the beginnings of modern drama) than he does about classical drama. The single piece that he devotes to

dramatic literature, 'Preface to Volume 11: the Dramas' is concerned entirely with Tolstoy's plays, which Bakhtin divides into two
groups: the 'carelessly constructed','insignificant' dramas written by
Tolstoy during his happy, life-affirming early period, before his
'crisis', and the plays written after this crisis, which Bakhtin further
divides into the 'folk dramas' and the dramas of withdrawal.[29]
Although Bakhtin concedes that Tolstoy's best known drama, 'The
Power of Darkness' 'in many respects deserves the epithet "peasant
drama"' and is, conceptually, a mystery play (and thus, as noted
previously, is formally if not profoundly, dialogic), his discussion of
Tolstoy's dramas, including 'The Power of Darkness', serves simultaneously to extend and confirm his dissatisfaction with both
Tolstoy and drama. The 'Preface to the Dramas' does, however,
contribute to our understanding of Bakhtin's resistance to drama,
while also suggesting that there is a dramatic realm, that of 'folk
drama' that might merit Bakhtin's – and our – interest and respect.

Ironically defending Tolstoy's dramaturgical failures, Bakhtin
clarifies his own resistance to drama with the claim that because
dramatic form 'must satisfy the demands of stageability, [it] is the
most difficult form to free from convention'. He then proceeds,
however, to turn the assault on Tolstoy, claiming that a key to
Tolstoy's difficulties in writing dramatic works during his early
period was Tolstoy's insistence on the transcendent and emphatic
role of the authorial voice. Tolstoy, the writer of novels and short
stories, aspired according to Bakhtin to 'complete freedom and autonomy' of the authorial voice. Without any hint that we might find
this disconcerting, given Bakhtin's consistent disavowal of drama
and celebration of prose fiction as the terrain where dialogism is
possible (although certainly not inevitable as the case of Tolstoy
demonstrates through Bakhtin's criticism), Bakhtin suggests that
this authorial self-assurance and certainty were far more difficult to
achieve in drama than in the novel.

The hint or clue to the way out of this apparent maze occurs in
Bakhtin's references to the 'almost' folk drama, 'The Power of
Darkness'.Tolstoy intended this play to be performed in the show-
booths as folk theatre, a form of theatre of which Bakhtin appears
to approve. But the intention that this work be a folk drama is not
fulfilled, by Bakhtin's analysis, because 'the deeply individualised
peasant language is no more than an immobile, unchanging background and dramatically dead shell for the internal spiritual deed of
the hero'.[30] Since all of Bakhtin's comments on Tolstoy's dramas

attend to the failures in these works, I can only infer what an authentic folk drama, according to Bakhtin, would be like .[31] It would reflect the 'real-life torrent of contradictory class evolution','the objective contradictions of reality itself' and would be mobile, dynamic and unfinalised.

To infer that such a drama is imaginable does seem to contradict Bakhtin's claim that I cited at the beginning of this piece. It is possible that Bakhtin only set up the idea of 'folk drama' as a foil for his critique of Tolstoy's plays; with the exception of his reference in the discussion of Tolstoy's dramas to mystery plays, Bakhtin does not cite any examples of 'folk dramas' that fulfil the criteria that Tolstoy fails to meet. We could also greet this apparent contradiction as consistent with numerous other apparent contradictions, modifications, variations in Bakhtin's writings – inconsistencies that other commentators on Bakhtin have variously addressed as reflections of particular and varying contexts in which Bakhtin was writing, as changes in Bakhtin's thinking, or as ironic confirmations of the double-voicedness in the theorist himself.[32]

I will not attempt to choose among these alternatives; my guess is that they all contribute to what may or may not be a 'problem' in Baktin's writings and our own critical endeavours. What I do want to do in moving towards a temporary stopping point (but not a conclusion) to my own reflections on these matters is to follow Bakhtin's example of a critical approach to the novel by contrasting two contemporary works that I believe suggest the difference between what a dialogic and a monological drama might look like in our own society.

Let me begin this endgame by restating that I believe there are a number of modern dramas that are arguably dialogic. My own, admitedly incomplete and contestable list would begin with Buchner's *Woyzeck* (a play well worth consideration as a Bakhtinian folk drama) and would include from the corpus of works usually judged to be major modern dramas: Jarry's *Ubu Roi*, much of Chekov, all of Beckett's dramas, most of Brecht's dramas, Pinter's *The Homecoming*, and several of Handke's plays. My list of dialogic dramas would be heavily weighted, however, by selections from black American drama and feminist drama. It is in these works, as I have discussed in several recent articles, that we find the most deliberate and conscientious assertions of polyphony, of refusals to finalise or assert dominant ideologies, of resistances to partriarchical authority and to a unified field of vision. That many of these works are American seems to me not coincidental; the doubleness of the consciousness of most Americans, including and perhaps especially the doubleness of being black and American and the bilingual experience of American culture is constituitive of the American experience. Similarly (but therefore expansively) as both Wayne Booth and I have urged, despite the overt sexism in the major texts that Bakhtin celebrates, there is a striking confluence between the attention to the construction of multivoicedness and hybrydisation in much of contemporary feminist writing and in Bakhtin's criticism.

Among the most striking examples of what I might call a feminist/Bakhtinian world view in modern dramas are Ntozake Shange's *for colored girls who have considered suicide when the rainbow is enuf* and *boogie woogie landscapes*, Caryl Churchill's *Top Girls, Cloud Nine* and *A Mouthful of Birds*, Megan Terry's *Mollie Bailey's Travelling Family Circus: Featuring Scenes from the Life of Mother Jones*, LeRoi Jones and Imamu Baraka's *Dutchman*, and Adrienne Kennedy's *The Owl Answers*. In each of these works, the spectacle and dialogue of theatre mediate but do not resolve differences; the essential strategy of these plays is to bring together diverse discourses in such a way that they interanimate each other and avoid an overarching authorial point of view. We can best understand this exceptional receptivity to dialogism by turning to the social and political contexts of these works. As Bakhtin implies about folk drama, the voices we hear in many black American dramas and feminist dramas are the voices of marginal folk, voices that are both in conflict with dominant ideological positions and resistant among themselves to the reductions of uniformity.

That this is not the case in all feminist drama, despite the contiguity between feminism and dialogism, and that Bakhtin's concerns about drama remain potent despite persistent attempts by men as well as women, white people as well as people of colour, to challenge the conventions of traditional drama becomes evident if we compare two ostensibly feminist works from contemporary literature: Maria Irena Fornes's *Fefu and her Friends* and *The Heidi Chronicles* by Wendy Wasserstein.

The Heidi Chronicles was first produced in April 1988 by the Seattle Repertory Theatre; on 12 December 1988 it moved to the Playwrights' Horizons in New York City; three months later, it reopened at the Plymouth Theatre on Broadway, where it quickly became one of the major hits of the season. Awards have poured down upon the play and its author: in addition to the Pulitzer Prize for drama and the Tony for best play of the season, *The Heidi Chronicles* won the Susan Smith Blackburn prize (a prize specifically meant to recognise outstanding work by women playwrights) and the Dramatists Guild Hull Warriner award which selects 'the best American play dealing with contemporary political, religious or social mores'. While my experience as a spectator is that audiences take the play lightly – they laugh, giggle and chat briefly after the performance about their own experiences growing up from the sixties to the eighties, experiences that the play recalls – both the wealth of awards and the passionately mixed reviews it provoked suggest that *The Heidi Chronicles* commands serious attention.

Working with the same kinds of characters she has created in previous dramas (*Uncommon Women and Others, Isn't It Romantic*), Wasserstein takes us along for the ride on a twenty-five year journey from adolescence to adulthood of two men and a woman, all bright, upper-middle-class people who begin to come to consciousness in the mid-sixties. (Heidi's friend, Susan, also makes the journey, but she is always a foil or adjunct to the affairs of the central three characters.) Heidi, who becomes an art historian, is ostensibly the protagonist of the drama (she appears in each of the play's 11 scenes and two prologues), although she is often dominated, dramatically and politically, by the two men in her life: Peter Patrone, a caring, intelligent man who becomes 'a liberal homosexual pediatrician', and Scoop Rosenbaum, already an aggressive entreprenuer at 19 who rises to become editor of *Boomer* magazine.

In a series of eleven anecdotes, these characters repeatedly re-encounter each other, at each instance addressing the vicissitudes of their own lives in the context of the changing values and mores of their society. None of these three main characters ever changes, but the play does build towards and away from two quasi-recognition scenes. In the first of these (scene 10), Heidi loses control of the keynote address she is delivering to a luncheon gathering at the Plaza Hotel and rambles towards a conclusion in which she confesses to the audience that she is 'just not happy', that she feels 'stranded' and disillusioned because she thought that the whole point of the women's movement 'was that we were all in this together' (scene 10). In the next scene (11), Heidi visits Peter at a children's hospital ward on Christmas Eve, and Peter reveals that he, the most prominent pediatrician in New York City, is living in an increasingly narrow world because so many of his friends are dying of AIDS. He confesses to Heidi that he is hurt because she does not understand him and is not authentically there for him as a friend. She immediately responds that she could 'become someone else next year'. The two briefly transcend their differences and embrace, but if there is recognition of self or other here, some traditional movement from ignorance to knowledge, the moment is explicitly presented as transitory and private. Heidi's offer to 'become someone else' is not a step towards a transformation of self but more like a proposal to wear a different dress tomorrow. Heidi neither knows what it means to 'become someone else' nor does she know what kind of person she would will herself to become. Her offer to 'become someone else next year' would be a good laugh line, even, perhaps, a parody of a dramatic transformation, were it not uttered in the context of Peter's suffering.

Gender – its roles and consciousnesses – provides the thematic thread that links the episodes in the twenty-five year time line of *The Heidi Chronicles*. Since there is neither beauty in the language nor surprise in the events or characters of this play, I can only surmise that it is the topical interest in gender issues that has called forth so much critical attention, both positive and negative. Those who praised *The Heidi Chronicles* found it to be 'enlightening' (Mel Gussow, *New York Times*) 'wise' (Howard Kissell, *Daily News*) and 'important' (Linda Winer, *Newsday*) in its depiction of feminism and feminists, and of men's and women's relations to each other. Negative commentary on the play, most thoroughly and bitingly presented in a long piece by Phyllis Jane Rose in *American Theatre*,[33] also focused on gender issues. 'The absence from the stage of images of women acting on their own beliefs in truth, beauty or justice implies that women do not act in this way in the world', writes Rose in her letter to Heidi. 'Or, if they do', Rose continues, 'it is not important enough to be dramatised. In your *Chronicles*, your struggle for women artists, your professed dedication to content over form, are secondary to your relationships with men. Your intelligence becomes wit in their presence. Your imagination settles for fantasy.'

The Heidi Chronicles is all, or worse, than Rose contends. And, here, Bakhtin comes to my aid in understanding why I find this drama – and its mostly celebrative public reception – so disturbing. It is precisely because this drama does not re-present the heteroglossia of the world, precisely because it is aggressively monologic, self-contained, a seemingly perfect picture without loopholes of a particular historic moment that it is so pleasing to some and distressing to others. Heidi does an adequate job of recuperating women artists, but even when she speaks of her subjects it is in the monologic discourse of professional academia. On the one occasion – a television talk show – where Heidi is explicitly positioned to speak her own different voice – she is silenced by the voices of two men, Scoop and Peter, her old friends who also appear on the show. Afterwards, she is angry, but even in her anger, we are given no sense of what her own voice might sound like. And, if we are meant to see this scene as a dramatisation of difference as absence, as an assault on patriarchical monology, such a vision is quickly undercut by the subsequent scene, a meeting among Heidi and her women friends, where the women's talk and ideologies are indistinguishable from those of Scoop and Peter. Heidi only briefly finds an alternative voice during her rambling speech at the women's luncheon, and that utterance is inaccessible because it is framed as the self-pitying ramblings of a woman in the process of a nervous breakdown.

The characters in *The Heidi Chronicles* neither acknowledge each other as other – indeed, their persistent attempt is to be like each other – nor do they, to use once more a Bakhtinian term, 'interanimate' each other. The world they comprise is coherent, consistent and stable, despite superficial changes from involvement in leftish politics and the women's movement to a kind of mushy humanism. Reaction is not revolution, as Rose urges, quoting Laurie Stone, and the world of *The Heidi Chronicles* is adamantly one of reaction, not revolution or change. When we meet Heidi for the last time, with her newly adopted baby, she is 'waiting' for something, perhaps for a new world and new generation in which her baby daughter's voice will be different and will be heard. Her world is not provocatively open, unfinalised; Heidi and her baby are just sitting there rocking, bathed in the nostalgia of an old fifties song. As my twelve-year-old daughter commented immediately after seeing the production, the play could have ended at any of several of its last few scenes. Had it done so, it would not have made any difference – to those on stage or in the audience.

In 'Discourse in the Novel', an essay that is central to his reflections, Bakhtin urges that 'this verbal-ideological decentring will occur only when a national culture loses its sealed-off and self-sufficient character, when it becomes conscious of itself as only one among other cultures and languages.'[34] In its refusal of such a 'de-centring',*The Heidi Chronicles* reveals a national culture that remains 'sealed-off', 'authoritarian','rigid' and unconscious of itself as only one among other cultures and languages. And it does so to a dangerous degree. There is no place in the world of this drama for the voices of women and men who can speak the discourses of feminism, there is no room in this drama for the poor, the marginalised, the inarticulate, for those who are not successes in the terms of the eighties, for those who wish to transform and not react. If this is what drama today is at its best, then it is less than that which Bakhtin claimed it to be initially.

This is, however, not all there is within the realm of contemporary drama. Maria Irene Fornes's *Fefu and her Friends*, first performed in May 1977 by the New York Theatre Strategy, and produced in numerous regional theatres throughout the eighties, offers a distinctly different way of thinking about both drama and its relations to gender. The play has received slow and steady respect from producers, audiences and critics, but has never received the loud public applause that greeted *The Heidi Chronicles* (or, notably, a comparably monologic prize-winning drama, Marsha Norman's *'night Mother*). Only recently, a production at my university was hesitantly supported, and the sounds of unease and perplexity in the small audience of mostly men at a dress rehearsal confirmed the difficulties *Fefu and her Friends* continues to pose for even sophisticated spectators.

Initially, *Fefu and her Friends* conforms to the conventions of traditional theatre. A small group of women come together for a reunion meeting to rehearse a series of presentations for a public event. The play preserves the unities of time, place and action: all events occur during one day, in one house, among a group of people who form a temporary community. From the start, however, the differences among the women's voices are striking, as are their abilities to reaccentuate each other's lives and the meanings of each other's utterances. Fefu opens the play, declaring to no one in particular, 'My husband married me to have a constant reminder of how loathsome women are'. 'What?' Cindy asks. 'Yup', Fefu responds. Often, one or another of the women do not understand each other, but what one says to an other changes the other before our eyes.

Central among these women are Fefu, the hostess in whose house the gathering occurs, and Julia, a friend of several of the women, including Fefu. Julia, for most of the play, is confined to a wheelchair, the result of a bizarre accident in which a hunter shot a deer, and, after falling as if shot herself, Julia found herself to be paralysed. Julia and Fefu are the most complex and perplexing of the characters, but the other women assembled each have their own specific voice, their own desires and differences. In a 1985 interview with Scott Cummings, Fornes described her relationship to these characters in the context of a change in style in her work: 'The style of *Fefu* dealt more with characters as real persons rather than voices that are the expression of the mind of the play.'[35] She goes on to say that instead of writing in a 'linear manner' she 'would write a scene and see what came out and then I would write another as if I were practising calligraphy'. This absence of 'voices that are the expression of the *mind* of the play' (emphasis mine) and the concomitant resistance to linearity point to precisely those attributes that Bakhtin uncovers in the heteroglossia of the novel.

It is not just, however, in the autonomy and multiple fields of vision of the characters that I find the dialogic imagination at work in Fornes's drama. The second act of *Fefu and her Friends* elaborates the differences among the voices of the women but also removes them and us to separate spaces. During Part II, four different scenes occur simultaneously in four different spaces – the lawn, the study, the bedroom and the kitchen. The audience is divided into four groups, each of which is guided to a different space where one or more of the women is speaking. After a scene is completed, the audience moves to the next space, and the scene that has just occurred in that space is repeated until all members of the audience have viewed all four scenes. The remarkable achievement of this device is to move the spectator from his or her single, unified perspective without, as Bakhtin worried, destroying theatre itself by removing the footlights. Fornes has created a dramatic correlative for the multiple points-of-view narrations of the modern novel or the parallel montages of film.

My experience as an audience member for several different productions of *Fefu and her Friends* is that we, the audience, are disconcerted, not only by being moved from our stable and familiar positions, but by our proximity to each other and to the characters; we are *in* their spaces but not *of* them. Their world remains separate from ours, and there is nothing we can do to make a difference in their world. We are thus not in the distracting position of the kind of interactive theatre that emerged in the sixties, where the divisions between the world of the stage and the world of the theatre were wholly destroyed and where I did not know to whom I was talking – an actor or a character.[36] Instead, in each viewing of each scene of *Fefu* our position as audience members is reaccentuated and our relationship to the characters is remediated. My experience is similar to that of my reading Faulkner's *The Sound and the Fury*; each character's telling of the tale remediates my relationship to all of the characters and their various meanings.

The most difficult and disturbing scene in Part II of *Fefu and her Friends* is that in which we witness Julia, lying on a mattress on the floor so that we must look down upon her; she speaks what the other characters refer to as her 'hallucinations'. The setting itself is a hybrid place, a mixture of cultural artifacts that do not normally belong together: *There are dry leaves on the floor although the time is not fall'*, the stage directions indicate. Julia speaks of 'they', they who clubbed her, tore out her eyes, took away her voice. Then her pronoun changes to 'he'. 'He said that women's entrails are heavier than anything on earth and to see a woman running creates a disparate and incongruous image in the mind. It's anti-aesthetic' (p. 24).[37]

Julia's hallucination is the discourse of an other, a male other, ventriloquated by Julia.[38] That this is a specifically and ominously gendered discourse we hear in an emission from Julia's lips that she calls a prayer:

> The human being is of the masculine gender. The human being is a boy as a child and grown up he is a man. Everything on earth is for the human being, which is a man. To nourish him. ... Women are Evil. Woman is not a human being. She is 1. A mystery. 2. Another species. 3. As yet undefined. 4. Unpredictable; therefore wicked and gentle and evil and good which is evil.
>
> (p. 25)

In the midst of these hallucinations, Julia has cried out of concern for Fefu, whom the other voices appear to be telling her they will have to kill. What 'they' want from Fefu is her light. Julia has become aware of herself as one among other cultures, but she also fears that that 'other' culture has good reason to dominate, control and destroy her own different voice. It is not anything that Julia has done or had done to her that makes her speak so strangely or that causes her paralysis. She is no more or less mad, no more or less paralysed than Hamlet. She is the figure whom Nietzsche presents in *The Birth of Tragedy*, the figure for whom Shakespeare's Hamlet stands as the paradigm, the one who experiences nausea in his own knowledge and in that knowledge cannot move. Like Hamlet, Julia is paralysed from too much knowledge, and she fears that Fefu is approaching the same state. Julia is always conscious of death; death is constantly present, and it is only because 'something rescues us from death at every moment of our lives' (p. 35) that she remains alive. But Julia is also threatened by the knowledge that 'they' who control insist that 'the human being is of the masculine gender', and she suffers because she can neither believe nor resist that dictum. Those whom she calls the 'judges' have told her that once she believes the prayer that denigrates women, she will be well. They tell her that all women have come to believe the prayer.

Until the last moment of the play, *Fefu and her Friends* is a dialogic drama, and is, more precisely in Bakhtin's terms, 'an intentional novelistic hybrid'. In 'an intentionally novelistic hybrid' differing points of view on the world collide within one cultural form; 'the novelistic hybrid is an artistically organised system for bringing different languages in contact with one another'.[39] The world that Fornes has created in *Fefu* is one in which not only Julia and Fefu herself but each of the women struggles with her own voice and brings into the conversation the diverse historical elements of her own linguistic consciousness. Emma, the incomparable performer, pontificates in the inflated rhetoric of a long passage from 'The Science of Educational Dramatics' by Emma Sheridan Fry; Paula weeps her contempt for 'those who having had everything a person can ask for, make such a mess of it' (p. 38). Her American 'plain style' tale of her own early envy of the rich might be heard as sentimental in another context, but here, as one utterance in an authentic conversation, it interanimates the whole of the drama.

To deliberately sustain this heteroglossia is dangerous, however; it is dangerous to the living of daily life and to drama itself. In the end, Fefu can no longer bear the multiple voices in her head. She goes outdoors and shoots a rabbit; indoors, blood appears on Julia's forehead, and Julia dies. The women surround Julia in a protective circle and the lights fade. Few in the audience agree on what this ending 'means'. Somewhat earlier in the play, yet another of the women, Christina, asked if she liked Fefu, said she did but that Fefu confused her. 'Her mind', Christina says, 'is adventurous. I don't know if there is dishonesty in that. But in adventure there is taking chances and risks, and then one has to, somehow, have less regard or respect for things as they are. That is, regard for a kind of convention, I suppose' (p. 22).

In Fornes's play, Fefu, the character, kills Julia and reconstructs the circle of monology only in the end and only as a last, desperate effort to ward off the threat to her own stability of consciousness. Other modern plays have ended similarly. Lula kills Clay at the end of Baraka's *Dutchman* because he has broken the conventions of his servile pseudo-discourse, the white middle-class discourse of the New York subway that still demands (even if it is now losing) its dominance. At the end of Beckett's *Krapp's Last Tape*, Krapp's lips move, but there is no sound: 'Past midnight. Never knew such silence. The earth might be uninhabited' (p. 28). Only the tape runs on in silence.

Beckett, perhaps not unlike Bakhtin, foresees, proclaims, the end of drama. Why? Because there are not two words, two different utterances to speak? Because if you kill the conventions you kill the form? Bakhtin proclaims the dialogic novel to be different, to transcend other forms because, for him, as rearticulated by Michael Holquist: 'Other genres are constituted by a set of formal features for fixing language that pre-exist any specific utterance within the genre.'[40] In contrast, Holquist argues, 'the "novel" is the name Bakhtin gives to whatever force is at work within a given literary system to reveal the limits, the artificial constraints of that system.'[41] Should we, then, give the name 'novel' to *Fefu and her Friends* or *Dutchman* or *Krapp's Last Tape* because they reveal the 'artificial constraints' of the system we call drama, reveal and disrupt those constraints?

Bakhtin would likely respond that these and other instances that you and I might cite of dialogic dramas are evidence that we are in an era 'when the novel becomes the dominant genre'.[42] At such a time 'all literature is then caught up in the process of "becoming" and in a special kind of "generic criticism". ... In an era when the novel reigns supreme, almost all the remaining genres are to a greater or lesser extent "novelised", drama (for example Ibsen, Hauptmann, the whole of Naturalist drama), epic poetry ... Those genres that stubbornly preserve their old canonic nature begin to appear stylised.'[43]

'What are the salient features of this novelisation of other genres suggested by us above?' Bakhtin asks. 'They become more free and flexible, their language renews itself by incorporating extraliterary heteroglossia and the "novelistic" layers of literary language, they become dialogised, permeated with laughter, irony, humour, elements of self-parody and finally – this is the most important thing – the novel inserts into these other genres an indeterminancy, a certain semantic openendedness, a living contact with unfinished, still-evolving contemporary reality (the openended present).'

The carnival spirit, the artistic representation of heteroglossia, is evident in modern drama, but if this is a sign of good living in the theatre, which I would take it to be, it is at best a weak sign struggling for acknowledgement. As *The Heidi Chronicles* attests, even in a world where the discourses of patriarchy and the discourses of feminism must encounter each other, they need not reaccentuate the other. The reason they do not is not a matter simply of formal attributes of a genre. Despite Bakhtin's claims about the rigid conventions of drama and their inherent resistance to polyphony, it is, paradoxically, central to Bakhtin's own theorising that literary genres do not transform themselves from within nor do individual authors and readers simply decide to write and read dialogically: 'This verbal-ideological decentring will occur only when a national culture loses its sealed-off and self-sufficient character, when it becomes conscious of itself as only one among other cultures and languages.'[44] As we well know, our own new technologies of communication offer decidedly alternative paths: one which would include and subsume into dominant Western patriarchical culture the diversity of voices that inhabit the earth; another that would break the seal and authoritarian self-sufficiency of its character and take on the adventure of speech diversity.

There is ample evidence that we live, more each day, not in a 'novelised, polyphonic' society but in what Raymond Williams once called a dramatised society, a world whose most succinct image is that of the self-enclosed living room in which every utterance completes a monologue. Our inclination has been to embrace and proliferate certain of the conventions of drama, to teach the foreign character who enters the stage for the first time the decorum of the given, wholly contained space which is the only space in which he can act.

This is not the only option, for ourselves or for our drama. When we approach drama in this way, we forget what Bakhtin also forgot in his initial pronouncements, that is, that while drama may press always towards a single field of vision, it is also the cultural space that most readily locates the viewer/reader outside, separate from an other. Drama, especially in its contemporary, televised form, may lure us to see and shape others as identical to ourselves, but that is not what its best work is ever about. In my own work over the last ten years, I have tried to recall drama's ability to enable us to acknowledge the otherness of others. With colleagues in the United States and in the Soviet Union, we have tried to do this by creating a new kind of stage, a stage that literally exists simultaneously in two cultures in a form of drama that has come to be called a 'space bridge'. When a space bridge occurs, two groups of people from two distinctly different cultures come together using satellite technologies for a conversation, nothing more or less but exactly that activity that Bakhtin locates as the essential site of dialogism (and which must be also the primary site of drama). In this context, we attempt what Bakhtin once urged: 'We raise new questions for a foreign culture, ones that it did not raise itself; we seek answers to our own questions in it; and the foreign culture responds to us by revealing to us new aspects and new semantic depths.'[45] Most often these 'space bridges' have been failures in any conventional terms of dramatic value: they have no clear beginning, middle or end, they lack a Unity of Plot, there are loopholes and misunderstandings and unresolved collisions. They are resisted and monologised by most American producers who demand total control of the event and who attempt to substitute the conventional drama of dispute for authentic dialogue. They are but whispers from the dialogic imagination, neither first words nor last words about novels or dramas, but words towards a genre in search of a name – and an audience.

'Nothing is absolutely dead: every meaning will have its homecoming festival. The problem of great time.' Thus Bakhtin ends his essay, 'Methodology for the Human Sciences'. In great time, the dialogic novel and the polyphonic drama may dance at their own homecoming festival amidst the laughter of a decentred society.

From *Modern Drama*, 34:1 (1991), 88–106.

NOTES

[I draw from the literary criticism of M.M. Bakhtin to argue that, contrary to Bakhtin's own judgements about most drama, feminist drama is, at its best, dialogic; that is to say that feminist drama is characterised by what Bakhtin calls dialogism, a form of ongoing polyphony with no single authoritative voice or resolution. After establishing the relevance of several of

Bakhtin's ideas, I use these to evaluate two controversially received plays by American women. The original article has been revised for this volume. Ed.]

1. M.M. Bakhtin's first book to be translated into English was *Rabelais and his World*, translated by Helene Iswolsky (Massachusetts Institute of Technology, 1968). In 1975, my colleague, Neal Bruss, brought this and other Bakhtin texts to the attention of an Amherst reading group of which I was a member. Included in the texts we read, in addition to Iswolsky's translation of *Rabelais and his World*, were unpublished translations of portions of the four essays orginally published in Moscow in 1975 in *Voprosy literatury i estetiki* and subsequently translated and published by Michael Holquist and Caryl Emerson as *The Dialogic Imagination* (Austin, TX, 1981) and translations of two works whose authorship remains a matter of dispute: *Marxisxm and the Philosophy of Language*, and *Freudianism: A Critique*, both of which are variously attributed to V.N. Voloshinov or M.M. Bakhtin or both.

2. Lest this seem to be an overstatement or an idiosyncratic judgement, I call attention to the 'Introduction' to M.M. Bakhtin, *Speech Genres and Other Late Essays*, translated by Vern W. McGee, ed. Caryl Emerson and Michael Holquist (Austin, TX, 1986) pp. ix–x. Holquist supports claims to Bakhtin's eminence with quotes from Todorov that hail Bakhtin as 'the most important Soviet thinker in the human sciences and the greatest theoretician of literature in the twentieth century'. Holquist also notes that the executive director of MLA in 1985 located Bakhtin among a pantheon of thinkers that included Karl Marx, Freud, Lévi-Strauss, Derrida and Barthes.

3. Wayne C. Booth, 'Freedom of Interpretation: Bakhtin and the Challenge of Feminist Criticism', in *Bakhtin: Essays and Dialogues on his work*, ed. Gary Saul Morson (Chicago, 1986), pp. 145–76. Originally appeared in *Critical Inquiry* 9 (September 1982).

4. J.L. Styan, *Elements of Drama* (Cambridge, 1960).

5. Helene Keyssar, 'Hauntings: Gender and Drama in Contemporary English Theatre', *Englische Amerikanische Studien* (December 1986), 449–68, esp. 456–7. I have taken the liberty of quoting extensively at this point from my own previous work since my guess is that this article, published in a German journal, has not been widely read outside Europe.

6. M.M. Bakhtin, *Problems of Dostoevsky's Poetics* (Manchester, 1984), p. 17.

7. See Tracy B. Strong, *The Idea of Political Theory* (Notre Dame, IN, 1990), pp. 45–6.

8. Aristotle, *Rhetoric and Poetics of Aristotle*, trans. W. Rhys Roberts and Ingram Bywater (New York, 1954), p. 234.

9. Ibid., p. 234.

10. Peter Euben, *The Tragedy of Political Theory* (Princeton, NJ, 1990), p. 100.

11. All citations in this section are from Aristotle, *Rhetoric and Poetics of Aristotle* (New York, 1954). On Peripeteia and Discovery, ch. 11; on avoidance of 'improbabilities', ch. 15; on the chorus, ch. 18; on Diction and Metaphor, ch. 22.

12. Euben, *Tragedy of Political Theory*, p. 108.

13. Ibid., fn 4, p. 97.

14. Ibid., p. 125.

15. Jean-Pierre Vernant, 'Greek Tragedy' in *The Structuralist Controversy*, ed. Richard Macksey and Eugenio Donato (Baltimore, 1970), p. 290.

16. Euben, *Tragedy of Political Theory*, p. 160.

17. Ibid., p. 161.

18. Bakhtin, *Problems of Dostoevsky's Poetics*, p. 17.

19. Ibid., pp. 17–18.

20. Mikhail Bakhtin, *Rabelais and his World* (Bloomington, IN, 1984), p. 7.

21. In the 'Notes' to 'Methodology for the Human Sciences', in M.M. Bakhtin, *Speech Genres and Other Late Essays*, Caryl Emerson and Michael Holquist cite an unpublished, internal review by Bakhtin of a book on Shakespeare as the source for the following brief yet comprehensive judgement of Shakespeare by Bakhtin:
    The stage of the Shakespearean theatre is the entire world (Theatrum mundi). This is what gives that special significance ... to each image, each action, and each word in Shakespeare's tragedies, which has never again returned to European drama (after Shakespeare, everything in drama became trivial) ... This peculiarity of Shakespeare's ... is a direct legacy of the medieval theatre and forms of public spectacles, determining the evaluative-cosmic colouring of above and below ... the main thing is the perception (or, more precisely, the living sense unaccompanied by any clear awareness) of all action in the theatre as some kind of special symbolic ritual.

22. Mikhail Bakhtin, *Rabelais and his World*, trans. Helene Iswolsky (Bloomington, IN, 1984), p. 34.

23. See Michael Holquist's 'Prologue' to *Rabelais and his World*, pp. xiii–xxiii, for a discussion of the role of the Soviet Revolution in Bakhtin's theory of communication.

24. Bakhtin, *Problems of Dostoevsky's Poetics, p. 69.*

25. See Tracy B. Strong, *The Idea of Political Theory* (Notre Dame, IN, 1990).

26. Jean-Pierre Vernant, 'Greek Tragedy,' in *The Structuralist Controversy*, ed. Richard Macksey and Eugenia Donato (Baltimore, MD, 1970), p. 284.

27. Ibid.

28. Helene Keyssar, *Feminist Theatre* (London, 1984, New York, 1985), pp. xiii, xiv; 'Hauntings: Gender and Drama in Contemporary English Theatre' (see note 5 above).

29. Mikhail M. Bakhtin, 'Preface to Volume 11: The Dramas', in *Rethinking Bakhtin: Extensions and Challenges*, ed. Gary Saul Morson and Caryl Emerson (Evanston, IL, 1989), pp. 227–36.

30. Ibid., p. 233.

31. See Helene Keyssar, 'Theodore Dreiser's Dramas: American Folk Drama and its Uses', in *Theater Journal* (Fall 1981), for a detailed discussion of modern folk drama. My comments on Dreiser's interest in the grotesque are especially relevant to Bakhtin's interests in carnival and folk theatre.

32. See *Rethinking Bakhtin* and *Bakhtin: Essays and Dialogues on his Work*, both cited above, as well as the various lengthy introductions to Bakhtin's works for some examples of these explanations of contradictions or complexities in Bakhtin. Also see David Lodge, *After Bakhtin* (London, 1990).

33. Phyllis Jan Rose, 'Dear Heidi: An Open Letter to Dr Holland', *American Theatre* (October 1989), 27–9, 114–16.

34. M.M. Bakhtin, 'Discourse in the Novel', in *The Dialogic Imagination* (Austin, TX, 1981), p. 370.

35. Scott Cummings, 'Seeing with Clarity: The Visions of Maria Irene Fornes', *American Theatre* (Summer 1985).

36. See Helene Keyssar, 'I Love You. Who Are You? The Strategy of Drama in Recognition Scenes', *PMLA* (March 1977), 297–306 for a fuller discussion of the significance of acknowledgement of otherness in theatre. While I hold to the position I argue in 'I Love You. Who Are You?' concerning the theatre's special ability to allow the spectator an intensification of the recognition of others as others, my more recent work, including this current essay, calls into question the claim I made in 1977 that the recognition scene clarifies the freedom of the audience.

37. All citations from *Fefu and her Friends* are taken from the playscript (1980).

38. See Michael Holquist, 'The Politics of Representation', in *Allegory and Representation: Selected Papers from the English Institute, 1979–80*, ed. Stephen J. Greenblatt (Baltimore, MD, 1981), pp. 162–83 for this specialised use of 'ventriloquation', a term I and others have come to use frequently as if it were one of Bakhtin's own terms.

39. Bakhtin, 'Discourse in the Novel', in *The Dialogic Imagination*, pp. 360, 361.

40. Michael Holquist, 'Introduction', *The Dialogic Imagination*, pp. xxix.

41. Ibid., p. xxxi.

42. Bakhtin, *The Dialogic Imagination*, p. 5.

43. Ibid.

44. Ibid., p. 412.

45. M.M. Bakhtin, 'Response to a Question from Novy Mir', in *Speech Genres and Other Late Essays*, p. 7.

6

Extremities and *Masterpieces*: A Feminist Paradigm of Art and Politics

TRACY C. DAVIS

In recent years, feminist critics have sought to identify what unites women's dramatic writing and distinguishes it from the predominant traditions. Several approaches are discernible. Janet Brown and Dinah Luise Leavitt codify characteristics of women's plays of the so-called second wave of feminism and study the political strategies of the groups that generated and performed the works, while Pattie Gillespie and E.J. Natalle stress the persuasive and rhetorical functions of feminist theatre.[1] Carol Gelderman and Nancy Reinhardt posit a feminist poetics (or anti-*Poetics*) of women's drama, concentrating on the formalistic components of texts and questioning how concepts of form, content, and excellence are gendered and how women's work is often devalued because it directly contravenes the tenets of Aristotelian critical theory.[2] More recently, however, Jill Dolan has led theatre studies into the discourses on representation of gender and sexuality, on subject and object, and on point of view that have preoccupied film theory and Marxian feminism. Specifically, Dolan considers how the content and style of certain performers relates to the maelstrom of feminist debate over pornography.[3]

Although Dolan takes her cues from performance art and satirical cabaret, these media do not monopolise theatrical efforts to question or protest the social origins of violence against women (which can take its most extreme form in pornography), nor is the

re-evaluation taking place only in fringe venues and alternative performance genres. A play that emerged from an English repertory
company, Sarah Daniels's *Masterpieces* (first performed at the
Manchester Royal Exchange in 1983 and subsequently at the Royal
Court),[4] reveals how feminist politics combine with women's
poetics in a 'mainstream' work that testifies to the effects of
pornography on women and argues that pornography is indissol-
ubly linked with masculine hegemony. *Masterpieces* is an exem-
plum of most of the common threads identified by Leavitt as well as
an excellent model of the rhetorical feminist writing described by
Natalle, and as such demonstrates the international applicability of
the findings of the American critics to a British play emerging from
a distinct political tradition. Daniels's accomplishment can be use-
fully contrasted to a play by William Mastrosimone, *Extremities*
(first performed at Rutgers in 1981 and subsequently on
Broadway).[5] Although the plays are remarkably similar in their
choice of subjects – the traumatisation of women, temporary over-
throw of power systems, and the justice of Justice – they are extremely dissimilar in their politics and formal dramatic techniques.
Extremities demonstrates that 'women's subject matter' does not
necessarily make a feminist play, and that unless challenges to form
and content converge, conventional dramaturgy can perpetuate and
replicate the ideology of domination even when the playwright's
personal view of sexual violence is one of abhorrence.

THE POLITICAL PARADIGMS

Mastrosimone is essentially conservative, espousing equilibrium,
psychological measures of 'normalcy', liberal humanist values, and
faith in the system. Daniels is the revolutionary because she questions one sex's right to dominate, rejects the notion that 'aware'
women are deviant, demonstrates that radical feminist analysis
(though widely shared by women) is incomprehensible to men who
live with, work with, and pronounce judgement over women, and
has no faith whatsoever in the system's fairness to both sexes. The
differences are also manifest in formal compositional elements of
structure and plotting devices, in imagery, and in the theatrical purposes of the two plays.

The apt title of Mastrosimone's *Extremities* is the author's
serious judgement on a victim of sexual assault, Marjorie, who at-

tempts to bypass the criminal justice system when she realises that she (not her attacker, Raul) could be convicted. By thwarting a rape and overcoming her attacker, Marjorie is forced into a paradoxical choice between extremes: if she sets Raul free he will return to kill her and her two female housemates (Pat and Terry), but if she calls the police Raul will argue that she (who is physically unharmed) was his assailant and she will be tried (not *with* her attacker, in the submission of her sexual history as admissable evidence, but *instead* of him). Marjorie rejects both choices and advocates a victim's justice that, if implemented, would be as extreme in its consequences as Raul's planned rape-murder. Mastrosimone seems to argue, along with the social worker/housemate Pat, that although the system is hard it is right, and that only the institutions of the police and courts can adequately mediate between the dialectical polarities that Marjorie and Raul embody as unlawful wielders of power. Neither the genderisation of sexual power nor institutional power are of concern to Mastrosimone. A man and a woman literally take turns exerting the power to torture, maim, and kill – both are extreme and therefore both are 'wrong' – and only the 'neutral' justice of the courts can resolve the stalemate.

Extremities commences with a solo mime. While caring for an ailing plant, Marjorie is attacked by a wasp and stung twice on her inner thigh. She viciously sprays the wasp with insecticide (well past the point of its death), scoops it up in a miniature gardening trowel, and deposits it in an ashtray. She settles down for a moment of leisure, lights a cigarette, looks at her wounds, scrutinises the wasp some more, and unthinkingly singes it. Thus, Marjorie's composite is succinctly drawn as a person who is compassionate toward inanimate objects, susceptible to sudden attack, capable of acting decisively and lethally, destructive beyond necessity, and ready to measure out death for minor attacks on her person. As Mastrosimone points out, this is best performed as a thoughtless action: 'I wanted to prepare the audience for the moment where she ties up another bug and tortures him, but I didn't want to suggest that it was out of sadism. Those things exist in all of us.'[6]

Raul enters, and the power immediately shifts. Now the wasp rather than the annihilator, Marjorie cannot flit to escape. Raul grabs her hair, knocks her down, muffles her, makes her comply verbally and gesturally to his whims, and orders her to scream to emphasise her isolation, entrapment, and helplessness. When she seems to be complying most (embracing him, volunteering expressions of love, and undoing his belt) she is preparing to regain power.

She sprays insecticide into his eyes. He screams. She breaks away, he catches her leg, she chokes him with the telephone cord, he screams again, and the stage blackens. By scene 3, Marjorie is triumphant: Raul is blindfolded, bound, and locked in the fireplace (a lifesize repository for embers and ashes, a crematorium, or a pyre). Still not satisfied, she prods him with a fire iron, douses him with ammonia, makes him believe he will be set alight, probes him with a shovel, saturates him with bleach, and demands his silence:

> **Marjorie** (*pulling him against bars by noose*) Talk again and I smash you like a fuckin bug!
>
> (p.24)

Considering that she has already decided to bury him alive, pulverisation seems a humane treatment. At the hands of this homicidal persecutor, Raul's fireplace prison becomes his fortress, a place of security and, ultimately, comfort.

Raul's ruthlessness is repeatedly demonstrated and his power (even in this predicament) is exercised whenever possible, but Mastrosimone's view is that Raul's evil manipulating genius is the product of a sick mind, and diagnoses untreated psychosis. A social cause of his behaviour is never posited. Thus, Raul deserves and gets sympathy because he acts out of illness. Like Raul, Marjorie is not content to thwart and capture her attacker and will stop at nothing until the victim has been maimed, humiliated, and murdered. She exerts power whenever possible, but Mastrosimone seems to argue that in spite of the legal Catch 22 her extreme actions are unnecessary and unjustified once she has captured Raul. Pat remarks that Marjorie will be 'crucified' in court (p. 32), while Raul exclaims 'Now I know how Christ felt' (p. 28), and later 'Give me a crown of thorns and finish me off!' (p. 54): common criminals can be nailed to a cross but only a messiah qualifies for Christ's full livery. Sympathy for Marjorie's seemingly unnecessary and barbarous course of action is minimal, for she is not a pathological miscreant incapable of helping herself, but is a normal healthy woman who goes too far in a moment of stress.

The plot of *Extremities* turns quickly when criminal justice, the presentation of evidence, and the demonstrability of guilt are introduced into the rhetorical argument. This is how Raul dissuades

Marjorie from summoning the police in Act I, scene 2; how the inevitability of Raul's release by the authorities secures Terry's tentative co-operation in Act I, scene 3; how Pat wins Marjorie's compliance in Act II, scene 1; and how the discovery of Raul's knife convinces Marjorie to submit to the law in Act II, scene 2 (it is the only proof of his intention to murder her). *Masterpieces*, in contrast, turns on sudden shifts in mood rather than shifts in power, for in feminist terms power is not a fluidly exchangeable prerogative.

Masterpieces commences with a restaurant scene, but before the pivotal characters are introduced the action freezes while three brief monologues by a millionaire pornography producer, a sex shop proprietor, and a consumer of pornography are delivered. The three central couples (Yvonne and Ron, Rowena and Trevor, and Rowena's mother and step-father, Jennifer and Clive) then engage in typical after-dinner conversation: the men take turns joking about women's compliance in rape, Jennifer tries a mild joke based on misunderstanding, and the conversation reverts to house repairs. For several minutes Yvonne remains still and silent. Her first utterance irrevocably changes the tone of the scene as well as the entire play. She asks:

> **Yvonne** How many men does it take to tile a bathroom? (*Pause*) Three but you have to slice them thinly.
>
> (p. 7)

Although the subject matter is always serious and tension steadily builds as the presence of pornography in men's lives is repeatedly shown to have effects on women's lives, Daniels frequently uses such quips (almost invariably humorous to women) to shift the mood and relax the tension.

Later in the first scene, for example, Jennifer's description of her menopausal guild members' competitive flower arrangements helps restore a civil (though for the men, embarrassing) state to the final moments of the dinner party:

> **Jennifer** Mine was a lovely dried number set in an oasis and for the base I used my diaphragm .... It seems a shame to think it was totally obsolete. And then Madeline grew mustard and cress in an empty pill packet.
>
> (p.13)

In the next scene (a preliminary hearing for a murder Rowena allegedly committed when a man approached her in an Underground tube station) Rowena's only comment on the didactic policeman's testimony has to do with the impossibility of travelling west on the one-way system of the Seven Sisters Road (p. 12). The midpoint of the play, a long monologue by Hilary on her contraceptive history (a history that results in single parenthood, state dependence, and the attention of the social worker, Rowena), is laced with ironic humour (scene 7). Rowena's interview with a psychiatrist who is double cast with Trevor, her husband, is a struggle of wits (scene 9); he believes she has lost her sense of humour, but her clever retorts are precisely what convey her sanity, wholeness, and perspicacity (as well as Jennifer's in scene 11).

Turnabout is Daniels's genius. The second dinner party (scene 12) is approached with foreboding because Yvonne hates her husband, but it quickly erupts into a shouting match because Rowena is furious at Ron for employing then raping Hilary. After the men leave, Rowena and Yvonne exchange four lines:

> Rowena   Ah well, Trevor never makes enough for four.
> Yvonne   I'm not very hungry.
> Rowena   What are you going to do?
> Yvonne   Leave him.
>
> (p. 60)

This suggests that a stormy encounter between Yvonne and her husband will follow, but instead the scene immediately changes to a lazy, relaxed, joyful picnic between Rowena, Yvonne, and Jennifer. The next three scenes have been fully prepared: the Underground incident that was described in scene 2 is enacted in scene 14, Rowena's conversation with Hilary about her rape was disclosed in scene 12 but is heard as a voice over in scene 15, and the final hearing of Rowena's case in court (scene 16) is a *fait accompli*. Judgment is not pronounced, though it is obvious from the summing up that the bench regards Rowena's submission on the sentencing rate for husbands' manslaughter of their spouses ('crimes of passion') as irrelevant, while the psychiatrist's description of her as 'removed, vague, uninvolved ... Prudish to the point of being sexually repressed – frigid' (p. 64) is indictable.

The final and most compelling turnabouts are reserved for the last scene, and are made more potent by the unprecedented calm of the three preceding scenes. Rowena and a policewoman (double cast with Jennifer) step forward, out of the courtroom. Rowena quietly describes the snuff film she viewed moments before pushing the man onto the Underground tracks. It is horrifying. A man actually cut up a living woman using a knife and an electric saw. The shocking effect of the film can only be conveyed by citing the speech in full:

> Rowena (*very quietly*) Well, the first part was badly made and like a lot of films it contained a good deal of violence and shooting. I think it was loosely based on the Charles Manson story. Then it changes, it becomes real. It's a film studio during a break in the filming. The director is near a bed talking to a young woman. He gets turned on and wants to have sex with her. They lie on the bed and he kisses her. She then realises that they are being filmed. She doesn't like it and protests. There is a knife lying on the bed near her shoulder. He pins her down as she attempts to get up. He picks up the knife and moves it round her neck and throat. There is utter terror on her face as she realises that he is not acting. She tries to get up but cannot. The film shows shots of his face which registers power and pleasure. He starts to cut into her shoulder, and the pain in her face ... it's real ... Blood seeps through her blouse. Her arm is held down and he cuts off her fingers. It is terrible. I have watched a woman being cut up and she is alive. He then picks up an electric saw. And I think no ... no he can't use it. But he does. Her hand is sawn off ... left twitching by her side. Then he plunges the saw into her stomach, and the pain and terror on her face. More shots of his face of power and pleasure. He puts his hands inside her and pulls out some of her insides. Finally, he reaches in again and pulls out her guts and holds them above his head. He is triumphant. (*Long pause.*) That's it. The end. And I kept forcing myself, to pretend that it was only a movie.
>
> (pp. 67–8)

The policewoman verifies that the description is not a fictive cinematic thrill, but that it is infused with reality for women of all ages; in the course of her work she has seen this reality confirmed in the mutilated bodies of hundreds of women. Elsewhere, Catherine MacKinnon (a feminist legal theorist and activist) makes the same point:

> One relatively soft-core pornography model said [in testimony relating to the Minneapolis Ordinance], 'I knew the pose was right when it hurt'. It certainly seems important to the audiences that the events in pornography be real. For this reason pornography becomes a motive for murder, as in 'snuff' films, in which someone is tortured to death to make a sex film. They exist.[7]

Rowena connects the snuff film to the sexual issues alluded to in the incidents of the play: 'I don't want anything to do with men who have knives or whips or men who look at photos of women tied and bound, or men who say relax and enjoy it. Or men who tell misogynist jokes' (p. 68).

Whereas *Extremities* explores the dynamics of a deadly personal sex war, *Masterpieces* depicts the hegemonic exertion of men's power over women, individually and generically. The hegemonic prerogative gives men superior control so that the victor in any contest is predetermined no matter how earnest the confrontation. The title is an ironic pun on the grim reality of a patriarchal culture as well as a reminder of men's centrality, women's customary marginality, and the wielders and genital weapons of power (the 'masters' and their 'pieces'). The martially extreme action Rowena takes in pushing a man into the path of an approaching tube train, and the maritally extreme action she, her friend Yvonne, and Jennifer take in denying their husbands conjugal access are more like the work of a covert guerilla resistance movement against a faceless regime of terror than the overt pitting of force and wits that Marjorie wages in her living room.

Both *Extremities* and *Masterpieces* depict women's response to male violence and the failings in criminal law; in one case this constitutes the mise en scène, and in the other it underlies the ideological issues that give the play meaning. Only Daniels proposes a radical critique that deeply questions the hegemony and demands change. By depicting what might be interpreted as the random, senseless, casual elimination of a man at the hands of a woman, Daniels shocks. The shock registers because it challenges the hegemonic order, but the impulse to label it extreme is checked by the contrasted example of a man's senseless, casual elimination of a woman in a snuff film. This is not a dialectic or a polarity. The shock registers because the slaughters are so similar: they are motivated by sexual loathing of a type, not an individual; they are witnessed; and they are truly arbitrary attacks by one sex upon the other.

PARADIGMS IN ART

Mastrosimone employs a single plot: Raul's attack and Marjorie's ensuing attempts to render justice to them both constitute the action. Previous and concurrent action is minimal and probably dispensable. *Extremities* is strictly a sequential linear rendering of the narrative line which is punctuated by several climactic developments culminating in the discovery of Raul's knife and concluding with a neat working out of conflict, restoration of order, and release of tension. Though its subject is somewhat unconventional, the plotting is typical of thriller, suspense, and revenge genres. It is, as Leavitt might describe, 'ejaculatory'; this is certainly the goal Raul has in mind, a man's sexual pleasure is sought at the expense of a woman's terror, humiliation, and physical trauma, and the plot leads up to a supreme moment of excitement followed by release. In accordance with Victor Turner's model of social drama, a 'breach of regular norm-governed social relations' commences when Raul refuses to leave the house, the breach widens in the crisis of the attempted rape and the ensuing reversal of power, Terry and Pat undertake redressive action in mediating between Marjorie and Raul, and in the fourth phase the disturbed group is reintegrated and the irreparable schism is legitimated.[8]

Masterpieces could not be more different. It is the *yin* to the *yang* of *Extremities*: cold, passive, and feminine instead of warm, active, and masculine. The story lines are multiple, though interconnected by characters and themes (like Richard Schechner's 'narrative nests').[9] Rowena is catalysed from numbness to assertive anger; Yvonne seems to progress through a similar course of feelings, also brought on by her awareness of pornography and its role in a coherent male socio-sexual system; Jennifer's enlightenment comes sooner, and she channels her radicalism into less destructive and avenging projects; and Hilary represents sexual victimisation of women who are not priviledged by class, education, marital status, or employment. The experiences of the four central women reveal their common group and further unite them (rather than separating them, which is the case in *Extremities*). By double casting the middle-class Yvonne with Hilary and defining Rowena as an ex-working-class social worker, Daniels shows the working-class woman as victim of her sexuality, and her sexuality as victim of patriarchal society (the Department of Health and Social Security welfare system and Ron the 'benefactor' rapist-employer) while women are powerless to give meaningful help. *Masterpieces* is episodic, asequential, multiply cast, employs direct address, voice overs, and many localities (indicated by musical motifs) – all experimental/Brechtian devices that promote objectivity, detachment, and the sort of stir and debate in spectators that the suspenseful thriller format of *Extremities* inhibits, or perhaps disallows. As Leavitt might observe, neither the plot nor the characters of *Masterpieces* are 'ejaculatory' (sexually or structurally) – the effect is quite the opposite, especially for the men.

Like other works by women in many literary forms, *Masterpieces* is cyclical rather than linear. Whereas Raul eventually subjugates himself to Marjorie's direction and sings a refrain from the song that suggests his withdrawal into juvenile dementia, Rowena's final moments show her at her most lucid, making explicit the connections between her imprisonment and her rejection of the sadism, pornography, coercive sex, and jokes that are equally prevalent and equally misogynistic. *Masterpieces* does not reassure and resolve – it provokes and revolves. The scenes go around and around motifs of dinners (contrasted with the serene picnic of scene 13); guilt, pornography, and the courts (contrasting the trials of Rowena and the Hughes boy in scene 3); psychiatric assessment of sanity; the working class and the middle class; men's solidarity in defending pornography and measuring women's sexual inadequacy; and women's 'crimes of disobedience' (ranging from Jennifer's flower arrangements to the Underground murder, the justification for which is partially laid in scene 5 when Rowena walks fearfully in the streets at the same hour of night). All previous action helps to explain and justify the stage action, with Yvonne's childhood, Jennifer's marital life, and Yvonne's withdrawal from Ron being particularly important. Rather than embodying the Greco-Roman structure defined by Turner, *Masterpieces* more closely emulates the Japanese aesthetic of *jo-ha-kyu* described by Schechner: a crisis, long in development, finally erupts in Rowena at the Underground station; this is followed by another slow phase on the swing and in court (scenes 15–16), and a very rapid rise to climax in the final scene.[10]

QUESTIONING REPRESENTATION AND THE PURPOSE OF ART

The cinematic and police-file apotheosis in *Masterpieces* is matched in *Extremities* when Marjorie holds Raul's deer-gutting knife to his scrotum and extracts a confession that he raped, mutilated, and murdered at least three women and that he intended to do the same to Marjorie, Pat, and Terry. This confession is Raul's *anagnorisis*, Marjorie's clemency, and *Extremities*' dénouement. But although motifs coincide in the two plays, Mastrosimone is consistently reticent over reflecting on the political context of sex and gender.

When Marjorie is released from blame and weeps at the conclusion of *Extremities*, it is not because she sees Raul as indicative of men's terrorisation of women or because she is struck by the realisation that he has many likenesses still free and roving, but because she is absolved of blame and feels she can live without fear of reprisals. According to Rowena's description of the snuff film, however, the rape-murder of a female victim means power, pleasure, and triumph for the man, while for the woman it brings terror, pain, and death; the grief and pain of the victim is shared by all surviving women, in perpetuity. According to Daniels, the different roles are wrought by gender, and cannot be reversed (as *Extremities* pretends to do) because the social reality is hegemonic. Time and again, motifs converge but are given distinct meanings by the two playwrights. Early in *Extremities*, Terry fears imprisonment because she accepts Raul's explanation that when his vehicle broke down outside and he innocently sought help from Marjorie, whereupon she behaved like a maniac; not dissimilarly, Rowena (the analytically clear Everyfeminist) is imprisoned for murder because she did not want to speak to a man. Her defence is not credible, as the judge states: 'the evidence you have put forward is nothing more than an irrelevant fabrication to further some fanatical belief that the laws concerning pornography in this country are inadequate. But that is of no concern here' (p. 66). Rowena's *anagnorisis* occurs in scene 8, when she gets her first glimpses of pornography, and culminates in viewing the snuff film. This exposure reveals her condition as a woman in a legally irresponsible, misogynistic society, leading to her rejection of patriarchy and culminating in *her* imprisonment for a heinous act against a random executive of the patriarchy.

By reversing the customary sexes of assailant and victim, Daniels reveals homicide as visible, heinous, and indictable. This gives rise to a series of questions. Why is Rowena gaoled but not the 'triumphant' film-maker? Why is it worse to murder a stranger than a wife who is 'neurotic' or 'nagging'? Why is the continuity of sexual objectification, exploitation, and brutality so acceptable to the sex that perpetuates it? Under what circumstances may women defend themselves, and at what point does self-defence become an offence? In *Masterpieces*, Daniels takes great pains to demonstrate that when Rowena acts, she acts for other women, not just herself, and sees the action through to completion, whereas in *Extremities* Marjorie is alone: she is a woman who is acted upon, who arrests this action, and who never carries out her own intent. In *Extremities*, the crimes are identified as assault and battery, mayhem, assault with a deadly weapon, imprisonment, and complicity to murder – all committed by one character upon another – whereas in *Masterpieces* the crimes are murder, rape, sado-masochism (S&M), bondage and degradation (B&D), and all forms of complicity in tolerating ritualised violence against any woman, wherever and whenever it is manifest, including the work place, in marriage, and in 'friendly' social relations. *Masterpieces*, thereby, would seem to indict *Extremities*.

Whereas *Masterpieces* informs spectators' perception of the causes and meanings of social phenomena, enhances sensitivity to the pervasiveness of men's hatred and violence toward women, and suggests that people can and should take action against the offenders (though not necessarily through random murder in urban subways), *Extremities* could cynically be summarised as a cautionary tale for women who spend time alone in isolated farmhouses. Mastrosimone was inspired to write *Extremities* after his girlfriend was raped,[11] yet the play serves to heighten women's fear of sexual attack and unrealistically compares women's actual helplessness and powerlessness against an armed attacker to a revenging powerhouse who happens to leave a can of insecticide within reach of her rape. *Extremities* might prompt some women to enrol in self-defence classes or to take stock of lethal household substances, but the overall effect is negative. Mastrosimone wrote a tight, exciting plot, not a Women Against Violence Against Women (WAVAW) pamphlet.

Masterpieces, like all feminist drama, has a social purpose to instruct and improve. Royal Court audiences generally took it as a springboard into debate, and despite its astounding final moments, ultimately it evinces positive effects related to social awareness, inviolable self-image, and self-assertion to everyone who can listen to it without total revulsion or withdrawal. In *Extremities*, violence against women isolates the women characters, but in *Masterpieces* resistance against the violence unites women – an effect that resonates in the audience. In *Extremities* the victims have names and they are victimised one by one, but in *Masterpieces* they are all women, all at once, actually not just potentially. The multiple casting and plotting help reinforce this message, implicating the collective experience beyond the confines of the dramatic fiction, the stage, and the theatre.

By shying away from all considerations of the social causes of sexual violence and allowing Raul to give his own explanations (because she was beautiful, she ignored him, and that annoyed him,

p. 21) Marjorie is portrayed as a provocateur, an impression enhanced by her costume (a bathrobe) at the outset of the play. So,
she 'asked for it' just as Terry believed she 'asked' for her rape years
before (pp. 45–6). Marjorie displays multiple rape avoidance strategies found in empirical research to be effective,[12] but Raul displays
most of the same behaviours: cognitive verbal techniques (logical
reasoning, conning, and stalling), utilisation of environmental intervention (Pat and Terry), and physical force (biting and grabbing).
Recent research shows that 80% of victims who thwart their rapists
feel embarrassment, fear, or anger immediately after the attack
while 75% deeply fear physical violence and 70% feel humiliated,
yet Marjorie evinces a single, lesser characteristic of the rape
trauma syndrome: the desire for revenge experienced by 65% of
women.[13] For all the accuracy with which the rapist is drawn,
Marjorie is allowed only a single trait of the victim's syndrome. In
this case, the revenge is both unlawful and psychically unhelpful for
Marjorie. Raul merges the characteristics of a power rapist and a
sadistic rapist – in this he is extraordinarily true to life.[14] Like
power rapists, he uses physical aggression to overpower and
subdue; he has concurrent consensual sexual relations with his wife;
he engages in assertive conversation, instructing Marjorie in what
to do; and he is inquisitive about her sexual life. Like sadistic
rapists, he perceives his victims as promiscuous, 'symbols of something he wants to punish or destroy',[15] the assault is premeditated;
he has taken precautions against discovery or interruption; he has
souvenirs of his victims (in this case, letters); the presence of the
knife strongly suggests that he intends to torture and destroy his
victims; and his attack on Marjorie is a serial offence. This is the
criminal profile that Mastrosimone manipulates his audiences into
admiring, pitying, or sympathising. The single positive aspect of
Extremities is that Marjorie is not raped (and, arguably, that Raul
is not murdered). Otherwise, details of the realism serve to eroticise
the torture in a prolonged aesthetic glorification of violence – first
upon Marjorie, then upon Raul – straddling the genres of erotic
thriller, social drama, and *Grand Guignol*.

One of the thrusts in feminist criticism has been to expose the
gendered nature of genres and styles in fiction, drama, and film. By
presenting the snuff film as the epitome of gendered violence,
Masterpieces participates in this critical project. Daniels names a
specific genre of film, categorises its typical technical and stylistic
features, and summarises its only content. This may seem like a pre-

sumptuous stroke for a play, but ultimately form is evaluated, rejected, and modified by artists, not critics, and there are precedents for satire, eulogy, or censure being used to point out the likeness of one medium to another. In this case, it is the snuff film that is under scrutiny, and it can be shown to be as closely dependent on long-established theatrical traditions as on film evolution.

	FICTION WITH SOCIAL REALITY		NON-FICTION
Theatre:			
1) *Grand Guignol*			
	→ 3) 'Therapeutic' Sex Theatre	→	Documentary
2) Burlesque			⇑
Film:			
	2) 'Roughies'		⇓
1) 'Nudies' →	→ 4) S&M/B&D	→	Snuff
	3) 'Kinkies'		(Pornography of death

The graphic macabre violence of *Grand Guignol* merges with the erotic rituals and costumed scenarios of burlesque dance to form the 'therapeutic' sex theatres of the Bizarre Theatre, Belle de Jour, and The Project, where participatory drama gives full rein to sado-masochistic enactments.[16] Similarly, films of nudity gave way in the early 1960s to genres Arthur Knight and Hollis Alpert call 'roughies' (films with female aggressors, such as *The Dirty Girls*), and then 'kinkies' with man-destroying Amazons, violence, and erotic realism (*A Smell of Honey*; *A Swallow of Brine*, and *The Mankillers* also known as *Faster, Pussy, Kill! Kill! Kill!*).[17] Later, S&M and B&D films became household items thanks to the popularisation of the home video recorder, with 104,000,000 rentals in the United States alone in 1986.[18] In these films, women are bound, suspended, probed, pinced, and beaten – supposedly for their own erotic stimulation.

The fictional enactments of cinema merge with the 'liveness' of theatre in two documentary forms; although these cultural artifacts are not Art, they are representations with social reality. The plotless *Faces of Death* montages of actual autopsies, gassings, electrocutions, alligator attacks, plane crashes, and suicides resemble snuff films in that they both test the limits of spectators' endurance of horrific documentary footage.[19] Unlike snuff films, however, the episodes in *Faces of Death* are neither caused for the sake of cinematic recording nor are they sexual. The sexual component of snuff films can also be contrasted to a suicide film Gary Jane Hoisington wrote about in 1976, which merges *Grand Guignol* with the film documentary, but in which eroticism is not involved:

> About six years ago a young German filmmaker ... sat down in a chair before his automatic camera, sliced himself open from throat to groin with a butcher knife, and pulled out his own entrails ... It was the first time an individual was killed for the purpose of filming death.[20]

Erotic celebration of torture and death is the *raison d'être* of *Snuff* and its inspirations, but like *Faces of Death* its fame spread by word of mouth, it had worldwide distribution within an unofficial counter-culture market, and it grossed enormous amounts of money.[21]

The film described in *Masterpieces* switches, mid-narrative, from a kinky format to S&M and then to snuff. By leaving the cameras rolling, the filmmaker switches from fiction to documentary. When the 'liveness' of this filmed death and the 'realness' of its *Grand Guignol* are described on stage, the social reality of theatrical 'fiction' documents the documentary. The irony that Daniels concentrates on is that the only 'true' victim society accepts is the Underground fatality; incest, threats, rape, sexual harassment, domestic violence, and sexual assault go unnoticed and unacknowledged, yet a fatal shove into the path of an oncoming train could not fail to be reported and successfully prosecuted. In the filmic product of this system, the director of *Snuff* is not prosecuted and the cinematic evidence is unsuppressed.

Both Rowena and the film director understand the masculine ideology of violence, though one is privileged by his sex to have a choice about being its executive and the other is doomed by her sex to have no choice about being its victim. Both are presented with a relevant stimulus (in one case a vulnerable woman, and in the other a non-specifically threatening man), both commit a spontaneous action from which there is no turning back, and both pass into the public realm for judgement. Unlike Mastrosimone, Daniels does not trust the legally democratic, responsible, and impartial institutions of society to render Justice. Any society that tries a woman for murdering her rapist in the process of a sexual assault upon her (as in *The Queen* v. *Clugstone*, Q.B. 1987) cannot render justice to Rowena.[22] Any society that turns *Extremities* into a film for general entertainment (directed by Robert M. Young) does not widely recognise the continuity of the documentary in the 'fiction'. Most importantly, Daniels exposes the all-pervasiveness of masculine hegemony by turning the tables and enabling the other sex to exert it briefly in a fictive setting.

Daniel was inspired to write *Masterpieces* by the long delayed appearance of *Snuff* in Britain in 1982. She used the theatre as a forum to oppose another public medium, the cinema, by exposing *Snuff* as an integrated (not aberrant) part of male hegemony wherein pornography is the revealed theory, but rape is not the only manifestation of practice. Resistance was needed, and resistance was ultimately facilitated by the content of *Masterpieces* and the argumentative rhetorical tradition of feminist theatre that it utilises. *Extremities*, in contrast, uses a conventionally sensational format with insensitive ideological miscalculation, aggresively denying the feminist critique of social power.

Both plays address issues of sexual politics within a violent culture, but only one tries to defuse the myths of sexuality and challenge their institutionalisation in the legal system and in personal relations. Unlike the lineally rendered plot of *Extremities*, the emergent story line of *Masterpieces* does not just juxtapose abstract points about the merits and demerits of society; its fluid plotting presents concrete images and details of the effects of sexual myths and pornographic mass culture on women. Like most feminist drama, *Masterpieces* is message-oriented – it attempts to prove an argument rhetorically – but it does this by fusing emotional responses to ideas that have been introduced but are not necessarily answered within the fiction of the play. In each of these respects, Daniels has fulfilled the description of feminist drama outlined by Natalle and Leavitt. While the post-production history of *Extremities* suggests that its sensationalism and conservative dramaturgy are more palatable than *Masterpieces*, Daniels's accomplishment is considerable and her contribution to the feminist canon is indisputable.

From *Modern Drama*, 32 (March 1989), 89–103.

NOTES

[This is a comparative critique of representations of violence and power in a British play, *Masterpieces*, by Sarah Daniels and an American play, *Extremities*, by William Mastrosimone. Davis shows how of two plays with similar subjects, one, Daniels's play, is feminist, and the other, Mastrosimone's play, is non-feminist, conservative and dangerous. Ed.]

1. Janet Brown, *Feminist Drama: Definition and Critical Analysis* (Metuchen, NJ, 1979); Dinah Luise Leavitt, *Feminist Theatre Groups* (Jefferson, NC, 1973); Patti Gillespie, 'Feminist Theatre: A Rhetorical Phenomenon', *Quarterly Journal of Speech*, 64 (1978), 284–94; Elizabeth J. Natalle, *Feminist Theatre. A Study in Persuasion* (Metuchen, NJ, 1985).

2. Carol W. Gelderman, 'The Male Nature of Tragedy', *Prairie Schooner* (Fall 1975), 220–36; Nancy S. Reinhardt, 'New Directions for Feminist Criticism in Theatre and the Related Arts', in *A Feminist Perspective in the Academy: The Difference it Makes*, ed. Elizabeth Langland and Walter Gove (Chicago, 1981), pp. 25–51.

3. Jill Dolan, 'The Dynamics of Desire: Sexuality and Gender in Pornography and Performance', *Theatre Journal*, 39 (1987), 156–74.

4. Sarah Daniels, *Masterpieces* (London, 1986). All further reference to this play is cited parenthetically.

5. William Mastrosimone, *Extremities* (London 1984). All further reference to this play is cited parenthetically.

6. William Mastrosimone, 'Interview', *Sexual Coercion and Assault*, 1:3 (1986), 105–7, 106.

7. Catharine MacKinnon, *Feminism Unmodified. Discourses on Life and Law* (Cambridge, MA, 1987), p. 159.

8. Victor Turner, 'The Anthropology of Performance', in *Process, Performance, and Pilgrimage* (New Delhi, 1979), pp. 63–4.

9. Richard Schechner, *Between Theatre and Anthropology* (Philadelphia, 1985), p. 233.

10. Ibid., p. 14.

11. Mastrosimone, 'Interview', 105.

12. Pauline B. Bart and Patricia H. O'Brien, 'Stopping Rape: Effective Avoidance Strategies', *Signs*, 10 (1984), 83–101. Curiously, Cohen reports that 'although victims who tended in general to be highly assertive women [such as Marjorie] were slightly more likely to have been injured during their [sexual] assaults, they had surprisingly, been LESS likely than unassertive women to have physically resisted.' Pearl B. Cohen, 'Resistance During Physical Assaults: Avoiding Rape and Injury', *Victimology: An International Journal*, 9 (1984), 128. Other findings accord with Marjorie's response.

13. Nicholas A. Groth, *Men Who Rape. The Psychology of the Offender* (New York, 1979); William Frederick Nobson, Cheryl Boland and

Diane Jamieson, 'Dangerous Sexual Offenders', *Medical Aspects of Human Sexuality*, 19 (1985), 104–9.

14. Judith V. Becker et al., 'The Effects of Sexual Assault on Rape and Attempted Rape Victims', *Victimology: An International Journal*, 7 (1982), 106–13; Michelle C. Lenox and Linda R. Gagnon, 'Psychological Consequences of Rape and Variables Influencing Recovery: A Review', *Women and Therapy*, 2 (1983), 37–49.

15. Groth, *Men Who Rape*, p. 45.

16. Catherine Burgheart, 'Sex Theatre', *Drama Review*, 25 (1981), 69–78; and Schechner, *Between Theatre and Anthropology*, pp. 298–302.

17. Arthur Knight and Hollis Alpert, 'The History of Sex in Cinema, Part 16, The Nudies', *Playboy*, 14 (June 1967), 124–36, 179–80, 182, 185–8.

18. Marshall Blonsky, 'On Looking at Pornography', a paper read before the Semiotic Society of America, 1987.

19. Annie Nakao, 'Faces of Death Video Outsells Even Sex', *San Francisco Examiner*, 20 July 1985, A-1, p. 2.

20. Gary Jane Hoisington, 'Hot Snuff', *Gay Community News*, 13 March 1976, p. 13.

21. Alan Shackleton, the distributor of *Snuff* in the United States, expected to gross $20,000,000. Hoisington, 'Hot Snuff', p. 9.

22. In October 1987, Janet Clugstone was tried at the Old Bailey for murdering a drunken man, Stephen Cophen, who had lured her into his home and raped her twice. The verdict was lawful self-defence, but while Judge Hazan remarked, 'he treated her like an animal, as an object for his perverted sexual lusts', he also qualified his ruling by saying that it was not to be regarded as a charter for victims of any crime to kill their attackers. Although Clugstone was acquitted, WAVAW criticised police for ever bringing the case to trial: 'We are outraged that a rape survivor who stabbed in self-defence has been made to go through the further ordeal of a murder charge. Self-defence is no offence.' (Angela Johnson, 'Woman who killed rapist is acquitted', *Manchester Guardian Weekly*, 11 October 1987, p. 40.)

7

Locked Behind the Proscenium: Feminist Strategies in *Getting Out* and *My Sister in This House*

PATRICIA R. SCHROEDER

During the 1970s feminist drama emerged as a potent force in the theatre world. In 1978, Patti Gillespie counted some forty feminist theatres in the United States alone, a large enough group for her to proclaim feminist theatre 'an example of a grassroots movement seldom witnessed in the American theatre'.[1] Just three years later, in 1981, Helen Krich Chinoy and Linda Walsh Jenkins listed 112 American feminist theatres.[2]

Defining exactly what feminist drama is, however, has become an increasingly difficult problem, despite some recent landmark studies of the plays, playwrights, theatres, and issues involved. For a few commentators, content alone can be the central defining quality. Playwright Megan Terry, for instance, defines feminist drama as 'anything that gives women confidence, shows them to themselves'.[3] Karen Malpede, another noted playwright, agrees, claiming 'Feminist theatre as I practise it is concerned with women *surviving* and creating new and human communities out of the wreckage of the past'.[4] Janet Brown, whose rhetorical model emphasises woman as the central 'agent' of a feminist play, claims that

155

'When women's struggle for autonomy is a play's central rhetorical motive, that play can be considered a feminist drama'.[5]

Other students of the 'phenomenon' (Gillespie's term) look more to structure and performance as the crucial defining elements of feminist drama. Helene Keyssar, for example, argues that feminist plays are based on 'strategies of transformation' rather than on the traditional – in her view, traditionally *male* – recognition scene.[6] And a large number of those exploring feminist drama focus exclusively on the experimental plays and productions of certain feminist theatres, whose ensemble strategies emerged (as Honor Moore has pointed out)[7] from women's consciousness-raising groups of the 1960s. For these scholars, only those theatre groups that employ such avant-garde techniques as improvisation, collective scripting, non-hierarchical production companies and non-linear dramatic form qualify as feminist.[8]

As this disagreement among scholars – and, indeed, among practitioners – of feminist drama shows, constructing an adequately broad yet still useful definition of feminist drama or feminist theatre is problematic. This difficulty is not surprising, given that (as many scholars have shown) women writers work simultaneously within two inherited traditions, the dominant male tradition and their own heretofore muted one.[9] It is crucial, of course, for feminists to define exactly what that alternative female tradition comprises, as many of the drama scholars mentioned above have been doing.[10] Yet in their enthusiasm to isolate what is unique about feminist drama, some scholars overlook or even reject the feminist possibilities inherent in more traditional dramatic forms. Even the astute Keyssar laments that certain predominantly realistic plays by women are not subversive enough in their dramaturgy.[11] Such criticism often implies, when it does not state outright, that women's plays which are traditionally constructed and produced cannot be feminist and have somehow failed – especially if they are commercially successful.

This undervaluing of conventional dramatic presentation raises a host of questions, two of which I plan to explore here. First, cannot the more traditional dramatic forms also support feminist values by depicting the entrapment of female characters in an unyielding, traditional society? Second, are the more realistic plays (that is, plays which do not depend on collective scripting, avant-garde production, and non-linear action) necessarily as conventional as they appear? For while it is clear that experiment feminist theatres have opened up new and exciting possibilities for the stage, traditional dramatic form is a flexible instrument that can also respond to feminist concerns.

Both Marsha Norman in *Getting Out* and Wendy Kesselman in *My Sister in This House* demonstrate the potential power of formal realism when appropriated for feminist purposes.[12] Both plays depend on formal realism and the picture-frame stage for their structure, using linearity and realistic detail to suggest the oppression of their female characters. Yet both plays combine this basic realism with experimental techniques (such as a divided protagonist, scenes presented out of sequence, and pantomime) to express the thwarted interior lives of the women they depict.[13] By using an imaginative combination of realistic and experimental techniques, these playwrights portray women's condition of being locked into limited social roles and powerfully explore the consequence – both personal and social – of that confinement.

Marsha Norman's *Getting Out* depicts the twenty-four hours following Arlene Holsclaw's release from a state prison. Although Arlene is legally free as the play begins, she is still surrounded by systems of enclosure. The set, which is divided into two parts, makes this point clear. The central performing area represents a cheap apartment, with conventional (if tawdry) accoutrements – bed, chair, sink, etc. – and the usual imaginary fourth wall. Around this realistic set, however, Norman erects yet another playing area, a catwalk of stairs and prison cells that completely surrounds the apartment. This playing area is both literal and metaphorical: it is used to enact remembered scenes from Arlene's prison days, but it also visually illustrates the restrictions placed on Arlene in the world outside the prison. By constructing a prison-like, interior proscenium arch to parallel the exterior arch of the stage, Norman has visualised in a theatrical context Arlene's continuing imprisonment in limited and limiting social roles.

The metaphor of theatre as prison is extended in the opening speeches. Each of the two Acts begins with prison announcements, broadcast throughout the theatre by an unseen prison official. Because the house lights remain up during these announcements, the audience is included among the prisoners who listen and must comply with the instructions. We cannot sit comfortably in the darkness, watching as outsiders, but must share the prisoners' degrading lack of privacy and individuality.[14]

The content of the announcements suggests the many subtle ways that Arlene and her fellow inmates are restricted, even beyond the physical confinement represented by the boxed-in set. First the announcer lists a series of prohibitions: no library hours, no walking on the lawn, no using the picnic tables. Prison excludes freedom of choice. The announcer next reports that the prison exercise instructor, Mrs Fischer, has given birth to a daughter. Her comment that Mrs Fischer 'thanks you for your cards and wants all her girls to know she had an eight-pound baby girl' reflects the prevailing paternalistic attitude towards the inmates, who are here equated linguistically with an infant. Then, after announcing three times that Frances Mills has a visitor, the broadcaster corrects herself: it is Frankie Hill, not Frances Mills, who has a visitor. This slip of the tongue reveals the loss of personal identity that accompanies the prisoners' loss of freedom.

Arlene's life outside the prison (at least, on this first day) remains uncomfortably like the life inside suggested by these announcements. When she wants to remove the burglar-proof bars that line her apartment window, she is told that 'The landlord owns the building. You gotta do what he says or he'll throw you out...'(p. 9). When Carl, her former pimp, arrives to entice her back to work for him, he scoffs at her plan to work at a legitimate job and spend her free time playing cards and watching television; 'Sounds just like the dayroom in the fucking joint', he remarks (p. 55). And when her neighbour Ruby, also a former prisoner, explains that life as a dishwasher is at least life outside a prison, Arlene retorts:

> Outside? Honey, I'll either be in this apartment or inside some kitchen sweatin over the sink. Outside's where you get to do what you want, not where you gotta do some shit job jus so's you can eat worse than you did in prison.
>
> (p. 59)

It is no wonder that Arlene feels as trapped outside a prison as she did inside one: her apartment and her limited opportunities represent continued imprisonment, reflected visually in Norman's doubled proscenium arch.[15]

The chronological plot, familiar characters, and conventional dialogue of Arlene's day of release – all devices of traditional stage realism – also underscore her ongoing confinement. Each visitor to her apartment reminds Arlene of her history of oppression and of the present restrictions to her behaviour. Benny, a former prison guard who has driven Arlene home, attempts to rape her, thereby recapitulating both her father's sexual abuse and the degrading voyeurism of the prison guards, who installed a two-way mirror in the inmates' shower. Carl, who accurately assesses Arlene's inability to earn a decent wage legally ('You come with me and you'll have money', he tells her. 'You stay here, you won't have shit' [p. 55]), recalls the economic powerlessness that first drove Arlene to crime. Her mother, appearing ostensibly to help Arlene get settled in her apartment, refuses to invite her home for Sunday dinner. Her explanation – 'I still got two kids at home. Don't want no bad example' (p. 23) – illustrates clearly Arlene's rejection by her family and by traditional society at large. Just as the set emphasises Arlene's continuing confinement, so the linear chain of the day's events suggests that her options are limited and that she will be forever imprisoned by others' expectations of her.

Within this realistic set and chronological plot, however, Norman has experimented with dramatic form in order to show Arlene's interior reality and the emotional effects of her lifetime of imprisonments. Most obvious is her creation of a separate, younger Arlene – the wild, incorrigible 'Arlie' – who, as John Simon puts it, 'rampages' through the prison scenes, in Arlene's memory, and on stage for the audience.[16] At the simplest level, Arlie represents Arlene's past. Although Arlie's words and actions are relegated to the prison 'surround' or are ignored by the characters who cannot see her in the apartment, she and Arlene both face the same sources of oppression, often suggested in parallel scenes of sexual, economic, or familial exploitation.

Arlie is more than an innovative expository device, however. Since she is played by a separate actor who often occupies the stage in conjunction with the actor playing Arlene, Arlie represents a split in Arlene, a fragmentation of personality that is the result of her oppression – what Rosemary Curb might call 'a mirroring of multiple selves in imprisoning cells'.[17] Arlie may well 'rampage' in Arlene's memory, but Arlene has had to develop a socially acceptable demeanour to escape at least literal incarceration. Arlie's presence on stage illustrates the repercussions for oppressed women of living in a double society, partly inherited from a patriarchal tradition and partly of their own making. By experimenting with this divided protagonist, Norman dramatises something expressed in feminist criticism:

> For women, then, existing in the dominant system of meanings and values that structure society and culture may be a painful, or amusing, double dance, clicking in, clicking out – the divided consciousness.[18]

Moreover, the achronology of the play that Arlie's appearances necessarily introduce, mirrors Arlene's memory rather than an externally verifiable sequence of events, moving Arlene to the subject position of the play. She becomes the producer of symbolic expression rather than the mere cultural construct that the play's realistic elements and the other characters demand she be.[19] As a result of Arlie's 'clicking in', we understand the past events and external forces that drove Arlene to crime; we see the psychological effects of abuse, restricted opportunities, and imprisonment embodied in Arlene's double consciousness; and we share in Arlene's past and present struggle to maintain some of Arlie's courage while developing a mature, autonomous identity.

By the end of the play Arlene does emerge as a mature character. She is no longer divided; Arlie, who sat centre stage in the opening scene of the play, has been banished to the prison catwalk of Arlene's memory, even though the play ends with Arlene (now centre stage herself) reminiscing about her younger avatar. Arlene is finally able to accept the conditions of her life and control them when possible, as we see when she firmly rejects both Bennie and Carl. What has brought about this change in Arlene? *Getting Out* abounds in images of entrapment and offers no real chance for escape. Where has Arlene gathered her new strength?

The answer to this question is twofold. First, Arlene has seen the value of autonomy. Although she recognises that she will not have extra money, fine friends, or the companionship of her family (even her son has been taken from her), she discovers that, on the 'outside', 'when you make your two nickels, you can keep both of 'em' (p. 59). Second, she learns the importance of female bonding. Despite her initial rejection of her neighbour Ruby's overtures, Arlene comes to value the companionship and sympathy of a woman who, like her, has lived a lifetime of varied imprisonments, and who will not exploit or demean her as every other character in the play attempts to do. As the play ends, Arlene accepts Ruby's supportive friendship. With Ruby's help, Arlene resolves to exercise those few options open to her and make the most of her meagre economic opportunities.

It is true, as Keyssar has pointed out, that a realistically constructed play can offer no solution or alternative to class- and gender-based hierarchies. *Getting Out* illustrates, however, that a flexible realism can depict the values encoded and disseminated by a patriarchal culture, assess the consequences of oppression by powerful cultural agents, and simultaneously support the alternative values – such as autonomy and female community – that feminism espouses.

Wendy Kesselman's *My Sister in This House* also uses an innovative combination of formal realism and experimental techniques to depict the harmful restricting of women's lives. In this play, based on the same true story that inspired Jean Genet's *The Maids*, the central characters are not literally imprisoned (as was Arlene Holsclaw), but the forces that entrap them are just as potent and even more pervasive, and the consequences – for them as well as for their society – are even more disastrous.

The central characters are sisters, Christine and Lea Lutton, who work as servants in the home of Madame Danzard and her daughter Isabelle. The four women could live together in harmony, and Kesselman uses a number of parallel scenes to establish the correspondences of taste, habit, and experience between them. Despite their similarities, however, the two sets of women inhabit different parts of the house, and the class distinction thereby preserved (and illustrated in the set) permanently segregates them. Like the set of *Getting Out*, that of *My Sister in This House* is a realistic representation of a divided world. One half of the stage depicts the elegant sitting/dining room of the Danzards; the other half, the kitchen where the Luttons work. Separating the two worlds is a staircase leading up to the tiny, unheated bedroom that Christine and Lea share. While their catwalk cell may not have the bars that Arlene's did, Christine and Lea are nonetheless imprisoned within its confines.

The basic plot, too, shares the fundamental realism of *Getting Out*. It comprises a linear sequence of causal events that lead inexorably to conflict between the two sets of characters, climax in the Luttons murdering the Danzards, and resolution in Christine's death sentence and Lea's term in prison, where, metaphorically at least, she has always been.

Within this realistic set and plot movement Kesselman, like Norman, has experimented widely. In contrast to Norman's innovative techniques, however, which primarily illustrate the psychological effects of prisons and traps on Arlene, Kesselman's theatrical devices and deviations from realism reiterate the restrictions of gender and class under which the Lutton sisters suffer, and predict their ultimate inability to escape confinement. For although Christine and Lea, like Arlene and Ruby, create a shared life (in their lesbian relationship) and devise moments of autonomy (such as wearing an inappropriate pink sweater while working or having their picture taken by an expensive photographer), their day of release will never come.

Kesselman uses a number of visual symbols to suggest the Luttons' hopeless condition and to predict their inevitable rebellion. The pink sweater mentioned above, the lacy undergarments Christine sews for Lea; and Madame Danzard's white glove (used to detect undusted spots) are obvious examples. The most potent of these significant props, however, is the blanket that the Luttons' mother crocheted for the infant Lea. Maman, like Arlene's mother, is implicated in her daughters' oppression: she confined Christine in a dreaded local convent when she was a young child, despite the girl's repeated attempts to escape; she denied Christine her wish, years later, to remain at the convent and become a nun; and she put both girls to work as domestics as soon as they could earn money for her. At the beginning of the play, Maman's crocheted blanket functions as a security blanket for Lea, who is homesick, and as a source of resentment for Christine, who has never forgiven Maman for undermining all her personal choices and taking all her hard-earned money. After they break off relations with Maman, however, the sisters unravel the blanket, symbolically unravelling their ties to their evidently greedy and manipulative mother. Nonetheless, escape is still impossible. As the stage directions reveal.

> *As the blanket unravels faster and faster, they run around the room. They are constricted by the confines of the narrow room. They wind the wool around the bed, under the sink. They wind it around each other.*

(p. 26)

Christine and Lea may feel that they have escaped their mother's domination, but the room in which she has placed them and the wool from her blanket keep them just as tightly locked in place as Maman herself ever did.

The most interesting of Kesselman's theatrical innovations is her extensive use of silence. Locked within the separate halves of the divided world they inhabit, the Luttons and Danzards never speak to each other until the final, climactic scene, the confrontation that leads to rage and murder. Their conversations remain strictly intrafamilial, alternating or even overlapping from within their separate realms. During the few scenes in which members of both families are on stage together (and not on opposite sides of the staircase), the Luttons always remain silent. Some scenes are therefore enacted entirely in pantomime, as Lea is silently ordered to pick up the seed pearls dropped by Isabelle, or Madame's dusty white glove speaks eloquently to the Luttons of their tiny domestic failures.

These scenes of total silence illustrate dramatically the inability of the two families to communicate with each other. The characters never know of the similarities among themselves (although Isabelle and Lea, both younger and less rigid than Madame and Christine, do silently share chocolates and hairbrushing, perhaps imagining the possibility of friendship). But the Danzards and the Luttons are in different social positions and do not, after all, share the same condition of voicelessness, as Kesselman dramatises powerfully in scene 13. In this scene Madame and Isabelle direct Christine in altering Isabelle's dress without ever speaking to either servant. Although Christine continues to make the required adjustments throughout the scene, '*Never, during any point in the scene, is a word addressed to Christine or Lea*' (p. 47). In fact, Madame Danzard refers to the silent Christine as 'she', even in her presence, asserting firmly that the dress will be ready on Friday because 'She hardly has anything to do' (p. 47). Despite Madame's repeated criticism of Christine's skilful alterations, the Lutton sisters must remain silent under her instructions, waiting until they are alone together to complain of Madame's increasing injustice. Their inability to speak in Madame's presence signifies their powerlessness in a world inexorably divided, and their frustration with their condition predicts the violence that will erupt when the women finally confront each other. For voiceless women imprisoned by an unjust society, anti-social actions become inevitable.

That the ability to speak is equated with power in this play is made quite clear by the two scenes enacted in front of the proscenium arch, outside the Danzards' prison-house: scene 9, in which the Luttons have their picture taken by a photographer, and scene 16, in which they are sentenced for the murders of the Danzards. Although they are outside the divided house in these scenes, the Luttons are still controlled by powerful social forces, represented by the disembodied male voices of the photographer, the medical examiner, and the judge. Although these male characters are never seen, their very voices restrict, define, and finally determine the fates of Christine and Lea.

This power of speech to define and control is only hinted at by the photographer, to whom the sisters, dressed alike, seem to be identical twins, as lacking in individuality as the inmates of the prison where Arlene was incarcerated (and, in fact, the male voice-overs in this play function similarly to the voice-over prison announcements with which *Getting Out* begins). By the end of the play the sisters, like Arlene, are literally imprisoned, and although the judge orders them to explain the murders, to speak in their own defence, the Luttons have learned well that to speak is futile in a world where their voices will never be heard. Christine's final speech is a cry to see her sister – a request which is, of course, denied. The play ends with the sisters standing 'as if framed in a photograph', that is, pictured as society has mandated they appear: silent.

Kesselman, however, has shown us another view of the Lutton sisters. By dramatising the inescapable condition of servitude and oppression under which Christine and Lea suffered, Kesselman engages our sympathy for them, making their eventual murder of the Danzards even more appalling. The voice of the medical examiner describes the scene of the crime in 'a flat, anonymous voice':

> a single eye was found, intact, complete with the optic nerve. The eye had been torn out without the aid of an instrument ... On the ground were fragments of bone and teeth ... The walls and doors were covered with splashes of blood reaching a height of seven feet.
>
> (p. 64)

With her innovative combination of realism and experimentation, Kesselman has dramatised the conditions that impelled these murders, making audible throughout the play 'that roar which lies on the other side of silence'.[20]

Getting Out and *My Sister in This House* both demonstrate that a modified realism can be an appropriate and powerful vehicle for staging feminist issues. While traditional theatre still depends to a lamentable extent on male-dominated hierarchical structures for production and funding, the proscenium stage offers playwrights built-in opportunities for dramatising the traditional systems of enclosure that restrict women. Michelene Wandor, defending the realism of her own feminist plays, has explained that 'artistic movements which seek to represent the experiences of oppressed groups reach initially for a realistic and immediately recognisable clarity'.[21] Perhaps this appropriation of the devices of realism will turn out to be only a small step in the history of feminist drama, but it is a step that should not be overlooked or undervalued. Depicting what is can help create what should be.

In fact, the variety of available theatrical forms is one of the strengths of the contemporary theatre, and feminists can and should take advantage of this variety. Eve Merriam recognised this fact when she described the generation of women playwrights that emerged with her in the 1960s and 70s; she said: 'first you had to write an Arthur Miller play, then you had to write an absurd play. Now there is a new freedom – you can write empathetic women characters.'[22] To deny women playwrights this freedom, to insist that their plays cannot be considered feminist unless they adhere to a particular ideological stance within feminism or that they take shape in a certain prescribed dramatic form, is to practise essentialism in its most insidious guise; such criticism only locks feminist playwrights into a new set of restrictions when our goal should be to empower them.

Feminist writers and scholars must, of course, continue to study, develop, and encourage their own separate tradition, in theatre as in all else. But an undeviating separatism of dramatic forms can only mean that fewer feminist concerns will be dramatised, fewer audiences will be reached, and feminist playwrights, like the women they often depict, may be left unheard, speaking softly to themselves at the margins of our culture.

From *Modern Drama*, 32 (March 1989), 104–14.

NOTES

[Schroeder argues that drama and theatre can be feminist within a variety of diverse forms and ideologies, including realism. She discusses Marsha Norman's *Getting Out* and Wendy Kesselman's *My Sister in This House* as positive examples of modified realism in feminist drama, as compared to my claims that *Getting Out* is not feminist and *My Sister in This House* is. Ed.]

1. Patti P. Gillespie, 'Feminist Theatre: A Rhetorical Phenomenon', *Quarterly Journal of Speech*, 64 (1978), 284–9, 284.

2. Helen Krich Chinoy and Linda Walsh Jenkins (eds), *Women in American Theatre* (New York, 1981), pp. 343–5.

3. Megan Terry, interview with Dinah L. Leavitt, *Women in American Theatre*, p. 288.

4. Karen Malpede, quoted in Elizabeth J. Natalle, *Feminist Theatre: A Study in Persuasion* (Metuchen, JJ, 1985), p. 41.

5. Janet Brown, *Feminist Drama: Definition and Critical Analysis* (Metuchen, NJ, 1979), p. 1.

6. Helene Keyssar, *Feminist Theatre* (New York, 1985). Rosemary Curb shares Keyssar's view that when recognition scenes exist in feminist plays they are qualitatively different from those in traditional, male-centred plays. She says: 'Recognition in woman-conscious drama does not unmask a personal flaw for which the individual character must make social restitution through personal suffering. Rather the necrophilia of patriarchy is unmasked.' See Rosemary K. Curb, 'Re/cognition, Re/presentation, Re/creation, in Woman-Conscious Drama: The Seer, The Seen, The Scene, The Obscene', *Theatre Journal*, 37 (1985), 302–16, 308.

7. Honor Moore, 'Woman Alone, Women Together', in *Women in American Theatre*, p. 185. Moore herself defines feminist drama more broadly than most students of feminist theatre troupes.

8. See, for example, Phyllis Mael, 'A Rainbow of Voices', in *Women in American Theatre*, pp. 320–4. Karen Malpede, 'Introduction' to *Women in Theatre: Compassion and Hope* (New York, 1983); Sylvia Virginia Horning Zastrow, 'The Structure of Selected Plays by American Women Playwrights: 1920–1970', unpublished dissertation, Northwestern University, 1975.

9. See Elaine Showalter, 'Feminist Criticism in the Wilderness', in *The New Feminist Criticism: Essays on Women, Literature, and Theory*, ed. Elaine Showalter (New York, 1985), pp. 261–5; Rachel Blau DuPlessis, 'For the Etruscans', in *The New Feminist Criticism*, pp. 271–91, and her *Writing Beyond the Ending: Narrative Strategies of Twentieth-Century Women Writers* (Bloomington, IN, 1985), especially p. 33; Judith Kegan Gardiner, 'Gender, Values, and Lessing's Cats', in *Feminist Issues in Literary Scholarship*, ed. Shari Benstock (Bloomington, IN, 1987), pp. 110–23.

10. For a helpful recent attempt to define a woman's dramatic tradition, see Sue-Ellen Case, *Feminism and Theatre* (New York, 1988), esp. chs 1 and 2.

11. See especially her ch. 7, 'Success and its limits'.

12. Marsha Norman, *Getting Out* (New York, 1978); Wendy Kesselman, *My Sister in This House* (New York, 1982). References to the plays will be cited in the text by page number.

13. In this way, they combine the two varieties of 'woman-centred drama' that Rosemary Curb calls 'Re/cognition' and 'Re/presentation'.

14. On this point I obviously disagree with Keyssar, who sees Norman's play as voyeuristic; see her ch. 7. See also Timothy Murray, 'Patriachal Panopticism, or The Seduction of a Bad Joke: *Getting Out* in Theory', *Theatre Journal*, 35 (1983), 376–88. Murray discusses in some detail the ways that the play encourages audience complicity with Arlie's behaviour and values.

15. Timothy Murray also discusses the implications of the prison for the theatricality of the play, concluding that 'getting out' is not much different from 'being in'.

16. John Simon, 'Theatre Chronicle: Kopit, Norman, and Shepard', *Hudson Review*, 32 (1979), 77–88, 84.

17. Curb, 'Re/cognition/', p. 308. Curb's comment does not explicitly refer to Norman's play but to one version of what she calls 'woman-centred drama'.

18. DuPlessis, 'For the Etruscans'. p. 285.

19. This discussion of feminist dramatic semiotics is indebted to Case, *Feminism and Theatre*, pp. 115–22.

20. George Eliot, *Middlemarch* (New York, 1977), p. 135.

21. Michelene Wandor, 'Introduction', in *Strike While the Iron Is Hot* (London, 1980), p. 11.

22. Eve Merriam, quoted in *The New Women's Theatre*, ed. Honor Moore (New York, 1977), pp. xxix–xxx.

8

Wordscapes of the Body: Performative Language as *Gestus* in Maria Irene Fornes's Plays

DEBORAH R. GEIS

I

If the stage is a place where (as Hélène Cixous has claimed) 'it is possible to get across the living, breathing, speaking body',[1] does that body constitute a 'text' in and of itself? In performance art an often-cited example of the female body 'as' text is Carolee Schneeman's *Interior Scroll* (1975), in which she appeared naked before her audience, extracted a long scroll from her vagina, and read aloud the words on the scroll.[2] More recently, Karen Finley has used her body as the site of transgressive (some might say counter-pornographic) acts: by arousing the mechanisms of disgust in her audience, her performances parody and subvert the associations between the female body and its role as sexually evocative signifier.[3]

Current theoretical discussions about staging the female body, however, return repeatedly to the question of whether privileging the 'textual' body is a reductive strategy that risks biological essentialism. The body's role in theatrical representation poses some particularly complex issues for materialist feminists because, despite the extent to which 'gender' and 'character' may be social and/or theatrical constructions, the facticity of the actor's biological sex always reinscribes the performer with the cultural codes associated with his/her gender. Jill Dolan has noted that 'the female body is not reducible to a sign free of connotation. Women always bear the mark and meaning of their sex, which inscribes them within a cultural hierarchy.'[4] At the same time, it is at the moment of entry into discourse (here, theatrical discourse) that the body acquires the multiple sources of signification associated with the *speaking subject*. Julia Kristeva, for instance, has emphasised the speaking subject's remarkable ability to 'multiply','pulverise', and 'revive' meaning.[5] However, Janelle Reinelt and others have criticised Kristeva's ultimate reliance on 'bipolarities' (male–female, maternal–paternal), which ignore the 'polyvocal' nature of the female subject.[6] Revisions of Kristeva favour polyvocality as a way of describing the processual nature of subjectivity; this metaphor of the voice, simultaneously bodied and textual, is an apt one for consideration of the theatre's unique status as an arena for the enactment or 'voicing' of multiple subject positions.

To show the subject-in-process or the non-unified subject, though, is to begin breaking the 'rules' of what happens to the speaking body onstage. Traditional theatre uses the actor's immersion in a character, and the audience's resultant empathy, as a way of closing up the occasional gaps between the languages of the body (both explicit and implicit) and the spoken language of the character: costumes, voice modulations, even lighting and music work to create an illusion of coherence, which is sustained by the spectators' complicity. Brechtian theory often serves as a paradigm for challenging or displaying these conventional strategies of representation. In Brecht's 'A-effect' the ongoing refusal to permit audience empathy – or the concomitant distinctions between actor/character and story/history – allows for a constructive disengagement (or, more accurately, a historicised 'reading') of the speaking body and its signifiers. Elin Diamond's feminist revaluation of Brecht proposes that the *Gestus* serves as an especially powerful agent for this spectatorial disengagement without wholly subsuming the possibility of spectatorial pleasure; her conclusion is that '[a] gestic feminist criticism would "alienate" or foreground those moments in a playtext in which social attitudes about gender could be made visible'.[7] It is in this realm of *Gestus* that I would like to accept Diamond's implicit invitation to explore new modes for a feminist theatrical *discourse*, as the term refers both to critical theory and to the dis-

cursive aspect of the female body as it appears within staged representation. As Brecht would have it, *Gestus* may occur through language as well as or instead of in the moment of physical enactment.
In fact, Patrice Pavis has described *Gestus* as the 'radical' displacement, or splitting, of the two elements:

> instead of fusing logos and gestuality in an illusion of reality, the
> *Gestus* radically cleaves the performance into two blocks: the shown
> (the said) and the showing (the saying). Discourse no longer has the
> form of a homogeneous block; it threatens at any moment to break
> away from its enunciator. Far from assuring the construction and the
> continuity of the action, it intervenes to stop the movement and to
> comment on what might have been acted on stage. *Gestus* thus dis-
> places the dialectic between ideas and actions; the dialectic no longer
> operates within the system of these ideas and actions, but at the point
> of intersection of the enunciating gesture and the enunciated
> discourse.[8]

Pavis's comments are pivotal for consideration in the context of
plays that prioritise monologues (particularly audience-addressed
monologues) and that downplay linear narrative forms. Monologic
speech could be described as taking on 'gestic' qualities as it sets up
the moment of 'splitting' between *énoncé* and *énonciation* Pavis describes. As an extended discourse, monologue continually threatens
to halt the 'continuity of action' and to 'break away from its enun-
ciator'. The gestic monologue is an almost-literal seizing of the
word. To take such a step can be, as Cixous and Ken Frieden have
argued in different contexts, a transgressive or 'deviant' act.[9]
Perhaps this is one reason why so many women playwrights have
been drawn to the monologue form: to some extent, the gestic
monologue marks a *locus* for the struggle for female subjectivity as
it enacts the 'drama' of the gendered speaking body and its polyvocal signifiers. The monologue's conquest of narrative space might
thus be viewed as a reification of the feminine 'subject-in-process'.

The plays of Maria Irene Fornes provide a striking opportunity
for illustrating the nature of gestic language, especially gestic monologue, in feminist drama. Her plays emphasise the creation of 'embodied' characters – that is, characters who enact the movements
toward and away from female subjectivity, in which corporeality
locates itself as the site of culturally-conditioned 'meanings'. While
these characters may reflect the 'broken'-ness and isolation that are
inevitable in their repressive environments (for example, Julia in

Fefu and her Friends, Sarita in the play by that name, or Marion in *Abingdon Square*), the fact that their 'impulses' as such are communicated in the gestic, self-narrated discourse of Brechtianism allows a partial recuperation of this fragmentation.

II

Surprisingly, despite Fornes's insistence that the Method helped her to locate an autonomy for her characters,[10] the figures that populate her earliest works (including *Tango Palace*, written in 1963 before Fornes studied drama formally) are noticeably *lacking* in corporeal identity: Isidore in *Tango Palace* is neither completely male nor completely female, the characters in *The Successful Life of 3* (1965) are identified by names that are at once universal and anonymous ('He', 'She', '3'), and the very plot of *Promenade* (1965) hinges on the notion that outer trappings determine and transform 'character', such as it is: '[C]ostumes/Change the course/Of Life', sing 105, 106, and The Servant.[11] At the same time, the physical movement and activity in these plays is nearly relentless, as if the characters were brought to life, puppet-like, only when they moved about onstage (a technique Fornes returned to in *Mud* and in *The Danube*). Similarly, the language used by the robotic characters in these early plays is continually mechanised, 'alienated', or formalised as a game or stage device; its failures and shortcomings are invoked repeatedly. Isidore in *Tango Palace*, for example, tosses out card after card upon which 'he' has written and (almost simultaneously) recites a multitude of clichés, anecdotes, and encyclopaedic information, so that the words which pour out of his mouth actually appear to fill up the stage space. At one point, Isidore tells a story about a man who loved his white rat, lost it, and fell in love with the rat's picture, then became desperate and smashed the rat's picture, thereby killing the rat, which had been hiding beneath the picture all along. Like the man in this story, the Jailer in *Promenade* confuses the signifier and signified when he arrests the Driver and Injured Man simply because they are wearing the jackets which have the numbers of the fugitives (105 and 106) on them. And, at the beginning of *The Successful Life of 3*, 3 says he is glad to have discovered that He (the other character) was waiting for 3 to drop his shoe because 'It starts action'. When He asks, 'What action did you start?' and 3 replies, 'We're talking', He retorts, 'That's nothing. We could as well be waiting for the shoe to drop'.[12]

Dr Kheal (1968), a piece for a solo actor, reflects an even more overtly metatheatrical direction, in which Fornes makes use of the potential for language to 'detach' itself from its speaker. The play itself consists simply of Dr Kheal's lecture to a classroom of 'students' (who may or may not be the members of the audience). Dr Kheal asks his listeners:

> But who, tell me, understands the poetry of space in a box? I do ... Abysmal and concrete at the same time. Four walls, a top, and a bottom ... and yet a void ... Who understands that? I, Professor Kheal, understand it clearly and expound it well.[13]

His description of the box – 'Four walls, a top, and a bottom ... and yet a void' – evokes an image of the theatre, or theatrical space; as the 'actor', Dr Kheal appears to 'understand' and 'expound' its function. Yet the more he says to 'expound' upon his points, the more obvious it becomes that Dr Kheal himself is an almost laughably insignificant figure in relation to 'the poetry of space in a box' itself, as is reinforced by the opening stage direction, 'He [Dr Kheal] is small, or else the furniture is large' (p. 129). In other words, as Dr Kheal's monologic discourse becomes increasingly circular and solipsistic in the course of the play, it reflects Kheal's own comment that 'words change the nature of things. A thing not named and the same thing named are two different things' (p. 132). In his encounter with the vision of Crissanda, she not only speaks a language which is incomprehensible to him ('She speaks in riddles, like the gods, "ksjdnhyidfgesles"'), but he lacks the language for recounting his experience of her: 'I know what happened and yet I cannot say. I do not know the words to speak of beauty and love. I, who know everything ... some things are impossible' (p. 133). The play, then, poses the possibility of a fundamental gulf between the apparent agent of signification (Dr Kheal) and the agent destabilised by Crissanda's alternate 'language'. In fact, Dr Kheal's words about the 'arithmetic of love' might be read as a gloss of this point:

> Don't you know that you can take a yes and a no and push them together, squeeze them together, compress them so they are one? That in fact is what reality is? Opposites, contradictions compressed so that you don't know where one stops and the other begins?
>
> (p. 134)

Like Brecht, Fornes refuses wholly to engage the language of these early plays in the seamlessness of traditional narrative – but she takes this to the point where the characters themselves seem at times to be oblivious to the 'story' that they are supposed to be in.[14]

III

Leopold in *Tango Palace* instructs Isidore to make his mind a blank, with the paradoxical advice, 'Don't imagine orange groves or anything';[15] Dr Kheal tells his audience that the moment one 'names' truth, it disappears (p. 132). Fornes's predilection for these slightly fractured moments of *énonciation* reflects her interest in the *im*possibilities of the discourse of theatre itself: how can theatre provide signs and assume they have stable referents? While her early works seem to address this question more generally, the plays dating from *Fefu and her Friends* (1977) locate the female speaking subject – itself a site for complex oscillations of signifier and signifieds – as a medium for pursuing this question at the level of theatrical language, especially monologic language.

Fornes has said that writing *Fefu* was, for her, a 'breakthrough' in her sense of her characters' autonomy; she comments, 'The style of *Fefu* dealt more with characters as real persons rather than voices that are the expression of the mind of the play.'[16] Much has also been made of the play's non-linear structure and its relation to a feminist perspective: after the first act, the audience divides into four groups and moves from scene to scene so that each group experiences the four scenes (each of which is repeated four times) in a different order; this structure is further complicated through the presence (made possible by meticulous timing) of two of the characters in more than one of the four scenes. As a result, when the spectators join back together as a single group to watch the third act of the play, they bring varying senses of the play's narrative to their experiences of the closing sequence.

Nearly all of the monologues in *Fefu*, up to Emma's lecture, dwell on the characters' senses of identity as defined in relationship to (or, more accurately, in contradiction to) their view of men. Cindy relates a dream in which she is being confronted and chased by a doctor, two policemen, and other figures; when she tells the doctor to stop cursing her, all present in the dream admire her forcefulness, but when she tries to determine 'whether the words coming out of my mouth were that I wanted to say',[17] she and her sister must run to escape being murdered by the doctor. Cindy's inability to control her own discourse in her dream typifies the way all of the characters have their language controlled or silenced by the patriarchal world represented by Fefu's husband and the other men, who remain outside the women's meeting place of Fefu's country house for the duration of the play. Emma, for instance, tells the story of Gloria, who was sent to a psychiatrist at school because the instructors could not believe the brilliant paper she wrote was indeed her own work.

The most extreme victim of this male-controlled discourse is Julia, who hallucinates that she has torturers who force her to utter and reiterate a 'prayer' consisting of precepts about the evils of the female gender:

> There are Evil Plants, Evil Animals, Evil Minerals, and Women are Evil – Woman is not a human being. She is: 1. A mystery. 2. Another species. 3. As yet undefined. 4. Unpredictable: therefore wicked and gentle and evil and good which is evil – If a man commits an evil act, he must be pitied. The evil comes from outside him, through him and into the act. Woman generates the evil herself ... Man is not spiritually sexual, he therefore can enjoy sexuality. His sexuality is physical which means his spirit is pure. Women's spirit is sexual. That is why after coitus they dwell in nefarious feelings. Because that is their natural habitat.
>
> (p. 25)

After she recites this monologue, Julia adds that she is supposed to be able to forget her torturers once she believes the prayer, and vice-versa: 'They say both happen at once. And all women have done it. Why can't I?' (p. 25). She is at once unable to resist and to acquiesce, and her paralysis between the two is reflected in the physical paralysis which confines her to a wheelchair. To some extent, Julia's condition is a representation of the oppression suffered by all of the women in the play; in this sense, her paralysis has a 'gestic' quality. Worthen, writing of the scar in Julia's brain (from a hunting accident), which apparently causes her spells of madness and her delusions of the speaking male 'guardians', states: 'The women of *Fefu and her Friends* share Julia's invisible "scar", the mark of their paralysing subjection to a masculine authority... . [Her] internalised "guardian" rewrites Julia's identity at the interface of the body itself, where the masculine voice materialises itself in the woman's flesh.'[18]

Indeed, the play resonates with instances of the division of the mind and the body caused by this 'authority', since the characters live in a society (the work is set in 1935) which insists on denying the validity of female sexual energy. When Emma remarks that heaven must be a place 'populated with divine lovers' ('[I]n heaven they don't judge goodness by the way we think', pp. 19–20), Fefu responds that she is visited by a foul, black cat, mangled and diseased, to whom she gives food because 'I thought, this is a monster that has been sent to me, and I must feed him ... I am afraid of him' (p. 20). The black cat is perhaps an extension of herself, the part of her that agrees with her husband's assessment of women as 'loathsome', her 'revolting' sexuality, which she must feed and yet finds frightening. Fefu, at the same time, seems somewhat cognisant of the challenges involved in acknowledging the existence of the female body in a society that views it as a decorative, useless, or inherently 'loathsome' commodity; after explaining to Christina and Cindy that she has learned how to fix a toilet herself, she leaves the room with the comment, 'Plumbing is more important than you think' (p. 13). The gestic implications of Fefu's proficiency as a plumber and of this line are apparent on several levels. Most literally, Fefu has learned a 'man's' activity and has therefore guaranteed herself a greater degree of autonomy. But 'plumbing', the inner pipes that sustain a system – here, specifically, the toilet – also represents the unmentionable and mysterious plumbing of the female body, which Fefu has in a sense reappropriated from the patriarchy by 'learning' its workings for herself. Finally, her admonition that it is 'more important than you think' suggests that the women as a group have been taught (as is evident in Sue's and Emma's anecdotes about their education) to undervalue their femaleness, their 'plumbing', in both the literal and the metaphorical senses.

Most of the characters in *Fefu* have difficulty accepting the body as a possible site for the inscription of their subjectivity because their bodies have already been (in)scripted for them with the male codes of their culture. The play's third act invites a possible re-inscription on their own terms, which will be accomplished through the ending of their physical/verbal paralysis and their joining together as a community of women. Emma has to some extent urged the dissolution of the artificial barriers of authority from the beginning of the play: when the women are discussing their upcoming fundraising presentation, she says, 'If we're showing what life is, can be, we must do theatre ... It's not acting. It's being. It's springing forth with the powers of the spirit. It's breathing' (p. 17). And Emma's monologue in Part Three, a lecture taken from Emma Sheridan Fry's 'The Science of Educational Dramatics', points out the direction for a new realm of subjectivity. Emma urges her listeners (the speech is actually part of the women's rehearsal, but here they listen to one another), to resist indifference, to give in to the 'Divine Urge', and to allow 'Environment' to come rushing in. Both of the Emmas (the author and the character) call for an end to the type of paralysis which Julia embodies. The 'lecture' demands, in effect, an awareness of 'acting' in both its theatrical and ontological senses: again, 'It's not acting. It's being.'

As they applaud Emma's speech, the other women share the sense of being a community of listeners (replicated to some degree by the intimacy that results from the small groups of audience members entering the characters' spaces in Part Two) who have much to give to one another. Such a community is transgressive, and it is capable of generating enormous power. In this sense Fefu's earlier comment that if women 'shall recognise each other, the world will be blown apart' (p. 13) proves to be somewhat prophetic as Julia, after refusing Fefu's exhortations to overcome her paralysis, 'dies' from an apparent gunshot wound at the same moment that Fefu shoots her gun to kill a rabbit. Perhaps, as Beverly Pevitts has suggested, this moment marks the new female identity defined by the end of the play, and this identity must emerge from the sacrifice of the old.[19] Evidently, in view of the odds these characters face, individual strength in itself is insufficient for the assertion of identity. Cecilia's words at the beginning of Part Three might serve as the keynote for the communal nature of such an assertion, bound as the women in this play are to their specific sociohistorical limitations and circumstances.

> We must be part of a community perhaps 10, 100, 1000. It depends on how strong you are. But even the strongest will need a dozen, three, even one who sees, thinks and feels as they do... . Thoughts, emotions that fit all, have to be limited to a small number. That is, I feel, the concern of the educator – to teach how to be sensitive to the differences, in ourselves as well as outside ourselves, not to supervise the memorisation of facts.
>
> (p. 29)

The last line of this speech gathers additional force though Cecilia's injunction to eschew the 'supervising' and 'memorisation' of the traditional (i.e. patriarchal) order. When the 'facts' that the characters must memorise – women are 'loathsome', 'the human being is of the masculine gender', etc. – are taken into account, it becomes clear that a community with an awareness of sexual differences refuses ultimately to 'supervise the memorisation of facts' and resists the coercion of dominant ideology.

IV

In *Mud* (1983), Fornes places a single female character, Mae, in a world that resembles the play's title: primitive, dingy, mundane, smeared and dulled by hopelessness and routine. The set itself is a run-down room filled with household items that suggest incompletion and brokenness (unpressed trousers, old shoes), attempts at creating a domestic space (stacked plates and spoons), and barely-suppressed brutality (an axe and rifle). This room is situated 'on an earth promontory ... five feet high ... red and soft ... [with] no greenery'.[20] This earthen setting (reminiscent of Hamlet's 'sterile promontory'?), along with the white mud-stained clothes worn by the characters in the original Padua Hills production,[21] gives the play a stylised quality in spite of the essentially naturalistic description of the room: these elements suggest that 'mud' has permeated the play at its essence and that the characters are visibly marked or stained with all that the mud comes to represent. As in *Fefu*, the structure of the play replicates or 'enacts' its content: at the end of each extremely brief scene, Fornes has the actors freeze for several seconds (in the 1983 Theater for the New City production, directed by Fornes, one could see the actors 'drop' their characters, then pick them up when the next scene resumed).[22] Although the original reason for this freeze-frame was a practical one, since the outdoor staging at Padua Hills prevented the use of blackouts or curtains between scenes,[23] the effect is of a series of cinematic-style 'shots' that reflect the repetitive, clumsily violent lives of the characters themselves. They not only enact a Beckettian tragicomic vaudeville, but the tableaux are also a reminder that the characters stand before us imprisoned in their bodies for the duration of each scene.

Mae, a woman with little education, seeks a way out of this imprisonment by learning how to read and write: 'I work', she says, '... I wake up and I work. Open my eyes and I work. I work' (p. 19). She lives with two men: Lloyd, who is essentially 'good-hearted' but who functions only at an animal-like level (p. 14), and

Henry, who initially possesses a scant amount of the 'knowledge'
Mae covets so earnestly but who becomes paralysed, inarticulate,
and helpless after he suffers a fall. When Mae decides that she has
had enough of Lloyd and Henry, she announces her intention to
leave them both, and Lloyd kills her with his rifle; the play ends
with the two men sobbing near Mae's body, which is outstretched
on the kitchen table.

The gestic quality of Mae's language in *Mud* emerges from her
efforts to achieve what she considers a more elevated form of discourse than her typical exchanges with Lloyd, 'Fuck you, Mae. /
Fuck you, Lloyd' (p. 18). Her duties in the house are to feed Lloyd
(and Henry), to wash and press their clothes, to attend to their
bodily needs. Written texts seem to her to be part of a realm of
knowledge and beauty into which she longs to escape. She cries
when Henry says grace ('For he satisfies the longing soul, and fills
the hungry soul with goodness') because, she says, 'I am a hungry
soul. I am a longing soul. I am an empty soul ... It satisfies me to
hear words that speak so lovingly to my soul' (p. 27). For Mae, language – which she connects with spirituality – is central to subjectivity to the extent that it takes on an almost material quality as
'food' for spiritual hunger, and yet its power for her lies in its
ability to let her transcend her earthbound existence. When, for
example, Mae struggles to read a passage about the starfish aloud
from a book, it is the very clumsiness and concentration of her
effort that allows the audience to feel the *physical* process by which
she tries to transform her world:

> The starfish is an animal, not a fish. He is called a fish because he
> lives in the water. The starfish cannot live out of the water. If he is
> moist and in the shade he may be able to live out of the water for a
> day. Starfish eat old and dead sea animals. They keep the water
> clean. A starfish has five arms like a star. That is why it is called a
> starfish. Each of the arms of the starfish has an eye in the end. These
> eyes do not look like our eyes. A starfish's eye cannot see. But they
> can tell if it is night or day. If a starfish loses an arm he can grow a
> new one. This takes about a year. A starfish can live five or ten years
> or perhaps more, no one really knows.
>
> (p. 27)

The luminousness of this moment comes not from the passage itself,
which resembles an excerpt from a biology textbook, nor from
Mae's skill in delivering it, for she can barely read. Yet Fornes indi-

cates in the stage directions that Mae's reading of the passage is 'inspired' (p. 27). In fact, it should be the very *difficulty* with which she reads that gives her recitation this quality. Similarly, Brecht has written that he found an 'almost unreadable "stumbling" ' translation of Shakespeare preferable to a smooth one for more aptly expressing the 'tussle of thoughts' in the gestic monologue.[24]

Just as Emma in *Fefu* urges the conflation of 'acting' and 'being', Mae acquires an identity and even a corporeality as she reifies herself through a text. Dolan has argued that Mae's 'entry into discourse' is in fact marked by Henry, who is able to move Mae with his language.[25] Certainly, Mae sees Henry as useful only to the extent that he can teach her or she can listen to his words; after Henry's fall distorts his ability to speak, she tells Lloyd, 'Kill him if you want.... He can't talk straight anymore' (p. 34). While Henry may indeed be a catalyst for Mae's inspiration, I would suggest that her point of 'entry into discourse' is, more fundamentally, the act of reading from her textbook. First, the stage language establishes Mae's centrality to the play and the centrality of the text both to Mae and to the staging. Fornes has said in an interview:

> I feel that what is important about this play is that Mae is the central character. It says something about women's place in the world, not because she is good or a heroine, not because she is oppressed by men or because the men 'won't let her get away with it', but simply because she is the *centre* of the play.[26]

Mae is 'framed' onstage by Henry and Lloyd because she differs from them in gender and her physical appearance onstage reflects the position of being 'at the centre of the universe', which Fornes says is integral to the portrayal of Mae's mind. Correspondingly, throughout the play, the audience is told that Mae's textbook is 'in the centre' of the kitchen table (pp. 27, 29).[27] To the extent that Mae refashions herself as a 'text', the parallel centricity is evocative, for this moment of *Gestus* embodies Mae's liberation from the representational limits within which she has been confined.

Dolan has claimed further that since Henry represents Mae's possibility for learning discourse, the accident that reduces him to a sexual body leaves Mae 'outside the register of language'.[28] Certainly, Mae's death occurs before she is fully able to find the realm of language she has been seeking, but her somewhat formally presented closing speech after she has been shot indicates that, to some extent, her text *has* 'given' her a language:

> Like a starfish, I live in the dark and my eyes see only a faint light. It
> is faint and yet it consumes me. I long for it. I thirst for it. I would
> die for it. Lloyd, I am dying.
>
> (p. 40)

This is a moment in which Mae experiences a brief flash of the lu-
cidity she has longed to attain. In the speech, her identification with
the starfish of her text (present to some degree in the earlier passages) becomes manifest, but it is infused with a voice that clearly
comes from her own associative and poetic powers and thus moves
beyond the mechanical prose of the biology textbook. This linguistic recourse allows Mae the power of self-demonstration, the ability
to articulate her bodied subjectivity. The somewhat 'presentational'
and overstated quality of the sequence as a 'closing speech' figures it
as a Brechtian-style didactic epilogue, as in *The Threepenny Opera*:
to some extent, Mae stands 'outside' of her character to reveal to
the *audience* the nature of her assimilation of language through the
starfish text, marking the speech as the closing *Gestus* of the play.

V

The Conduct of Life (1985) is set in the more overtly political
context of an unnamed Latin American country where prisoners are
tortured routinely and where those who are victims of oppression
become, in an endless cycle, oppressors themselves. Orlando, an
army lieutenant later promoted to lieutenant commander, tortures
political prisoners, maintains his marriage to Leticia only because
she keeps house for him, and has as a secret prisoner an impover-
ished young girl named Nena, whom he uses to satisfy his sexual
appetite. Leticia, Nena, and Olimpia (the maid) are all women who
must exist within the power structures of both Orlando's dominance and the ongoing repressive violence in the country itself. As
in *Mud*, Fornes uses monologic discourse to show the gestic role of
language in the constitution of the subject-in-process. Again, female
subjectivity is constricted by powerful social and historical forces,
and yet there are ways for the speaking subject to emerge.

Unlike *Fefu* or *Mud* (except perhaps for Lloyd's brief self-
introduction near beginning of the latter), this play includes
monologues spoken by a male character that counterpoint the
use of discursive language by the female characters. Orlando's
monologues differ from those of the three women in *Conduct*

because he uses language to justify a previously defined and cir-cumscribed identity or 'role' rather than creating subjectivity *out* of language. He 'narrates' or 'performs' himself with Brechtian aplomb, and the result is an elaborate series of rationalisations for his own behaviour:

> Man must have an ideal, mine is to achieve maximum power. That is my destiny – No other interest will deter me from this – My sexual drive is detrimental to my ideals. I must no longer be overwhelmed by sexual passion or I will be degraded beyond all hope of recovery.[29]

The irony, of course, is that the more Orlando tries to control his actions by setting them forth in language and then expecting his body (i.e. his 'sexual passion') to follow suit, the more obvious it becomes to the audience that Orlando's own words betray him. Although he uses Nena to satisfy his sexual desire, the result is the very degradation he has tried to avoid. He attempts to justify his brutalisation of Nena as 'love' (p. 82), just as he rationalises the death of a political prisoner whom he tortured as being due to 'fear, not from anything I did to him' (p. 79).[30] He believes, then, that he can change an actuality simply by expressing it in different words; one might say that he tries to exert the same domination over lan-guage that he does in 'marital' terms over Leticia and in sexual terms over Nena. Olimpia's description of Orlando is amusing, but apt: 'Like an alligator, big mouth and no brains. Lots of teeth but no brains. All tongue' (p. 79).

As the maid, Olimpia is the play's most 'invisible' character, but she is the speaker of its longest monologue, a lengthy narrative about the tasks she has to complete every morning:

> You can't just ask me to do what you want me to do, and interrupt what I'm doing. I don't stop from the time I wake up in the morning to the time I go to sleep. You can't interrupt me whenever you want, not if you want me to get to the end of my work. I wake up at 5:30. I wash. I put on my clothes and make my bed. I go to the kitchen. I get the milk and the bread from outside and I put them on the counter. I open the icebox. I put one bottle in and take the butter out. I leave the other bottle on the counter. I shut the refrigerator door. I take the pan that I use for water and put water in it. I know how much. I put the pan on the stove, light the stove, cover it. I take the top off the milk and pour it in the milk pan except for a little ... Like this. For the cat. I put the pan on the stove, light the stove. I put the coffee in

the thing. I know how much. I light the oven and put bread in it ... [she continues in detail]. I go upstairs to make your bed and clean your bathroom. I come down here to meet you and figure out what you want for lunch and dinner. And try to get you to think quickly so I can run to the market and get it bought before all the fresh stuff is bought up. Then, I start the day.

(p. 71)

The amount of detail which accumulates in Olimpia's monologue renders it humorous in effect, especially as it is followed by Leticia's 'So?' and Olimpia's response, 'So I need a steam pot' (p. 71). At the same time, the delivery of the speech is deliberately difficult and un-aesthetic to listen to; the stage directions indicate that Olimpia has a speech defect and that she speaks the monologue 'in a mumble' (p. 71). In the 1987 Organic Theatre production in Chicago, the actress who portrayed Olimpia used an atonal voice resembling that of a deaf person, and the repeated lines ('I know how much ...') took on the quality of an untuned musical instrument repeating an off-key chorus. Again, Fornes's emphasis on the 'unlistenability' of the monologue – its rough and grating rhythms and sounds – resembles Brecht's insistence that the *Gestus* not be created through smoothly-flowing poetry. Here, the gestic quality of Olimpia's monologue is shaped out of her insistence on transforming domestic space into narrative space to affirm her place in an environment where (as the servant) she is marginalised. One might say that Olimpia's use of language is the opposite extreme of Orlando's: while the latter attempts to make his behaviour follow from his language, Olimpia's language *is* her behaviour. Perhaps more so than any of Fornes's characters, Olimpia depends upon her discourse (which embodies her actions, and vice-versa) to establish that she even exists – hence her monologue's repeated invocation of the actual and grammatical subject, the 'I'.[31]

Although she is impatient with Olimpia's monologue, Leticia, too, struggles to find ways of 'speaking herself'. She resembles Mae in *Mud* in her desire to 'be knowledgeable', for she equates appearing as an 'ignorant person' with 'being ignored' (p. 70). Indeed, her most powerful desire is to command an audience; she tells Orlando's friend Alejo, 'I would like to be a woman who speaks in a group and have others listen' (p. 70). At moments Leticia does attempt to enter this taboo territory, such as when she speaks movingly and eloquently (but to no effect) to Orlando and Alejo about the condition of their country, 'We're blind. We can't see beyond an arm's reach . . .' (p. 75). But, for the most part, Leticia's only opportunities to speak for an audience are when she talks to her friend Mona on the telephone; at one point she even pretends to speak 'to Mona in her mind' (p. 81) in order to express herself. Even her monologues, then, are thwarted and reshaped as incomplete dialogues. When Leticia endeavours – like Mae, or like Marion in *Abingdon Square* – to memorise a passage from a book, the audience sees the cumulative effect of her frustration (as well as, perhaps, the limitations of Leticia's own class consciousness) when she slaps Olimpia for pretending to know how to read in order to help with the memorisation. At some level, Leticia's furor at Olimpia masks her rage at herself for her own lack of knowledge and her inability to receive sufficient attention.[32]

In the 'legal, social superstructure' which Dolan characterises as the source of hierarchical power in Fornes's works,[33] Nena is most overtly and painfully a victim of oppression. Orlando controls her to such an extent that at first she is unable even 'to speak words' and only 'whimpers'.[34] In a scene with Olimpia, though, Nena gives voice to a narrative about her earlier experiences doing ironing to earn her keep and about her grandfather's life in a camp for the homeless. Her description of the ways she would like to fix up the box where her grandfather stays is, once again, an effort at existing (or, in her case, *surviving*) through the creation of a linguistic 'reality'; her verbal construction of the box is like an architecture of the self. Yet even her ability to reside within this verbal framework has been destroyed, for her narrative turns into a re-evocation of her imprisonment and rape by Orlando. He beats her, she says. because '[t]he dirt won't go away from inside me' (p. 84). Nena's speech (and the scene itself) ends with the chilling words:

> I want to conduct each day of my life in the best possible way. I should value the things I have. And I should value the kindness that others bestow upon me. And if someone should treat me unkindly, I should not blind myself with rage, but I should see them and receive them, since maybe they are in worse pain than me.
>
> (pp. 84–5)

The moment is particularly unsettling because Fornes seems to be deliberately unclear about whether Nena is reciting words that Orlando or another authority figure has taught her to believe or whether the passage emerges from Nena's own idea that she should pity those who victimise her because they are probably victims themselves. Worthen describes the speech as emblematic of Nena's learned helplessness: 'Rather than taking a resistant, revolutionary posture, Nena accepts a Christian humility, an attitude that simply enforces her own objectification, her continued abuse. ... [She] finally adopts a morality that – grotesquely – completes her subjection to... [Orlando] and to the social order that empowers him.'[35] Perhaps, though, Worthen stops a bit short in pinpointing Nena's 'acceptance' and 'adoption' of the doctrine that her words announce. Apparently Nena, like Julia in *Fefu*, possesses a fragment of 'text' to which she must cling for survival, even if the text itself perpetuates her oppression. So great is the gulf between Nena's text and what the audience knows of her physical brutalisation by Orlando that Nena must disconnect herself from her body and from the pain which Orlando inflicts upon it. Her sense that she is indeed (as Orlando says) 'dirty' reflects the extent to which she has had to alienate herself from the physical and to hold tightly and desperately onto language because it is all she has. The *spectator*, though – one might assume – remains aware of the disjunction of *logos* (Nena's words) and gestuality (the physical moment of her enunciation), and so the speech is a gestic one in spite of or even because of Nena's inability to own her body – or even her language, if the words she speaks are ones she has been forced to learn.

VI

Jeanie Forte, writing about debates over the use of the female body in performance art, has argued that 'through women's performance art, the body speaks both as a sign and as an intervention into language; and it is further possible for the female body to be used in such a way as to foreground the genderisation of culture and the repressive system of representation.'[36] Forte's point, which emphasises that the (re)inscription of corporeality in the female speaking subject is not *a priori* 'biological essentialism', is applicable to Fornes's work. Whereas a more self-consciously Brechtian feminist playwright such as Caryl Churchill might choose to alienate the gendered body as a social formation existing almost solely in the realm of language,[37] Fornes allows the potential readings and misreadings of the body-as-sign to counterpoint and participate in the linguistic emergence of the subject. She recognises language as a crux of subjectivity, but just as language creates and deploys a body/corpus of words, the body/corpus creates and deploys a 'language'. As a final example, at one point in *The Danube* (1983) Eve says:

> I feel how my face quivers. And my blood feels thin. // And I can hardly breathe. And my skin feels dry. // I have no power to show something other than what I feel.[38]

Eve is using language to 'give voice to' her body: she suggests that her body has a sign-system (face quivering, blood feeling thin, difficulty breathing, skin dry) of its own, yet it is actually at the moment of transference to language that her body becomes the site of a readable text. The moment also is a gestic one because in the context of the play these 'symptoms' figure both Eve's perceived pain in her alienation from Paul and her radiation sickness from what can be assumed is a nuclear explosion. Thus, Eve's decoding of her body foregrounds Fornes's larger indication of nuclear war's ability to encode, to usurp control of the body.

Fornes, then, presents what Catherine Belsey has called the 'crisis of subjectivity',[39] a crisis set in motion at the moment of entry into the symbolic order embodied in the mode of performance. A reclamation of the speaking body's ability to 'act' (in its dual theatrical/existential senses) comes through recodifying this symbolic order; as Belsey says, 'in the fact that the subject is a *process* lies the possibility of transformation'.[40] The *Gestus*, with its multivalent moments of highlighting the competition of *logo* and gestuality, insists on an attention to this process. The female bodies onstage in Fornes's plays may not 'speak' with the comic literalness of Schneeman's interior scroll, but her theatricalisation of the subject-in-process through the use of gestic monologues suggests a similar preoccupation with the scripting/inscription/conscription of a textualised 'voice', playing ironically, like Schneeman, off the notion that language 'originates from' the body of the speaking subject.

From *Theatre Journal*, 42:3 (October 1990), 291–307.

NOTES

[The author presents a careful analysis of Fornes's plays from a Brechtian/feminist perspective. This piece exemplifies claims in other essays in this *New Casebook* of the power of Brechtian devices as deployed in dramas by and about women. Ed.]

1. Hélène Cixous, 'Aller à la mer', trans. Barbara Kerslake, *Modern Drama*, 27 (1984), 547.

2. For a description of Schneeman's performance, see Lucy Lippard, *From the Center: Feminist Essays on Women's Art* (New York, 1976), p. 126 and Moira Roth (ed.), *The Amazing Decade: Women and Performance Art in America, 1970–1980* (Los Angeles, 1983), pp. 14–15. For a discussion of the implications of Schneeman's body/text, see Jeanie Forte, 'Women's Performance Art: Feminism and Postmodernism', *Theatre Journal*, 40 (1988), 221–3; and Sue-Ellen Case, *Feminism and Theatre* (New York, 1988), pp. 57–8.

3. See Jill Dolan, *The Feminist Spectator as Critic* (Ann Arbor, MI, 1988), p. 66; and Janelle Reinelt, 'Feminist Theory and the Problem of Performance', *Modern Drama*, 32 (1989), 55.

4. Dolan, *The Feminist Spectator as Critic*, p. 63.

5. Julia Kristeva, 'Oscillation du "pouvoir" au "refus"', trans. Marilyn A. August, in *New French Feminisms*, ed. Elaine Marks and Isabelle de Courtivron (New York, 1981), p. 165.

6. Reinelt, 'Feminist Theory and the Problem of Performance', p. 52. See also Sue-Ellen Case, 'From Split Subject to Split Britches', in *Feminine Focus: The New Women Playwrights*, ed. Enoch Brater (Oxford, 1989), pp. 126–46.

7. Elin Diamond, 'Brechtian Theory/Feminist Theory: Toward a Gestic Feminist Criticism', *The Drama Review*, 32 (1988) 91.

8. Patrice Pavis, 'On Brecht's Notion of *Gestus*', trans. Susan Melrose, in *Languages of the Stage: Essays in the Semiology of the Theatre* (New York, 1982), p. 45.

9. Hélène Cixous, 'Le rire de la méduse', trans. Keith Cohen and Paula Cohen, in *New French Feminisms*, p. 251; Ken Frieden, *Genius and Monologue* (Ithaca, NY, 1985), p. 20.

10. Scott Cummings, 'Seeing with Clarity: The Visions of Maria Irene Fornes', *Theatre*, 17 (1985), 52–3.

11. Maria Irene Fornes, *Promenade and Other Plays* (New York, 1987), p. 24.

12. Fornes, 'The Successful Life of 3', in *Promenade and Other Plays*, p. 49.

13. Fornes, 'Dr Kheal', in *Promenade and Other Plays*, p. 130. Subsequent references to the play are to this edition and will be indicated in the text.

14. William Worthen has suggested the possibility that Fornes in these works is refusing to 'assimilate' the various 'enunciators' of the stage (character, plot, language, etc.) into a coherent whole the way the tra-

ditional theatre would advocate, choosing instead to 'suspend the identification between the drama and its staging'. It is especially striking that Worthen goes on to characterise this process, in his discussion of 'Tango Palace', as 'the dialectical tension between fiction and flesh' (W.B. Worthen, '"Still Playing Games": Ideology and Performance in the Theatre of Marie Irene Fornes', in Brater, *Feminine Focus*, pp. 168, 171).

15. Fornes, 'Tango Palace', in *Promenade and Other Plays*, p. 78.

16. Cummings, 'Seeing with Clarity', p. 53.

17. Fornes, 'Fefu and her Friends', in *Wordplays 1: An Anthology of New American Drama* (New York, 1980), p. 17. Subsequent references to the play are to this edition and will be indicated in the text.

18. Worthen, 'Still Playing Games', p. 176.

19. Beverly Byers Pevitts, 'Fefu and her Friends', in *Women in American Theatre*, ed. Helen Krich Chinoy and Linda Walsh Jenkins (New York, 1987), pp. 316–17.

20. Fornes, 'Mud', in *Plays* (New York, 1986), p. 15. Subsequent references to the play are to this edition and will be indicated in the text.

21. Kathleen Betsko and Rachel Koenig, *Interviews with Contemporary Women Playwrights* (New York, 1987), p. 61.

22. Dolan, *The Feminist Spectator as Critic*, p. 109.

23. Betsko and Koenig, *Interviews with Contemporary Playwrights*, p. 161.

24. Bertold Brecht, 'On Rhymeless Verse with Irregular Rhythms', in *Brecht and Theatre*, ed. and trans. John Willett (New York, 1964), pp. 115–16.

25. Dolan, *The Feminist Spectator as Critic*, p. 109.

26. Betsko and Koenig, *Interviews with Contemporary Women Playwrights*, p. 166.

27. For a discussion of 'centring', see Rudolf Arnheim, *The Power of the Centre* (Berkeley, CA, 1982), pp. 72–3, 75.

28. Dolan, *The Feminist Spectator as Critic*, p. 109.

29. Fornes, 'The Conduct of Life', in *Plays*, p. 68. Subsequent references to the play are to this edition and will be indicated in the text.

30. See, for instance, Elaine Scarry:'[T]he translation of pain into power is ultimately a transformation of body into voice, a transformation arising in part out of the dissonance of the two, in part out of the consonance of the two ... [P]ower is in its fraudulent as in its legitimate

forms always based on distance from the body.' *The Body in Pain* (Oxford, 1985), pp. 45–6.

31. See, for instance, Catherine Belsey, *Critical Practice* (London, 1980), p. 59. Olimpia is also the only character who stands up to Orlando, as she turns his own vocabulary of torture back on him: 'You are a bastard! One day I'm going to kill you when you are asleep! I'm going to open you up and cut your entrails and feed them to the snakes. (*She tries to strangle him.*) I'm going to tear your heart out and feed it to the dogs! I'm going to cut your head open and have the cats eat your brain! (*Reaching for his fly.*) I'm going to cut your peepee and hang it on a tree and feed it to the birds!' (Fornes, 'The Conduct of Life', p. 80).

32. Possibly because Leticia remains further outside the realm of discourse than she desires, she tries the alternate escape route of taking a lover (though the lover's existence, admitted under torture from Orlando, is never verified by the play and thus may be a choice Leticia has made by means of the language of her imagination). Orlando's torture of Leticia in his interrogation, which resembles his treatment of his political prisoners, ends with the obverse of *Mud's* finale, as she responds by shooting him. Her final act of handing the gun to Nena, saying 'Please ...' (p. 88) is left open for multiple interpretations, enacting the Brechtian legacy of avoiding catharsis and closure. Gayle Austin has interpreted this final gesture as Leticia's request that Nena shoot her, thus 'asking help of her double in ending her own torment' (Austin, 'The Madwoman in the Spotlight: Plays of Maria Irene Fornes', in *Making a Spectacle: Feminist Essays on Contemporary Women's Theatre*, ed. Lynda Hart [Ann Arbor, MI, 1989], p. 84). Dolan, though, has argued that Leticia is forcing Nena to accept the blame for shooting and thus that the moment is part of a larger social *Gestus* of historicised violence (Dolan, *The Feminist Spectator as Critic*, p. 108).

33. Dolan, *The Feminist Spectator as Critic*, p. 108.

34. See, for instance, Elaine Scarry: 'Intense pain is ... language-destroying: as the content of one's world disintegrates, so the content of one's language disintegrates ...' (*The Body in Pain*, p. 35).

35. Worthen, 'Still Playing Games', p. 174.

36. Forte, 'Women's Performance Art', p. 227.

37. See, for instance, Elin Diamond, '(In)Visible Bodies in Churchill's Theatre', *Theatre Journal*, 40 (1988), 188–204.

38. Fornes, 'The Danube', in *Plays*, p. 53.

39. Belsey, *Critical Practice*, p. 88.

40. Ibid., p. 65.

9

Unmasking the Minstrel Mask's Black Magic in Ntozake Shange's *spell #7*

KAREN CRONACHER

'the minstrel may be banned as racist/but the minstrel is more powerful in his deformities than our alleged rejection of him',[1] writes
Ntozake Shange in her foreword to *spell #7*. In the foreword, she
reveals that the audience at the original production of the choreopoem at the New York Shakespeare Festival (1979) failed to detect
her ironic, critical use of the minstrel tradition; rather, they de-
lighted in and 'grandly applauded'[2] the familiar spectacle of the
minstrel's singing, dancing, and posing as Al Jolson and Bert
Williams. Minstrelsy, then, had not lost its psychic power or its entertainment value for the dominant culture. As Tania Modleski
points out, the minstrel tradition is still operative in contemporary
Hollywood films.[3] If minstrelsy is still a popular form of entertainment, what constitutes the 'pleasurable' appeal of this banned form
of theatrical performance?

A 'huge black-face mask hanging from the ceiling of the theatre'
literally and figuratively dominates the scene of *spell #7*, confronting the audience with the minstrel mask's historical role in the
American theatre, and the question of its enduring power.[4] This
minstrel mask, a sign of white domination in the field of entertainment,[5] compels the audience to *face* the mask and unmask the *face*
underneath the mask. The face underneath the mask of blackface is
always already white, in the sense that minstrelsy is a white male

tradition, a white disgrace, a white issue. Minstrel shows reveal nothing whatsoever about African Americans; they do, however, reveal something about the dark continent of the white male phobias and desires, and 'the horror, the horror' of the white male's experience of gender and racial difference.

Minstrelsy was founded by a white man, and the short plays are traditionally written and performed by white men. Minstrel shows are written in an imitation of black dialect, and while the set-up is obviously a joke upon African-American men, the dialogue consists of jokes about women, jokes that play upon gender difference among whites. I write 'gender difference among whites' rather than 'gender difference' because Hortense Spillers points out that during the time of minstrelsy's popularity, the late nineteenth century, African-American women, unlike white women, were not 'gendered' (i.e. culturally produced as female subjects); rather, they occupied subaltern status for white men as property, chattel.

White women and African-American men are 'present' in traditional minstrelsy as the degraded objects of the joke(s) (they are not physically present in the spectacle, but present as referents), while African-American women are conspicuously absent, doubly excluded from this spectacle of white men posing as black men to make fun of white women, doubly excluded from the dubious pleasure of being in on the joke. It is in the *face* of this double exclusion that Shange, an African-American heterosexual feminist, appropriates the minstrel mask to investigate its multifarious signifying potentialities; and it is in the face of this exclusion that I, a heterosexual white feminist, also want to examine, historically, who has been playing jokes on women, and what exactly, is so funny? Shange's play addresses this absence of a subject position for African-American women by reclaiming and rewriting the legacy of minstrelsy, writing herself back into a history in which she was excluded by virtue of her sex and implicated by virtue of her race.

There is a sense in which I am addressing Shange's work because Shange's work addresses me, as a white female subject – not 'me' personally, but my historical position as a subject with different racial, cultural, political, and class privileges. In *spell #7*, when Natalie pretends to be a white woman, she delivers a fiercely satiric and historically accurate account of white women's complicity in racism and imperialism that calls attention to the different positions of power occupied by white and African-American women.

As a white heterosexual feminist, I am missing the joke of minstrelsy, and missing *in* the joke of minstrelsy; and when a feminist is *missing* something, it behooves her to turn to psychoanalysis. When the British feminist film theorist Laura Mulvey turned to psychoanalysis to explain the heterosexual male's experience of visual pleasure afforded by dominant narrative cinema, she discovered that where there is male heterosexual pleasure, there is the fetish.[6] Similarly, when British post-colonial critic Homi Bhaba turned to psychoanalysis to explain the condition of the colonised citizen as a 'mimic' of the coloniser, as a person who is 'almost the same, but not quite', he discovered that the logic of the fetish underwrites colonial discourse.[7] More recently, the American psychoanalytic feminist film theorist Tania Modleski applied Homi Bhaba's insights regarding the fetish to the American tradition of minstrelsy. Modleski names minstrelsy as a fetishistic enterprise, and explains the logic of the fetish as a process of disavowal:

> We need, then, not just to analyse the function of mimicry on the part of the colonised people, but to understand its role in the life and art of the *coloniser* – to understand, that is, the function of minstrelsy... Minstrelsy would be a method by which the white man may disavow – acknowledge and at the same time deny – difference at the level of the body; as a process of fetishism, it seeks, like all fetishes, to restore the wholeness and unity threatened by the site of difference... The concept of fetishism enables us to understand why minstrelsy has never really died out.[8]

One of the theoretical tasks of this article is to explain, from a psychoanalytic point of view, the white male experience of minstrelsy as a discourse of desire. The purpose of this paper is to ask different questions that reformulate previous queries, such as, what do white men want when they don masks of black cork? This investigation relies upon the work of African-American feminist theorist Hortense Spillers, who points out that the symbolic order (the language, kinship system, cultural traditions, representational systems, and legal order) of the United States remains white, segregated, and unchanged. Spillers maintains that the original theft of the African-American body during the slave trade, and the subsequent coding of the African-American body as a profitable piece of property during slavery, is still compulsively repeated in the current symbolic order.[9] Because the African-American woman lacks a subject position in the current symbolic order, her body is still missing, or stolen, as the site of an embodied subject. The minstrel mask is the sign of this symbolic order that has not accommodated the changes of history, the sign of a representational system in which African Americans are still missing as subjects.

The characters of *spell #7*, all unemployed actresses and actors, must live under the spell of a theatre industry that excludes them, a theatre industry that reflects their status as 'missing subjects' in history. In that sense, the performers live under the spell of the minstrel mask, which functions as an overseer of their acts. The persistence of minstrelsy's fetishistic appeal illustrates an historically unchanged symbolic order, in which whites still laugh at blackfaced entertainers, although they may 'know better', and even though minstrelsy was banned during the Jim Crow laws. The legacy of the traditional, theatrical minstrel shows not only lives in the film industry (one of the earliest sound films, *The Jazz Singer*, features Al Jolson singing in blackface), but also in 'empirical' government documents such as the 1965 Moynihan Report. Minstrelsy, then, has affected what I call 'the colonial frame of representation', the symbolic order of the white coloniser that currently endures.

In her foreword to the play, 'uncovered losses / black theatre traditions', Shange reveals that she has been influenced by Frantz Fanon's theory of 'combat breath', the lived struggle of the colonised subject contending with foreign surveillance. Shange notes the similarity between Fanon's description of life in French-occupied territory and her own experiences living as an African-American woman in the United States. Shange implies that she, too, lives and breathes in 'occupied territory':

> In everything I have ever written... I have made use of what Frantz Fanon called 'combat breath', although Fanon was referring to fran-cophone colonies, the schema he draws is sadly familiar... 'combat breathing' is the living response / the drive to reconcile the irreconcil-able / the black & white of what we live n where... my characters [respond] to the involuntary constrictions n amputations of their hu-manity / in the context of combat breathing.[10]

The American stage is an agent of colonialism, not in the sense that it is owned and controlled by foreign, European agents, but in the sense that it perpetuates traditions and stereotypes that cause one of its best playwrights to consider the stage as a territory occupied by foreigners.

Shange exorcises the spell of minstrelsy's powerful legacy in *spell* #7 by using African-American rhetorical devices such as the signifying monkey, irony, and satire, the formal rhetorical strategies and traditions that Henry Louis Gates, Jr describes as unique to African-American discourse.[11] Precisely because of the experience Shange describes, in which the audience interprets the minstrel show literally, missing the social critique, Shange's work calls for a contextual reading such as Gates provides, a reading that illuminates the specific codes, tropes, and signifying practices of African-American discourse. Gates's work allows the critic to understand the complexity of Shange's signifying strategies without being 'signified upon'. In *spell* #7, Shange reveals the many ontological, political, and historical connotations of blackface. In so doing, she demystifies minstrelsy's unconscious appeal, by demonstrating how this white man's joke still haunts the lived, conscious experiences of black performers.

Whites are the Other in *spell* #7. Shange foregrounds 'whiteness' as an ethnic category, decentring the construction of whites as natural, inevitable subjects.[12] Richard Dyer, in 'White', notes that the power of white is consolidated through the effacement of its construction as the norm: 'the strength of white representation... is the apparent absence altogether of the typical, the sense that being white is coterminous with the endless plentitude of human diversity'.[13] 'Whiteness' effects this naturalistic illusion of centrality by disappearing behind the construction of other identities, as whites disappear beneath the black cork in the minstrel show: 'whiteness both disappears and is subsumed into other identities'.[14] When whites put on black face for a minstrel show, they conceal the fact that they are dramatising their own anxieties by displacing the construction of their own identities onto the degraded representation of African Americans.

Although African-American men and women are under the spell of the black minstrel mask, they dis-spell the spell through black magic.[15] In *spell* #7, Shange reclaims the notion of magic, transforming the negative signification of 'black magic'. Lou appropriates the roles of the magician and the minstrel, so that his black magic transforms the black-cork of the minstrel from the sign of a mere mask into the sign of African-American being and lived experience. Lou asserts: 'this is blk magic / you looking at / & i'm fixin you up good / fixin you up good & colored / & you gonna be colored all yr life / & you gonna live it' (p. 8).

The performance of the constitutive traits of 'white experience' is another form of black magic. The notion that whites are 'naturally' clean and sanitary is undercut by Lily's description of Madison Square Garden as the sullied space of white entertainment. The 'latino chic /... rastafare... outer space funk suits' (p. 19) of 'ethnic' cultures add beauty to the space defiled by the 'cheap beer' and 'nasty smellin bano' accompanying white entertainment. African Americans wearing gold in their hair and silks and satins on their bodies transform Madison Square Garden, 'this barn / this insult to good taste' into 'a foray into paradise' (p. 17). Shange wonders at the customs of the white patrons of Madison Square Garden, who exhibit an appetite for blood but no sense of colour: 'madison square garden... the temple of the primal scream / oh how they love blood / & how they dont even dress for the occasion / all inconspicuous and pink' (pp. 15–16). Lily juxtaposes an account from a slaver's logbook describing Africans wearing rings in their noses and quills in their ears with this construction of badly-dressed whites attending violent sports events at Madison Square Garden. Hortense Spillers points out, 'the visual shock waves touched off when African and European "met" reverberated on both sides of the encounter'.[16]

In the plays of Amiri Baraka and Ed Bullins, the white woman functions as a sign for the United States. 'America' is feminised, constructed as a seductress uttering racial slurs as she projects her own voracious sexuality onto the African-American male.[17] For Shange, the white woman symbolises the relations between white women and women of colour. In *spell #7*, Natalie pretends to put on 'white-face', the mask of naiveté that prevents white women from confronting their complicity in racism and colonialism. 'i cd push the navaho women outta my way in the supermarket... i cd smile at all the black and puerto rican people / & hope they cant tell i want them to go back where they came from' (p. 47). Natalie also implicates white women as ideologically complicit in a fascist eugenics: 'those poor creatures [women of colour] shd be sterilised' (p. 49).

In Natalie's satiric mockery of the white woman, she performs the history of the unequal distribution of labour between white women and African-American women. From the African-American woman's perspective, the white woman appears lazy. 'like if i do anything / anything at all i'm extending myself as a white girl' (p. 49). Shange does not construct the white woman as essentially, or naturally lazy; Shange exposes 'laziness' as an historically persistent component of the dominant ideological construction of femininity. bell hooks points out that in the nineteenth century, the cult of true womanhood coded white women as angels in the house, while black women, as field labourers, were denied this ideological effect of gender differentiation.[18]

Glenda Dickerson describes the ideals of passivity defined by 'the cult of true womanhood' as it applied to the woman of leisure, and the exclusionary effects of the cult upon African-American women:

> at the turn of the century a dangerous little idea took hold in this country. It was called 'The Cult of True Womanhood'. Some of the attributes necessary to gain admission to the 'cult' were domesticity, submissiveness, piety, and purity. The ideals set up for 'true women' were in actuality a fanatical method of sexual oppression by white men to oppress and control women... The 'cult' became virtually synonymous with the upper class because only they had the luxury of leisure. Women of colour were triply locked out; by class, by race, and by history – they had been made the mule of the world in slavery, how could they now aspire to silk parasols and satin dresses.[19]

Dickerson reveals that the cult of true womanhood serves the interests of the white man as a discourse of power over women. The irony of the cult of true womanhood is that no woman could ever accede to such a position of docile passivity; the cult is a white male fantasy that obscures the truth of women's activity and labour.

When Lou promises the audience hair ribbons, '3 wishes is all you get / scarlet ribbons for your hair' (p. 8), he is referring to the sign of femininity defined by the cult of true womanhood. bell hooks notes that the ribbons were used as bribes to tempt African-American women who felt demoralised by their exclusion from the coding of femininity: 'White male slaveowners and overseers found that slave women could best be manipulated by promises of a new dress, a hair ribbon.'[20] When Ross and Natalie explain that they have not been paid for their performances, Bettina refers to the history of African Americans' exclusion from the dominant mode of monetary exchange. African-American women were forced to depend upon a system of bribes and barter: 'maybe they think we still accept beads & ribbons' (p. 14).

In the nineteenth century, the cult of true womanhood excluded African-American women from the domestic space, confining them to the fields.[21] In the 1970s, the period of *spell #7*, the cult of true womanhood operates differently; women of colour are frequently employed as *domestic* labourers. Natalie imagines being unable to leave the home until her domestic labourer arrives: 'i wonder why the colored lady hasn't arrived to clean my house yet' (p. 48). Shange's point is that the liberation of white women in the 1970s was accomplished at the expense of African-American women.[22] Shange parodies the Women's Liberation Movement of the 1970s as a monolithic, predominantly white organisation composed of isolated housewives whose estrangement from economic and political realities allowed them to privilege sexual difference above racial and class differences. Natalie complains, 'all of this is the fault of the white man's sexism' (p. 48).

Natalie constructs white women as vain, vapid, and drugged on valium: 'the first thing a white girl does in the morning is fling her hair... with 2 valiums slugged awready' (p. 48). The reference to hair-flinging mocks the privileged vanity of white women, who are constructed as the universal object of desire. 'i can assume since i am a white girl on the streets / that everyone notices how beautiful i am' (p. 48). The differences between heterosexual white women and heterosexual African-American women arise due to the historical exclusion of African-American women from the dominant ideological ideal of beauty. Lou remarks: 'the whole world knows that nobody loves the black women like they love farrah fawcett-majors' (p. 36).

Natalie also addresses the tensions between heterosexual African-American men and heterosexual white women, whose coupling represents a threat to white patriarchy. Historically, the white male's phobia that African-American heterosexual males desire white heterosexual women motivated and justified the castration and lynching of African-American men. This phobia produced symbolic violence as well as physical violence. Whites constructed the African-American male as the exotic, primitive Other, the site of an excessive sexuality represented in myths of the large phallus. Natalie satirises the heterosexual white woman for whom sexual desire itself has been coded as savage and dark, so that she associates the 'blackness' of her desire with desire for the African-American man while remaining ignorant of the sexist and racist material conditions constructing her desire: 'if i was one of those white girls who loves one of those grown black fellas / i cd say i didn't know / i can't / i dont know how / cuz i'm a white girl' (p. 48).

The differences between African-American men and white women were exacerbated by the publication of Susan Brownmiller's *Against Our Will*. While this text addressed the issue of rape, it also assumed that all feminists were white. Brownmiller described how she used the smile of the white woman to ward off cat calls from African-American men on the street, for that smile represented a death warrant for African-American men after the Emmett Till murder. Natalie alludes to Brownmiller's racist comment: 'i can remember emmett till & not haveta smile at anybody' (p. 49). Natalie's performance charts the complex historical effects of class, race, and gender differences as they affect the constructions of African-American and white women and men.

In *spell #7*, Shange deconstructs the humanistic assumption of character as a stable identity by foregrounding the role of narrative in the construction of a subject. The plot of the play consists of actors and actresses taking up the position of narrator as the remaining cast enact the story, so that the actors and actresses do not retain fixed identities, but are subjects-in-process confronting the constraints of a hegemonic system of representation. This strategy allows Shange to reveal the effect of gender differences upon the subject of narration. As Elin Diamond notes, 'feminist artists... turn to narrative as a means of incorporating and critiquing the problem of female identity and history'.[23] Alec and Natalie collaborate in the construction of Sue-Jean's narrative. While Alec constructs Sue-Jean as a erotic siren, conceiving her sexuality within masculine parameters, 'her legs straddled and revealing red pants' (p. 28), Natalie constructs Sue-Jean as a woman whose autonomous sexual pleasure exists outside of the phallic economy : 'i laughed and had a good time masturbating in the shadows' (p. 29).

spell #7 is a choreopoem, a collection of related poems combined with song and dance, influenced by the works of Sonia Sanchez, Beah Richards, Alexis DeVeaux, and Judy Grahn. The choreopoem allows the different characters to express their material, historical situation in an emotional, lyrical, dance performance that makes use of African-American movement and gestures. Each of the many characters erupts as a dynamic presence, a strategy that foregrounds the performative nature of identity. Richard Dyer points out that white hegemony works through effacing the constructed nature of the installation of the white man as the natural, inevitable, central subject of all discourse. Shange's choreopoems do not use the same humanistic strategy responsible for consolidating white male dominance; her characters take up positions, a strategy that emphasises the constructed nature of identity rather than naturalising identity.

Glenda Dickerson, theorising about formal strategies for the expression of African-American experience, quips, 'Aunt Jemima tapped my shoulder and told me that "well-made" – in my case – was a phrase which modified beds', not plays.[24] The choreopoem's formal structure contrasts with that of the well-made realistic play, in which dramatic elements support one issue, one protagonist, and one narrative, a monolithic strategy that subsumes difference. Shange's characters tell many different stories, all imaginative constructions of the devastating effects of racism. This strategy of multiple stories and positions subverts the possibility of any one image of an African-American character becoming representative of the entire race.

The choreopoem is a uniquely African-American formal strategy that deconstructs the binarisations between the material and the spiritual, objective and subjective reality, psychological realism and Brechtian alienation. As Sandra L. Richards points out, the choreopoem resists the rationality and empiricism of the well-made play, the coloniser's aesthetic.[25] Shange's choreopoem uses the spirituality of the African tradition to counteract and disrupt the coloniser's system of Enlightenment thought. Within the African tradition, language, music, and dance are *mojos*, spiritual force-fields of energy. Shange's emphasis on *mojos* challenges a western, Eurocentric system of aesthetics privileging the spoken word.

The visual appearance of Shange's text, the way she marks the page, registers the African-American subject's alienation-insignification. As Hortense Spillers implies, the African-American subject's experience of acceding to the Lacanian symbolic order is doubly alienating in that white slave traders destroyed the language, culture, kinship system and legal order of the African subject, and white slave owners 'replaced' the African symbolic order by destroying kinship ties and renaming their 'property'. Paulette Williams's decision to rename herself Ntozake ('she who comes with her own thing') Shange ('she who walks like a lion') suggests a feminist reclamation of the African symbolic order. In the foreword to *spell #7*, Shange calls attention to her experience living and writing within an alien symbolic order: 'i have viscerally wanted to attack deform n maim the language that i was taught to hate myself in.'[26] Shange writes in black dialect, she uses abbreviations, lower-case letter, and poetic slashes to signify the historical connotations that the coloniser's language (Received Standard English) evokes for her.

Shange's most striking formal innovation in *spell #7* is her appropriation of the role of the interlocutor from the traditional minstrel show. Traditionally, the interlocutor did not 'signify' but was 'signified upon'. The interlocutor plays the 'straight man' to the two 'end men', who speak in an imitation of African-American dialect and play the bones and the tambourine. The interlocutor feigns a dignified air and is responsible for setting up jokes and regulating the pace. Shange's interlocutor, Lou, uses the African-American formal strategy of signifying, when one, as Kimberly Benston notes, 'tropes-a-dope'.[27] Lou is not a straight man, but a trickster figure who fools the whites in the audience with the trope of the minstrel show. Lou performs as Bert Williams and abruptly, as Shange's stage directions read, 'speaks now... to the same audience who fell so easily into his hands & were so aroused by the way the black-faced figures "sang n danced"' (p. 9). Lou intervenes between the audience's complicit acceptance of the minstrel show by confronting them with the implications of racism and citing African-American history. 'why dont you go on & integrate a german-american school in st. louis mo. / 1955' (p. 9).

Lou functions as a Signifying Monkey, the master trope of African-American discourse whom Henry Louis Gates, Jr describes as, 'a figure who seems to be distinctly Afro-American... the Signifying Monkey exists in the discourse of mythology not primarily as a character in the narrative but rather as a vehicle for narration itself.'[28] Lou is a magician practising black magic who can make the minstrel mask appear and disappear. Shange writes, 'it is only thru him that we are able to know these people without the "masks"' (p. 27). In the narrative poems of the African-American tradition, the signifying monkey is able to signify upon his enemy, the lion, because the monkey and the lion do not speak the same language. Gates notes: 'The monkey speaks *figuratively*, in a symbolic code; the Lion interprets or "reads" literally and suffers the consequences of his folly, which is a reversal of his status as King of the Jungle.'[29] The relationship between the monkey and the lion parallels the relationship between Lou and the whites in the audience. The whites in the audience are duped into taking the minstrel-show performance literally, as a form of entertainment, rather than as a satiric comment upon the history of African-American representation.

Shange uses the feminist political strategy that Teresa de Lauretis advocates, one that is 'a politics of experience... which later then in turn enters the public sphere of... creative practice... [and] establishes the semiotic ground for a different production of reference and meaning.'[30] For both Shange and de Lauretis, the appeal to 'experience' is not a mere rejection of sign-systems. Both are interested in exposing how 'woman' and 'black' function as signs, as fictional constructs, the vanishing points upon which the white hegemonic system of representation depends. Lou reveals how African Americans as historical beings are affected by the sign of the minstrel mask, and how this mask masks the differences among African Americans as well as the material circumstances of African-American history. If the minstrel show allowed whites to *represent* African Americans, Lou asks the whites in the audience to imagine a literal minstrel show in which they *lived* African-American experience: 'be a lil too dark / lips a lil too full /... why dontchu c'mon & live my life for me.../ i didn't want certain moments at all' (p. 9).

Lou deconstructs the ontological ramifications of the minstrel mask, subverting the binarisations between being and appearance, and exposing the intersections between representation and experience. As a masquerade, the psychic power of black-face is the suggestion that it is a put-on, a semblance concealing a white being; so Lou tells the story of an African-American third-grader who 'asked to be made white / on the spot' (p. 7). The third grader's desire reveals that the minstrel show visually associates 'being' with whiteness, as the central subject of ontological and humanistic thought is always presumed to be white. If 'being' connotes 'whiteness', and 'appearance' connotes 'blackness' or 'woman', then Lou's function in the play is to subvert this dominant sign system, alluded to when the cast takes a bow 'a la bert williams' (p. 9).

Bert Williams, the first African-American entertainer to participate in the Follies company, is an historical figure who represents the impossibility of African Americans acceding to ontological status upon the colonised stage. Bert Williams's act reveals how both gender and racial difference function only as a conflated sign of 'appearance'. His act incorporated woman-as-sign; it was strangely reminiscent of a woman's strip-tease, a performance for the Other's pleasure: 'First a long white-gloved hand with slowly moving fingers would protrude from the wings, followed by a long black-suited arm.'[31] The mere appearance of his white-gloved hands would cause the audience to howl; his hands, like the bodies of women, became fetishised. The spectacle of a black-faced African-American man performing in 'drag' obliterates the lived experience of all women and all African Americans. Like the white minstrels, Bert Williams entertained in black-face, a circumstance that consolidates the association of black-ness with illusion, semblance, mere appearance – a mask.

Bert Williams's act, as a kind of drag show, is a symbolic repre-sentation of the ungendering of the African-American subject. Hortense Spillers, in 'Mama's Baby, Papa's Maybe: An American Grammar Book', argues that gender difference was not always op-erative in the context of the colonisation of African Americans. Spillers's reading is an important one for the creation of an African-American female subject position because she uses white European psychoanalytic theory in order to dismantle the very foundation upon which such a discourse rests – sexual difference. Spillers points out that the historical circumstances of the capture and theft of the African-American body, and its subsequent status as cargo, obliterated the possibility of gender differentiation. 'Under these conditions, we lose at least *gender* difference *in the outcome*, and the female and male body become a territory of cultural and politi-cal manoeuvre, not at all gender-related.'[32]

The 1965 Moynihan Report represented the African-American family as a matriarchal structure in which the economic and political power of African-American women posed a threat to the masculinity of African-American men. This 'objective' report, produced by white males, reveals much about white male phobias and desires and nothing whatsoever about the African-American family. Hortense Spillers reads this report as a misnaming that conflates and degrades both male and female African-American subject positions. The repre-sentational strategy of the Moynihan Report, an empirical govern-ment document, is the same as that of the Bert Williams act: '"Sapphire" enacts her "Old Man" in drag, just as her "Old Man" becomes "Sapphire" in outrageous caricature.'[33] The Moynihan Report and the Bert Williams act are constructions produced by white men which privilege and exploit gender difference, rather than racial difference, as a primary source of conflict. Both of these con-structions depend upon the efficacy of the prior representations of the traditional white minstrel show, in which jokes about gender dif-ference (at the woman's expense) were conventional. In all three dis-courses, the Name and Law of the Father are displaced, as Spillers notes, onto 'the territory of the Mother and Daughter'.[34] The 'missing phallus' in such 'stunning reversal[s] of the castration the-matic'[35] is white male patriarchy, which is nowhere visible amidst black-corked faces or black female matriarchies, but is hiding behind the curtain, producing the entertainment.

Both Hortense Spillers and Homi Bhaba use psychoanalytic discourse as a political tool, subjecting colonial discourse to analyses emphasising the overdetermination, condensation, and displacement constitutive of representation. Given the phantasmatic quality of representations such as Bert Williams's act, minstrel shows, and the Moynihan report, psychoanalytic discourse becomes a strategy that exposes the repressions, anxieties, and ambivalences produced by the colonial encounter. Both theorists re-read the castration motif, with a difference; they reconceptualise the process of fetishisation and disavowal as it applies to racial difference, rather than applying it to sexual difference. The use of the castration motif also has different historical implications for Spillers and Bhaba than it does for Freud. According to Freud, the young male spectator imagines castration as an act once inflicted upon the mother. As Bhaba 'recognises' in a footnote, the compulsive repetition of the castration complex as the primal scene of sexual difference is in itself a form of fetishisation that consolidates the definition of the spectator as male.[36] Within the context of American history, however, castration is not *an imagined fantasy* inflicted upon the mother in the unconscious mind of the male spectator but *an historical reality* inflicted upon African-American men.

Homi Bhaba reads the racial stereotype as a discourse of fetishism, an ambivalent mode of knowledge that simultaneously recognises and disavows difference. The stereotype functions as a fetish, a substitute for the recognition of difference that restores a fantasy of an original, whole presence. The stereotype sutures over any culturally defined site of 'lack' that activates the fantasy of wholeness and racial purity. According to Freud, fetishism is the male subject's response to sexual difference, his strategy for combating anxiety; for Bhaba, the stereotype is the white subject's response to racial difference.

> For fetishism is always a 'play' or vacillation between the archaic affirmation of wholeness / similarity – in Freud's terms: 'All men have penises'; in ours 'All men have the same skin / race / culture' – and the anxiety associated with lack and difference – again, for Freud 'Some do not have penises'; for us 'Some do not have the same skin / race / culture'... the scene of fetishism is also the scene of the reactivation and repetition of primal fantasy – the subject's desire for a pure origin that is always threatened by its division... The stereotype, then... is the scene of a similar fantasy and defence – the desire for an originality which is again threatened by the differences of race, colour and culture.[37]

Bhaba's psychoanalytic strategy allows him to account for the appeal of the racial stereotype, given that 'the body is always simultaneously inscribed in both the economy of pleasure and desire and the economy of discourse, domination, and power'.[38] The minstrel shows, as popular, entertaining spectacles, call for an analysis that charts the inscription of the coloniser's desire upon the colonised subject. Bhaba emphasises the necessity of analysing the productive power of overdetermined colonial texts such as the minstrel show:

> In order to understand the productivity of colonial power it is crucial to construct its regime of 'truth', not to subject its representations to normalising judgement. Only then does it become impossible to understand the *productive* ambivalence of the object of colonial discourse – that 'otherness' which is at once an object of desire and derision, an articulation of difference contained within the fantasy of origin and identity.[39]

The legend of the minstrel show, with its obvious castration motif, exposes such 'a fantasy of origin and identity'. According to the legend, the white 'father' of American minstrelsy, Thomas Dartmouth 'Daddy Rice', copied the gait of a limping African-American stable boy singing a nonsense song about Jim Crow.[40] The jumping Jim Crow gait became a hallmark of minstrelsy. The legendary limping leg functions as a sign which, again, as in the Bert Williams act and the Moynihan Report, conflates sexual difference and racial difference. The leg signifies castration, so that in the minstrel show the African-American male is 'feminised', constructed as the site of a double 'lack'. The white minstrels use their own bodies as fetish-substitutes that suture over this 'lack', so that their bodies oscillate between denial and recognition: the blackface and the mimicked gait deny absence and difference, while the fact that they are neither black nor differently-abled registers the recognition of absence and difference. The stereotype functions to cover up the white male's desire for a body which is ungendered and 'racially pure', a body representing the wholeness of the imaginary order: 'Black skin splits under the racist gaze, displaced into signs of bestiality, genitalia, grotesquerie, which reveal the phobic myth of the undifferentiated white body.'[41]

The use of blackface in the nineteenth century represented the immigrants' anxieties surrounding their own disrupted origins: they desired a fantasy of the whole white body in the face of cataclysmic changes. As Bhaba notes, minstrelsy functions as an 'other' scene that exposes and subverts the white man's desire for authenticity: 'The colonial discourse that articulates an *interdictory* "otherness" is precisely the "other scene" of this nineteenth-century European desire for an authentic historical consciousness.'[42] In minstrelsy's most popular period, between 1840 and 1870, the majority of its stars were European immigrants contending with economic hardship worsened by the economic depression of the 1870s. In *This Grotesque Essence*, Gary Engle notes that the minstrel functioned as a scapegoat that relieved the anxieties of thwarted expectations for social mobility. Blackface visibly signified both the certainty of African origin as well as the fixity of social immobility, thus representing a fantasy of stability and certainty to which immigrants experiencing social, cultural, and economic upheaval responded.

The minstrel show as colonial discourse disrupts its own authority, for these texts register an American concern with the plural nature of its own origins in the face of European 'purity'. Minstrel shows parodied the institutions of high art prevalent on the European stage – Shakespeare productions, melodrama, romance, opera, and ballet. The juxtaposition of the white man's imitation of African-American dialect with the 'high poetry' of Shakespeare, as in the minstrel show 'Desdemonum', became a convention of minstrelsy that represented the fears of immigrants trying to establish new class hierarchies.[43] As Homi Bhaba observes, within the representations of dominant culture, skin becomes the fixed signifier of the signifieds 'of racial topology, the analytics of blood, ideologies of racial and cultural dominance or degeneration'.[44]

Shange's political, resistant strategy in *spell #7* entails the deconstruction of the dominant representation of the 'black experience', revealing blackface as an overdetermined text signifying the phobias and desires of white experience. In the minstrel show, blackness is always already a sign that whites have manipulated to their own ends. When asked to write a play for an all-black cast, Jean Genet asked, 'But what exactly is a Black? First of all, what's his colour?'[45] Shange's play, like Genet's question, reveals the difficulty of conceiving African-American experience when the dominant representational mode is white. African-American experience appears in the Symbolic order only as negation, as the stereotype of the minstrel blocks the possible play of difference within the symbolic order.

Like the black minstrels, Lou, Natalie, and Eli use the strategy of mimicry to subvert the colonising history of the stage. In 'Of Mimicry and Man: The Ambivalence of Colonial Discourse', Homi

Bhaba reveals that the strategy of regarding the colonised subject as a mimic-citizen of the colonising state, 'as a subject of difference that is almost the same, but not quite', inadvertently ruptures the authority and power of the state.[46] Bhaba reveals the effects of mimicry upon both the colonising power and the colonised subject. The colonised subject becomes a 'partial presence', incomplete and virtual, a text capable of exposing the disavowals, projections, and indeterminacies upon which a discourse of authority depends. The colonising power produces 'another knowledge of its norms', an awareness of the limits of Enlightenment discourse.[47] Mimicry calls into question the central tenets of humanism and Enlightenment thought subverted by the material circumstances of colonialism: the belief in an essential, stable identity, and the faith in civil liberties, so that within colonial discourse, as Bhaba notes, 'the great tradition of European humanism seems capable only of ironising itself'.[48]

The character Eli in *spell #7* exposes his own interpellation within a white symbolic order as a form of mimicry. As a mimic-subject he exposes the dominant culture's ideal of homogeneity. Eli imagines himself as the protector of imaginary boundaries which demarcate his pure, whole, sanitary space. He disrupts the authority of the coloniser's discourse by revealing it to be founded upon the repetitive warding off of what Julia Kristeva calls 'the abject', that which calls into question the established binary oppositions necessary to sustain the illusion of a system's totality. 'It is thus not lack of cleanliness or health that causes abjection but what disturbs identity, system, order. What does not respect borders, positions, rules. The in-between, the ambiguous...'[49] Eli exposes the white nationalist's solution to immigrants who pose the threat of abjection: 'aliens / foreigners / are granted resident status / we give them a little green card / as they prove themselves non-injurious / to the joy of my nation' (p. 13). Eli also plays out the denial of abjection through the compulsive reinstatement of the structural opposition between dirt and cleanliness. Eli, as a colonised subject, must remind the audience that he is not a foreigner, that he speaks perfect English, that he is capable of mimicking whites: 'our toilets are disinfected... leave nothing out of place / push no dirt under my rugs /... no fingerprints / clean up after yourself in the bathroom' (p. 13). Homi Bhaba notes that mimicry is a mode of colonial discourse 'construed around an ambivalence; in order to be effective, mimicry must continually produce its slippage, its excess, its difference'.[50] Eli's defensive posture becomes an excessive performance of the denial of his own difference; he epitomises the subject split within an alien symbolic order. Eli exposes fear as the basis for white obsessions with maintaining distinctions between inside and outside, between self and other: 'MY kingdom / there shall be no trespassers... the burgler alarm / armed guards vault from the east side... i sustain no intrusions' (p. 12).

Spillers argues that the Moynihan Report repeats the effacement of the material, historical conditions of the African-American community because it is the symbolic order, in contrast with the order of human agency, which has not changed, but remains grounded in colonial mutilations. Liberation is not complete unless the politics of representation dramatised in *spell #7* are changed. In contrast to empiricist and humanist assumptions of liberal ideology which address only the material, social politics of agency, Spillers calls attention to the sphere of representation, the power of words and images as they affect the interpellation of the subject.

> Even though the captive flesh / body has been 'liberated', and no one need pretend that even the quotation marks do not matter, dominant symbolic activity, the ruling episteme that releases the dynamics of naming and valuation, remains grounded in the originating metaphors of captivity and mutilation so that it is as if neither time nor history, nor historiography and its topics, shows movement, as the human subject is 'murdered' over and over again by the passions of a bloodless and anonymous archaism, showing itself in endless disguise... We might concede, at the very least, that sticks and stones might break our bones, but words will most certainly *kill* us.[51]

In *spell #7*, Shange posits a subject always already inscribed within representation. The framework of representation, which, in drama, is more than words but consists of a racist and sexist apparatus comprised of casting policies, historical images, and the conventions of stage and film, literally degrades the material lives of the struggling entertainers depicted in the play. Dahlia, a singer/dancer, drinks too much; Natalie, an actress, describes how her poverty compels her to perform with a tambourine, a convention of minstrelsy: 'i had to go around wit my tambourine just to get subway fare' (p. 14). The entertainers are unsuccessful because they must continually confront the limits of representation opportunities imposed upon them within the historical context of white hegemony. Alec tells Dahlia, 'if you didn't drink you wd remember that you're not workin' (p. 13). For Alec, as for Spillers, the symbolic order has not registered the effects of social change: 'i cd always black up again & do minstrel work' (p. 46).

Shange foregrounds the conditions of representation in the theatre by portraying actresses struggling with directors who will cast them only as stereotypes inherited from the stage and film industry, or who will allow them to pass for white. Bettina is forced to play the 'mammy' stereotype: 'but if that director asks me to play it any blacker / i'm gonna have to do it in a mammy dress' (p. 46). Lily, an unemployed mulatto actress, cannot pass for black and white: 'they say i'm too light to work / but when I asked him what he meant / he said i didn't actually look black... I said so let me play a white girl... he said that wdnt be very ethical of him. can you imagine that shit' (p. 47). Shange points out a contradiction: a white director believes it is unethical to have an African American cast as a white, although the American theatre has its roots in whites passing for blacks. The symbolic order is still segregated; integration has only affected the arena of human agency.

By referring to filmic stereotypes in her play, Shange foregrounds what Barbara Freedman calls 'the implacability of the law of place and frame', and points to both 'the potential of theatre for revisioning it and/or the complicity of theatre in this frame-up'.[52] Shange's play reveals how the frame-up of representation, here the racist apparatus of the entertainment industry as it is haunted by the minstrel mask, functions to freeze-frame the possibility of change.[53] For Shange, as for Glenda Dickerson, 'the image of the African-American woman has been sullied on the world stage'.[54] Dickerson uses the womanist strategy of re-appropriation to counteract the colonial history of the stage.

> The trick for her now is to reclaim that image through self-definition, using Nommo, the magic power of the word; uncategorically rejecting the stereotypes which are not 'my shame' (as Harriet Tubman said), they are the shame of the perpetrators.[55]

Shange's strategy is informed by both a womanist strategy of reclamation and by a postmodern refusal to provide an essentialised, unified, transcendental subject position for African Americans. Although the actresses and actors wearing blackface masks in *spell* #7 eventually remove the masks, ostensibly to speak of their 'true', essential selves, they immediately begin to construct imaginary characters and experiences. The characters are continually engaged in the process of representation, revealing how representation influences and is influenced by experience and history. Shange does not merely create positive images for African Americans; her strategy is more daring, in that she recognises the mediating power of the symbolic order, the effect of representational systems upon the subject as it is inscribed within history.

The legacy of the minstrel show's representational strategy recently ghosted the Anita Hill/Clarence Thomas fiasco. The trials performed the findings of the 1965 Moynihan Report for its television audience. Anita Hill was cast as the legendary matriarch wielding economic and political power who 'castrated' the masculinity of Clarence Thomas with her eloquent testimony regarding his sexual harassment. George Bush revealed himself as the author of the spectacle by publicly endorsing Clarence Thomas during the trial. The Moynihan Report, the Hill/Thomas trial, and the minstrel show all displace the issue of racial difference onto the issue of gender difference, so that the guilty party is always female. Hill became prey to a representational system in which she functioned as a sign of a familiar 'threat' to 'African-American' manhood, while, as in the Moynihan Report, such a sign system expresses the phobias and desires of white male patriarchy, and serves its interests. Unlike the legacy of the minstrel's representational system, Ntozake Shange's *spell #7* clarifies the difference between white male fantasies and the lived experience of African-American women and men.

From *Theatre Journal*, 44 (1992), 177–93.

NOTES

[Cronacher draws on the work of feminist theorist Hortense Spillers and culture critic, Homi Bhaba to argue that Ntozake Shange reveals the 'absence' for African-American women of a subject position in American society. Cronacher's approach recalls Freedman's use of feminist understandings of psychoanalysis, but Cronacher also deploys African-American history to explain the use in Shange's play of the minstrel mask as a sign that 'African-Americans are still missing as subjects'. This piece positions Shange in relation to feminist theatre on one hand, and on the other hand, to a provocative array of writings about the legacy of the minstrel shows in late twentieth-century America. Ed.]

1. Ntozake Shange, 'unrecovered losses/black theatre traditions', in *Three Pieces* (New York, 1981), p. xii.

2. Ibid.

3. In the chapter entitled, 'Cinema and the Dark Continent: Race and Gender in Popular Film', Modleski writes: 'The concept of fetishism enables us to understand why minstrelsy has never really died out – why it lives in a different form in the "trading places" and "black like me" plots with which Hollywood is enamoured, the most recent example being Paul Mazursky's *Moon Over Parador* (actually an instance of "brownface"), in which the Richard Dreyfus character ... is pressed into masquerading as the leader of a Central American country.' (Tania Modleski, *Feminism Without Women* [New York, 1991], p. 119).

4. Ntozake Shange, 'spell #7', in *Three Pieces*, p. 7.

5. The minstrel mask is also a sign for whites' appropriation of black cultural traditions. Margaret B. Wilkerson notes that the minstrel mask in *spell #7* 'evokes a potent symbol of the exploitation of black music ... initially the "music" of the minstrels, played by whites in black face, was an imitation of jigs and songs created by southern slaves.' Margaret B. Wilkerson, 'Music as Metaphor: New Plays by Black Women', in *Making a Spectacle*, ed. Lynda Hart (Ann Arbor, MI. 1989), p.64.

6. Laura Mulvey, 'Visual Pleasure and Narrative Cinema', *Screen*, 16 (1975), 6–18.

7. Homi K. Bhaba, 'Of Mimicry and Man: The Ambivalence of Colonial Discourse', *October*, 28 (1984), 126.

8. Modleski, *Feminism Without Women*, p. 119. See also Sylvia Wynter, 'Sambos and Minstrels', *Social Text*, 1 (1979), 149–56.

9. 'First of all, their [African people's] New World diasporic plight marked a theft of the body – a wilful and violent ... severing of the captive body from its motive will, its active desire ... this body ... focuses a private and particular space, at which point a convergence of biological, sexual, social, cultural, linguistic, ritualistic, and psychological fortunes join.' Hortense Spillers, 'Mama's Baby, Papa's Maybe: An American Grammar Book', *Diacritics*, 17 (1987), 67.

10. Shange, 'unrecovered losses/black theatre traditions', pp. xii–xiii.

11. See Henry Louis Gates, Jr (ed.), *Black Literature and Literary Theory* (New York, 1984); Henry Louis Gates, Jr (ed.), *'Race', Writing and Difference* (Chicago, 1985); Henry Louis Gates, Jr, *The Signifying Monkey: A Theory of Afro-American Literary Criticism* (New York, 1988).

12. See David Savran, *Breaking the Rules: The Wooster Group* (New York, 1988), p. 33. In this discussion of the Wooster Group's use of blackface in *Route 1 & 9*, Savran points out that the Wooster Group

critiques and deconstructs the liberal humanist perspective on black-face, 'the very desire of humanism to penetrate the black face is revealed to be an indignity, because it assumes that the humanity beneath it is white.'

13. Richard Dyer, 'White', *Screen*, 29 (1988), 47.

14. Ibid., p. 45.

15. See Langston Hughes and Milton Meltzer, *Black Magic* (New York, 1967).

16. Spillers, 'Mama's Baby, Papa's Maybe', p. 69.

17. See Paul Carter Harrison, *The Drama of Nommo* (New York, 1972), p. xx.

18. See bell hooks, *Ain't I a Woman* (Boston, 1981). pp. 22, 47–9. See also Hazel Carby, *Reconstructing Womanhood: The Emergence of the Afro-American Woman Novelist* (New York, 1989). Carby calls attention to the historically produced political differences between white female slaveowners and Afro-American female slaves, noting that reproducing heirs of property is a different female experience than reproducing 'property'.

19. Glenda Dickerson, 'The Cult of True Womanhood: Toward a Womanist Attitude in African-American Theatre', in *Performing Feminism: Feminist Critical Theory and Theatre*, ed. Sue-Ellen Case (Baltimore, MD, 1990), p. 110.

20. hooks, *Ain't I a Woman*, p. 48.

21. For an account of the differences between white and African-American women in the nineteenth century, see Aida Hurtado, 'Relating to Privilege: Seduction and Rejection in the Subordination of White Women of Colour', *Signs*, 14 (1989), 833–55.

22. See Paula Giddings, *Where and When I Enter: The Impact of Black Women on Race and Sex in America* (New York, 1984), p. 384. Giddings argues that 'the fundamental goals of white feminists have been historically defined through the Black movement'. While African-American women were instrumental if unrecognised leaders in the Civil Rights Movement, to which both the Black Power movement and the Women's Liberation movement of the 1970s owe their existence, both of these later groups excluded African-American women through their racist or sexist monolithic strategies.

23. Elin Diamond, 'Refusing the Romanticism of Identity: Narrative Interventions in Churchill, Benmussa, Duras', in *Performing Feminisms*, p. 94.

24. Dickerson, 'The Cult of True Womanhood', p. 115.

25. See Sandra L. Richards, 'Conflicting Impulses in the Plays of Ntozake Shange', *Black American Literature Forum*, 17 (1983), 73–8.

26. Ntozake Shange, 'unrecovered losses/black theatre traditions', p. xii.

27. Kimberly Benston, quoted by Henry Louis Gates, Jr, 'The Blackness of Blackness: A Critique of the Sign and the Signifying Monkey', in *Black Literature and Literary Theory*, ed. Henry Louis Gates, Jr, p. 286.

28. Gates, 'The Blackness of Blackness', p. 287.

29. Ibid., p. 289.

30. Teresa de Lauretis, 'Feminist Studies/Critical Studies: Issues, Terms and Contexts', in *Feminist Studies/Critical Studies*, ed. Teresa de Lauretis (Bloomington, IN, 1986), p. 10.

31. Hughes and Meltzer, *Black Magic*, p. 58.

32. Spillers, 'Mama's Baby, Papa's Maybe', p. 67.

33. Ibid., p. 66.

34. Ibid.

35. Ibid.

36. See Bhaba, 'The Other Question. . .', p. 18, note 1. In a footnote that is an ambivalent mode of knowledge registering the recognition and disavowal of feminist interventions, Bhaba admits: 'despite the subject's problematic accession to sexual difference which is crucial to my argument, the body in this text is male. Realising that the question of woman's relation to castration and access to the symbolic requires a very specific form of attention and articulation, I chose to be cautious till I had worked out its implications for colonial discourse.'

37. Bhaba, 'The Other Question. . .', p. 27.

38. Ibid., p. 19.

39. Ibid.

40. Huges and Meltzer, *Black Magic*, p. 12.

41. Bhaba, 'Of Mimicry and Man: The Ambivalence of Colonial Discourse', p. 133.

42. Ibid., p. 132.

43. See Gary Engle, *This Grotesque Essence* (Baton Rouge, LA, 1978).

44. Bhaba, 'The Other Question. . .', pp. 27–8.

45. Jean Genet, quoted by Mance Williams, *Black Theatre in the 1960s and 1970s* (Westport, CT, 1985), p. 11.

46. Bhaba, 'Of Mimicry and Man', p. 126.

47. Ibid.

48. Ibid., p. 128.

49. Julia Kristeva, *Powers of Horror*, trans. and ed. Leon S. Roudiez (New York, 1982).

50. Bhaba, 'Of Mimicry and Man', p. 126.

51. Spillers, 'Mama's Baby, Papa's Maybe', p. 68.

52. Barbara Freedman, 'Frame-Up: Feminism, Psychoanalysis, Theatre', in *Performing Feminisms*, p. 56.

53. Timothy Murray calls attention to the ways in which African-American dramatists such as Ntozake Shange, Adrienne Kennedy, and Amiri Baraka expose the media as an ideological apparatus that reinforces dominant power relations. Murray writes: 'the contemporary (technological) image ... [is] both a structure of representation and a device or apparatus (tool and *episteme*) lending itself naturally to our struggles for power and authority... to speak of the technological image in view of contemporary American drama is to unfold theatre's aesthetic and ideological garments of confrontational strategy and enactment. In regarding contemporary American drama, moreover, I find myself dwelling on how the complexity of technological confrontation developed with particular care and concern by Black American theatre, by a play world suggesting that the marvellous technicolours of the media have yet to escape from their white against black fundamentals.' Timothy Murray, 'Screening the Camera's Eye: Black and White Confrontations of Technological Representation', *Modern Drama*, 28 (1985), 110–11.

54. Dickerson, 'The Cult of True Womanhood', p. 111.

55. Ibid.

10

Chicanas' Experience in Collective Theatre: Ideology and Form

YVONNE YARBRO-BEJARANO

In preparation for this article I spoke with a number of Chicanas and Latinas involved in collective theatre, with the idea of making the piece itself more collective and experiential: Evelina Fernández, Ana Olivares and Socorro Gamboa of El Teatro de la Esperanza; Olivia Chumacero and Diane Rodríguez of El Teatro Campesino; Sylvia Wood, formerly of Teatro Libertad in Tucson, Arizona; Wilma Bonet of the San Francisco Mime Troupe and Cara Hill de Castañón, formerly of Teatro Latino and Valentina Productions. I also spoke with Rose Cano, a Peruvian actress working in commercial theatre in Seattle, and Yolanda Broyles, a professor in the Foreign Languages Department at the University of Texas at San Antonio who has spent the last year and a half collecting data on Chicanas in theatre. These conversations form the basis for this article although we should keep in mind that the ideas expressed by these women represent where they are at this moment in time and should be put in a larger perspective. We look forward to the fruits of Yolanda Broyles' research which, carried out over a long period of time, will give us a more balanced picture.

I

Any discussion of working in collective versus commercial theatre must take into account certain economic and social factors specific

213

to Chicanas. Because of their class, race and culture, Chicanas have historically been shut out of commercial theatre. The tracking prevalent in the educational system effectively discourages Chicanos in general from going into theatre. The percentage of Chicanas with sound professional training in acting, directing or playwriting is abysmally low and reflects the general economic exploitation and racial discrimination that characterises the experience of Chicanos as a group. The fact that now and then a particularly determined individual may 'make it' through the system does not alter the systematic exclusion of Chicanos as a whole from mainstream theatre.

Chicanos as a social group have been excluded not only from theatre, but from all middle-class forms of literary production. The reasons for this are historical, social and economic. Since 1848, the history of Chicanos in this country has been one of economic oppression and social inequality. The vast majority of Chicanos in the United States belong to the working class, and the absence of upward mobility together with linguistic discrimination have resulted in severely limited access to literacy and education. As a result, Chicano literary expression has been largely popular in form, and oral in transmission.

One of the projects of the Chicano movement in the late '60s and early '70s was to validate popular and oral forms of cultural expression, and to counter the lack of access to the mainstream literary establishment with the creation of a Chicano communications network. This network included community newspapers featuring local, grass-roots poets writing in Spanish or bilingually, as well as Chicano literary magazines and publishing houses. Dozens of Chicano theatre groups sprang up, inspired by the example of the Teatro Campesino.

This group, founded by Luis Valdez in 1965, was extremely important in providing a specifically Chicano alternative to mainstream theatre. Initially made up of and directed at farmworkers, the Teatro Campesino contributed to the struggle headed by César Chávez to form a farmworkers' union. It is difficult to overestimate the significance of this group's exuberant validation of bilingual Chicano speech and cultivation of a rough, funky and funny, extremely dynamic style, drawing on popular Chicano and Mexican culture.

The majority of Chicanas in theatre became involved during this period, working with collective theatre groups that saw both their function and structure as part of a political struggle. All of the women I talked to spoke of their experience in collectives in very positive terms. Many cited as a major plus of collective work the opportunity to develop themselves in different areas, including acting, writing, directing, administration and workshops. Although in practice, the experience may vary because of the definition and organisation of the particular collective, many remain committed to the idea of direct and equal participation as a member of a unified and supportive group in the creation and development of characters, scripts and mise-en-scènes, as well as the work's political statement and the general policies of the group.

In opposition to the hierarchical division of labour characteristic of commercial theatre, the collective gives Chicanas and Latinas the chance to share responsibility for decisions, to have input into the entire process, to spearhead projects and assume leadership positions. The collective lifestyle in itself is seen as part of a political process, providing the opportunity to work out in the daily practice of human relationships the ideology underlying the plays. Some women spoke of the importance of participating in progressive or liberal activities and organisations, and practising collectivism in workshops, classes and performances at festivals. As opposed to the individualism of commercial theatre, the subordination to decisions coming down from on high, the concentration on money and the star mentality, the collective provides a supportive structure for the personal needs of the individuals as well as a forum to air criticisms. These women also appreciated the goal of catering to a specific audience in the attempt to create a truly Chicano theatre, one that would address the problems and general reality of a specific community.

The commitment to the dreams and aspirations of Chicano theatre, in which not only the plays but also the group organisation attempted to oppose the dominant ideology of a capitalist, sexist and racist society, has helped women endure the economic sacrifices and heavy demands of extended collective work.

II

From 40 to 50 groups at its height, the number of Chicano theatre groups has dwindled to a mere handful. Of the surviving collectives, the San Francisco Mime Troupe and the Teatro de la Esperanza offer viable options for Chicanas and Latinas, though of course they are not without problems and contradictions. Besides incorporating a child care policy in their structure, Esperanza struggles to reconcile women's issues with a progressive analysis of the social and economic problems of the Chicano community.

The San Francisco Mime Troupe, which has a long history of political theatre work, is currently engaged in the struggle to maintain a progressive orientation in their plays given the varying levels of political consciousness of the different members of the company. The pressure of creating new shows for the free theatre in the parks during the summer, and the indoor performances and touring during the year has led to the unfortunate situation in which the play is often still being written while the actors are in rehearsal, seriously reducing the opportunity to research and discuss the politics of the piece as a collective. It is embarrassing for some that not all members of the group can field questions about the political issue dramatised by the play. The lack of ideological cohesiveness in the group has led to what some see as a softening of the politics in their work. The theme of factory shutdowns in their recent work, *Steeltown*, suggests a continuing commitment to exploring pressing political problems.

The San Francisco Mime Troupe is, nevertheless, one of the few multi-racial and multi-ethnic collectives, and has been so since the early '70s. An Asian-American has recently joined the black, Chicano and white members of the group as musician and actor. Wilma Bonet is the only Latina in the Mime Troupe, hired to replace the Chicana actress, María Acosta Colón, who decided to develop her skills in administrative work within the group.

As the only Latina, Bonet has the sense of representing her community in the group. She serves as a moderator for all Latin roles, making sure they are not stereotypes. With the Chicanos in the group, she has been instrumental in bringing about open discussions of racism within the collective, including problems in the area of casting and relationships between white and non-white members. These discussions have greatly helped in dealing with racism in the company, a problem confronted by the group as one of extreme importance since the 'Minstrel Show'. Although Bonet feels personal and economic pressures, she stays with the group because of the rewards of having equal input into the creative process, and augments her income with commercials, ads and any other work she can find in which she can use her acting skills. She is pleased with the roles she has played, including a character in their play, *Last*

Tango in Huahuatenango, based on Nora Astorga, and her most recent work in *Steeltown*, in which she plays the wife of a laid-off steelworker who drinks and abuses her. The character is passive at the beginning, but undergoes a change within the play. Although she felt she had to prove herself first, Bonet has been successful in her struggle to play non-Latina roles, such as her hilarious robot in *Fact-Wino vs. the Moral Majority*, and her portrayal of Laurencia in *Fuenteovejuna*.

Some Chicanas and Latinas have formed collectives made up exclusively of women. Teatro Raíces, in San Diego, does popular political theatre in the *acto*, or Chicano agit-prop, tradition. Valentina Productions, composed of women in San José, performed a polished collage of poetry, dance, music and pantomime called *Voz de mujer* at the 11th Chicano/Latino Theatre Festival in San Francisco in September 1981. Valentina's goal was to provide a support group for women in theatre and to explore women's issues through theatre. Although the response to the show was very positive, the group disbanded shortly after the festival, succumbing to the major problems that beset all collectives – extreme shortage of time and money. Most of the members worked full time, many had children, and the demands became too great. An additional problem, which hastened their demise, was the lack of ideological cohesion within the group. Members were brought together around the idea of doing women's theatre, but they all had different perspectives on women's issues. Since they were at different levels, *Voz de la mujer* sought the lowest common denominator, treating 'safe' themes, for example the exaltation of motherhood and the analysis of male–female relationships, with an emphasis on solidarity with men and the desire not to offend or alienate them. Some women wanted to present more controversial issues, but the group as a whole was not ready.

Olivia Chumacero, of the Teatro Campesino, has been exploring other options. The Teatro Campesino has concentrated on a cultural nationalist analysis of the Chicano experience, blending *indigenismo* and religious elements in their post-political phase. Founder Luis Valdez' turn toward commercial theatre in *Zoot Suit* and the establishment of a new theatre in San Juan Bautista, has been accompanied by an emphasis on cultural identity at the expense of a materialist analysis of the concrete conditions that create the oppression and exploitation of Chicanos as a largely working-class group. The work of Luis Valdez with the Teatro Campesino can generally be characterised as male-oriented. The central characters are always men, while the women revolve around them on secondary levels. In the *actos*, their peripheral status is propagated through stereotyped gender roles. They are the mothers, sisters, girlfriends or wives of the main male characters. The *mitos* of their religious phase added the Virgin of Guadalupe to the roster of stereotyped role models. This tendency to relegate women to secondary levels of importance is seen clearly in *Zoot Suit*. Besides the usual polarisation of portraying Chicanas as either whores or virgins, the play establishes an opposition between Della, Henry's *pachuca* girlfriend, and Alice, a Jewish woman who played a crucial role in the defence committee. The politically unsophisticated Chicana stands in contrast to the progressive white woman, but in the long run, Alice fares no better than Della. Alice's politics – based on the radical commitment of a real person – could have helped in giving the play the ideological clarity it lacks; instead her politics are played for laughs. As the play progresses it becomes evident that the main function of the two women is to provide the male character with the romantic dilemma of whom to choose. This depiction of women is accompanied by the text's subtle message that the white lawyer is the saviour of the Chicano youths, an insinuation captured in the paternalistic scene in which the lawyer, raised a good few feet above the youths by the blocking, convinces them to have faith in the American system of justice.

Could the portrayal of women in the work of the group heavily dominated by Luis Valdez or in the work of Valdez himself have something to do with his declared assimilationist goals? According to Valdez, he is not doing 'Chicano' theatre, but rather 'New American' theatre, and he envisions the '80s as a new period of integration for minorities, who would nonetheless maintain a sense of cultural pride and dignity (*Mother Jones*, June 1979). More recently he declared that 'We're working on our reality and commitment as Americans. . . . It took us a while to call ourselves Americans' (*San Francisco Examiner*, 9 August 1981). Is this 'New American' theatre just another way of talking about commercial theatre, as opposed to 'Chicano' theatre, which has long been understood to be part of a larger political struggle? *The Rose of the Rancho*, to cite but one example among the shows which have been produced since *Zoot Suit* at the new theatre in San Juan Bautista, was performed July and August of 1981 at $7.50 top ticket to a predominantly Anglo, middle-class audience. The treatment of women in the play – the domineering mother, the submissive, childlike servant, the incredibly foolish and unappealingly flirtatious title character – is completely consistent with the assimilationist revision of the Mexican-American war that the play presents. Valdez' most recent commercial venture, *Corridos*, has come in for heavy criticism from women who object to the choice of ballads that depict women as victims of rape and murder. The section celebrating the role of women in the Mexican revolution concentrated on their duty to 'follow their men' and make them their coffee and tortillas. Once again, the notion of the white saviour appears: the character of John Reed is the only male who is depicted as having some sensitivity for the women's predicament.

The Teatro Campesino produced their last collective work, the *Carpa de los Rascuachi*, in '75–'76, although *Fin del Mundo*, which toured in 1980, was also somewhat collectively elaborated. The recent development toward commercial theatre has reduced the opportunities for some of the women members of the company, who have turned to other venues. Chumacero has been working on her own, depending on grants to develop community theatre workshops. She has maintained a social and political focus, and is currently involved with theatre workshops with battered women and youth involved with drugs.

Sylvia Wood, formerly of Teatro Liberted of Tucson, Arizona, is working part time at Pima Community College, writing and staging one original script a year. Although she is happy to be concentrating on her writing, she feels isolated, and misses the experience of working collectively. Working part time to develop her writing has not relieved the economic pressures of doing theatre.

After working with Valentina, Cara Hill de Castañón participated in *Tongues of Fire*. Although *Tongues of Fire* was not produced by a collective, it represents the range of experimental options for Chicanas and Latinas outside commercial theatre. The *teatropoesía* piece was created and performed as part of a conference on Chicanas in 1981 at Mills College in Oakland, with grant money available to bring together writer, director and actresses. *Tongues of Fire* broke ground in Chicano theatre for its depiction of Chicanas and its ideological analysis of their specific problems. The play centred on the Chicana writer, analysed in terms of sex, class, race and culture. Based on the collection of writings by radical women of colour *This Bridge Called My Back*, *Tongues of Fire* explored the personal and collective history of Chicanas, contradicting gender stereotyping through irony and humour.

De Castañón also recently worked with the Teatro de la Esperanza. The progressive orientation of the Teatro de la Esperanza throughout the 12 or 13 years they have been in existence has functioned as a kind of cement which holds the group together and allows for continuity in spite of turnover in personnel. Having a common ideological base enables the members of Esperanza to feel responsible for the political as well as the artistic dimensions of their work, and they screen for politics in auditioning for the collective. Besides offering consistent analyses of the relationship between the discrimination and exploitation of Chicanos in this country and the larger structures of imperialism and corporate capitalism, they have broken ground in the creation of female characters in Chicano theatre and in the area of gender stereotyping in general. It is not uncommon for women to play male or androgynous roles in Chicano theatre, as in the Teatro Campesino Socorro Valdez' portrayal of Death, the Devil, a lowrider, etc., or Ana Olivares' General Rata in *The Octopus*. But in their last two works, Esperanza has men playing female roles, for example, the spunky older woman character in their musical show, *La muerte viene cantado*.

The group experimented with a collective protagonist in their first play, *Guadalupe*. In their next three plays, *La víctima*, *Hijos* and *The Octopus*, a limited male protagonist is countered by a strong female character who functions as a catalyst transforming the consciousness of the male characters or bringing their contradictions to a point of maximum tension.

Although de Castañón values collective work in Chicano theatre, she pointed out the scarcity of available groups and her own geographical limitations. Since having a baby, she is forced to look for work exclusively in San José. Like Olivia Chumacero, she has partially resolved the problem by working on her own, performing and touring a one-woman show based on the life and writings of Sor Juana Inés la Cruz. She has also auditioned for the upcoming season in San José's repertory company.

III

It is within a context of crisis, then, that we must place the experience of Chicanas and Latinas – a crisis that is linked to the waning of the Chicano movement and the economic recession, accompanied by a swing to the right politically in the US. The few collectives that still exist face a daily struggle for survival, paying extremely low wages and becoming increasingly dependent on grants and touring. The rewards of doing popular political theatre have been drastically reduced by the lack of connectedness to a broad-based political or social movement and the failure to develop a working-class Chicano audience in their base communities, due largely to the necessity to tour in order to survive. While the rewards have dwindled, the demands have increased.

Many women have expressed a sense of frustration and exhaustion. Although people continue to validate the opportunity to participate in all aspects of theatre work, the shared responsibility of many different tasks demands enormous quantities of time and energy. Collectives such as the Teatro de la Esperanza are understaffed and overcommitted, simultaneously producing shows, touring, organising, attending festivals and building networks with the popular political theatre in Latin America. Members of collectives can hardly subsist on the extremely low wages paid by collectives, when wages are paid at all.

The collective structure often makes the decision process maddeningly show. Equally slow is the artistic process of collective creation which, in some cases, leads to artistic stagnation and makes the beginning of every tour extremely hectic as the group struggles to finish the show before they hit the road. Acutely aware of technical deficiencies, especially in the area of playwrighting, many have taken leaves to study and improve their skills. The necessity of regular touring has been very draining as well as a strain on personal relationships, and people at times find it difficult to balance the pros of a collective lifestyle and the need for privacy.

While these problems are common to both men and women working in collectives, there are others that are specific to women. In some mixed collectives, Chicanas and Latinas have struggled against contradictions between the supposed progressive orientation of the group and the perpetuation of social and cultural attitudes about gender roles. A sexist double standard exists within many groups, affecting everything from behaviour on tours to the existence of the 'double day' for women, who must bear the additional responsibilities of home and family. While calling themselves a collective, in some cases the real power has been exercised by one man, severely limiting the input of Chicanas into the decision-making process. Many women have dropped out of theatre work altogether because of the frustration of not having their insights and

personal experience taken into real consideration. Many were critical of the kinds of roles they were asked to play, yet were unable to
influence the development of female characters when they voiced
their opinion that the group was seriously lacking in their theatrical
representation of Chicanas.

For many social and cultural reasons, it has been harder for
Chicanas and Latinas who have children – especially single mothers –
to work in collectives. Women with children face pressure from
spouses and lovers to stop doing theatre and attend to 'motherly
duties', while most collectives do not provide for child care or see it as
a political problem. Women have had to struggle, not always successfully, to make their collectives recognise the special problems of
women with children, who restrict their time and energy and make it
difficult for them to tour. Now the San Francisco Mime Troupe provides extra financial support for people with children, although
because of their overall economic situation the extra $20 only
amounts to a symbolic recognition of the problem. The difficulties of
women with children become most acute when touring; the options
are to leave the children behind or take them along, both of which are
problematic. Sylvia Wood, formerly of Teatro Libertad, attempted to
partially solve the problem by writing her children into the scripts, so
at least they would learn something since they had to be at rehearsals
anyway. The Teatro de la Esperanza is unique in incorporating child
care into its policy. Anyone who joins the group, whether they have
children or not, is required to do his or her share of child care.

Many women have become disillusioned with male dominance in
mixed collectives and their unwillingness to develop strong female
roles or address women's needs. Others have become dissatisfied
with what they feel was an excessively rigid concept of collectivity,
submitting everything to consensus while actually concentrating
power in male hands and stifling the individual development of
other members. In her research on women in theatre, Yolanda
Broyles has found that in situations where men dominate as power
holders, Chicanas and Latinas are not stagnating. They either struggle to influence the collective by staying in it or branch out to
explore other options. Some women point out that in the past, they
have been severely limited by youth, inexperience and lack of ideological and theoretical sophistication, factors that contributed to the
predominance of male leadership. Some feel that by striking out on
their own, they will gain strength and experience that will place
them in a better position to increase women's voices in collectives.

IV

If Chicanas decide they are tired of working in a collective, what alternatives do they really have? Chicanas and Latinas are usually only hired for 'ethnic' parts, usually terrible stereotypes, reinforcing the image of the Latina as sex bomb, or relegating her to typecast roles such as maid or mother. In much commercial theatre, being brown is bad, and lighter-skinned Chicanas and Latinas will be chosen for parts over darker ones, except when the role calls for Indian features. Wood remarked that in casting for the few productions employing Chicanas or Latinas, Latinas are often chosen over Chicanas, because they tend to have more training. Even in commercial productions of Chicano theatre, such as Luis Valdez' *Corridos*, Chicanas and Latinas with collective experience auditioning for roles felt they were passed over because they were not the right 'type'.

Diane Rodríguez, veteran of the Teatro Campesino, has had experience both in regional and 'downtown' commercial theatre. She has been in three shows at the Old Globe Theatre and was recently in a commercial production in San Francisco, *Women Behind Bars*, by Tom Eyen (of *Dream Girls* fame). On the whole, Rodríguez has found this experience positive. She spoke of being stretched in her exposure to other directors and actors, which has enabled her to identify the areas she needs to work on as an actress and has encouraged her to take more risks with her art. She is making good money and enjoys working with a cast of mature women. At the same time, there are negative aspects to her experience in non-collective theatre. She must struggle with the added pressure of reviews and the producer's power – the producers can remove you from the show if they don't like your work. Rodríguez finds herself confronted by dilemmas expressed by many Latina and Chicana actresses: enjoying the luxury of confining her participation to performing her part and picking up her check, yet missing input into the creative process; wanting to express herself politically and socially in her theatre work, yet playing stereotypes of Latin women; wanting her own career, yet still being committed to the collective process.

Rose Cano is a Peruvian actress who has lived in Seattle since she was a child. She is a recent graduate of the Cornish Institute's Professional Training Programme. So far, commercial theatre has been a viable option for her. She recently performed a one-woman

show in the Broadcloth series of The Women's Theatre in coopera-
tion with the Women's Programmes of Seattle Central Community
College, and plans to tour the show. Severely limited in the market
by her colour, Cano is aware that directors will not cast Latinas for
non-Latin roles, and is fighting against the perception that she 'can't
do' Noel Coward and other theatre classics. There is no Chicano or
Latino theatre in Seattle – although there is an Asian-American
theatre company, and The Group, the resident company at the
Ethnic Cultural Theatre of the University of Washington, is multi-
racial, and tries to do colour blind casting for plays that have
some social and political content.

Still, Cano feels that if she wants good roles, she will have to
write them herself. Her training at Cornish included playwrighting,
and her one-women show, *Self-Portrait*, is her latest attempt to
fight the obstacles for Latinas in commercial theatre. In *Self
Portrait*, Cano was inspired by her family to explore her self and
her cultural roots. She creates five female characters who have most
influenced her life: Angelita, the mentally challenged 11-year-old
sister; Carmen, her older Americanised sister; Mrs Johnson, the
Mexican-American cleaning woman; her mother, the rock of the
family, and her 88-year-old grandmother. Each character speaks to
Dolores, the character representing Cano, and at the end, she is
pulled between the 'demands of family and cultural values and the
need to establish her own life and separate self'.

It is interesting to see how Cano resolved the problem of dramatising a bilingual experience for a monolingual audience. The play is
bilingual; some 30% of the text is Spanish. The grandmother
speaks only Spanish, but Cano treats her character in a highly gestural fashion. The others mix Spanish and English, but anything important in Spanish is also said in English. The linguistic aspect of
the work includes the recreation of Mrs Johnson's speech, which is
neither English nor Spanish, but a creative hybrid of both. Cano is
motivated by the desire to share her ethnic background with Seattle
audiences, who are largely unfamiliar with other cultures. In her
treatment of her Americanised older sister, Cano critises Latinas
who accept the media's image of 'woman', which involves a rejection of who they really are. In the character of Mrs Johnson, the
cleaning woman, Cano juxtaposes Peruvian and Mexican cultures,
and although she shows their differences, she is aware of the
common problems of being non-white in a white society and of
maintaining a Latin cultural identity within the dominant culture.

V

Collective theatre certainly does not have a corner on formal experimentation. But the groups discussed display a spectrum of forms that respond to the goals of Chicano and/or popular political theatre through the miming of working-class culture. The San Francisco Mime Troupe has a long tradition of using popular forms, including the minstrel show, western, melodrama, spy thriller and recently the comic book in the Fact Person/Wino series. *Tongues of Fire* uses the *teatropoesía* form, which has some history in the Chicano theatre movement. But instead of presenting a collage of relatively unrelated poetic texts in a stage setting, Barbara Brinson-Pineda, who scripted the show, created a structure with five sections, grouping the poems around particular themes. The unifying thread that ties the sections together is the character of the Chicana writer.

The Teatro Campesino is responsible for the creation of forms and images that have influenced a whole theatre movement. Drawn loosely after the agit-prop model, the *acto* combined satire, bawdy humour and stock characters with a broad playing style characterised by its funky dynamism and expressive use of gesture and body movement. In their religious phase, the company created the *mito*, such as *Fin del mundo*, which served as a vehicle for the expression of universal truths of Catholicism and indigenous philosophies. At the same time, the group experimented with *corridos*, which entailed the simultaneous singing and dramatisation of the popular ballads of Mexican and Chicano oral tradition. The Teatro Campesino has created a whole repertory of characters that have given Chicano theatre a specific visual imagery all its own; the *calaveras*, or skeletons, based on Jose Guadalupe Posada's lithographs, represented an attempt to express certain indigenous attitudes toward life and death, but this ideological content is not necessarily tied to the form. Its link with Mexican popular art of a satirical nature makes it a perfect springboard for rapid character changes. Other characters are equally expressive of Chicano urban lifestyles, for example, the *pachuco*, or its contemporary equivalent, the *cholo*. Another form developed by the Teatro Campesino, which I call the historical procession, tracing the history of Chicanos back to pre-Colombian times, through the Conquest, Independence and Revolutionary Mexico to the United States, initiated a tradition within the Chicano movement as well, influencing

the Mexican group Mascarones, now Teatro Zero, which participated in the Chicano theatre movement. Valentina also used the
historical procession form to give shape to their selection of poetic
texts, dance and mime.

After an initial phase of developing *actos*, the Teatro de la
Esperanza created the docudrama form that they used in their first
three plays. This form combines drama and documentation,
framing the action with quotes and statistics, scene titles and
musical commentaries in the attempt to demystify certain aspects of
theatre. This form reflects their adaptation of Brechtian principles
within a Chicano cultural context, and also reveals similarities with
the Joker system developed by Brasilian post-Brechtian Augusto
Boal, who has also worked closely with the Chicano theatre movement. Not content to rest on their laurels, the company abandoned
the docudrama form in their fourth play, *The Octopus*, to experiment with political allegory enclosed by a cabaret/circus frame. For
their latest two efforts, Esperanza works within a Chicano theatre
tradition, using the same form and characters as the Teatro
Campesino, but with political content and more sensitivity to
women's issues. Their musical show, *La muerte viene contado*, uses
the *corridos* form, but the choice of texts avoids the pitfalls of the
Valdez production. Esperanza selected a *corrido* that tells the story
of a woman who shoots a captain who has raped her and killed her
brother. Other sections celebrated the role of women in the
Nicaraguan revolution and dramatised Domitila's famous speech at
the Women's Conference in Mexico City.

Esperanza's latest show, *Lotería*, works with another form of
Mexican popular culture, the lottery, which is played like bingo but
with figures instead of numbers: the sun, the little old lady, the
drunk, the dandy, etc. The show's characters are built around the
figures of the lotería, in the creative development of popular political theatre that works within a collective visual imagination.
Esperanza has been working closely with the new theatre movement
in Cuba and Latin American for several years now. The members
remarked on the difference between the definition of collective that
they have been trying to work with – where everything is done collectively, including writing and directing – and the kinds of collectives they have come in contact with in Latin America. The Cubans,
for example, tend to delegate certain functions according to
people's strengths. After collecting data on the chosen topic directly
from their target community, one person will write the script, after

the topic has been discussed and/or improvised by the collective. This text is then submitted to extensive collective improvisation and continually rescripted to accommodate audience reactions.

This ongoing interchange within a network of popular political theatre is bound to have an invigorating effect on the Chicano theatre movement. While this moment is a difficult one, I would agree with Yolanda Broyles that Chicanas and Latinas are not stagnating or dropping out. I have the impression that they continue to search for a theatrical practice that will reconcile individual and collective needs.

From *Women and Performance: A Journal of Feminist Theory*, 2:2 (1985), 45–58.

NOTES

[This is one of the first of several articles by Yarbro-Bejarano that focus on the history and process of Chicana theatre as compared to Chicano theatre. Yarbro-Bejarano contrasts the powerful objectification of the Chicana woman in the most well-known Chicano theatre productions to the alternatives created in the mid-eighties by Chicanas who worked in a much more collaborative fashion than did their male counterparts. The article points both to the internationalisation of feminist theatre and to the particular issues that have emerged in the conjoining of feminism and the Chicana–Chicano political movement.

11

Contemporary Women's Voices in French Theatre

JUDITH GRAVES MILLER

In the Provençal village of Villeneuve-les-Avignon, the local museum features a remarkable composition entitled 'Le Couronnement de la Vièrge' (The Coronation of the Virgin). This fifteenth-century painting by Enguerrand Quarton depicts identical images of God the Father and God the Son crowning a sunken and passive Mary. The Dove-Spirit, final member of the Trinity, hovers directly over the Virgin's head. While gripping the diadem in its beak, the holy bird extends its wings from the lips of the Father to those of the Son. Thus is Mary dominated by three manifestations of metaphysical authority, each bearing down on her with a collective 'tongue'.

Submerged in the multiplied voices of the Lord and, one might infer, deprived of her own speech, Quarton's Mary stands – with few exceptions – for the place of woman's voice in the history of French theatre. Throughout the 'grand' theatrical tradition in France, the producing, writing, or originating voice of the text has primarily been male. Major women playwrights appeared only after World War II. And there has not yet been a re-evaluation of the canon which has discovered or recuperated lost women playwrights whose interest can be termed other than 'socio-historical'.[1] Rather, as might be expected from a country which so much enjoys debating and prizing 'the feminine' and 'femininity', the place of women in theatre has mainly been as flesh and blood image, as representation; that is – as actress.[2]

One can indeed speak of a distinguished tradition of female performers from the seventeenth century to the present. These include the independent Béjart women of Molière's company and the grand tragedian La Champmeslé in the seventeenth century, or the theatrical innovators Adrienne Lecouvreux and Mlle Clairon and the exquisite comique talent Mme Riccoboni in the eighteenth century, or the respective queens of melodrama and classical tragedy – Marie Dorval and Rachel – and the invincible Sarah Berhardt of the nineteenth century, or contemporary greats Maria Casarès, Madeleine Renaud, Jeanne Moreau, and Delphine Seyrig. However, despite their verve and their vocal gifts, despite their physical dexterity and remarkable memories, these women have excelled for the most part in materialising the imaginative constructs of male authors and male directors, in telling the 'great story of MANkind'.[3]

With the re-energising of the women's movement in France after 1970, women writers did, nevertheless, begin to make their voices heard in theatre. Many of these women, like their counterparts in North America and elsewhere in Europe, came to feminism or to 'women-centred' projects directly out of anti-war protests or from other forms of political activism. There was consequently, particularly in the mid 1970s, a flurry of agit-prop or consciousness-raising types of theatre work, much in the style of progressive theatre pieces of the late sixties and early seventies. For example, the Parisian troupe La Carmagnole, which took its name from a song popularised during the French Revolution, worked up a series of sketches foregrounding forms of patriarchal oppression. Their performances encouraged the audience to discuss with the actors the ramifications of the use and abuse of power within the domestic arena.[4] A company which continues to draw attention through an agit-prop format to patterns of dominance in the family is the Reims-based La Théâtrelle. La Théâtrelle creates sketches, such as a 1985 piece on housework, from interviews with local women. The audience thus engages with domestic scenes it may itself have generated.[5]

Other groups seeking a feminist theatre practice, notably Les Trois Jeannes (The Three Joans), evolved trenchant cabaret pieces which teased – and continue to chide – their public in send-ups of everyday sexism, as for example, in their 1977 satire *Je te dis, Jeanne, ce n'est pas une vie la vie qu'on mène* (I'm telling you, Joan, this is not life we're living). Since the mid-seventies women's cabaret shows, frequently written and performed by an actress working alone, have accounted for almost twenty per cent of the programming at Parisian café-théâtres.[6] As explained by the actress Liliane Rovere, who wrote and acted in the one-woman show *Lili* (1984), these pieces allow actresses to take risks, to put their 'selves' in danger in ways which conventional theatre, with its play of masks, refuses.[7]

In 1977, Hélène Cixous, one of the first and most provocative theoreticians of 'l'écriture féminine' or feminine writing, declared in *Le Monde* (28 April 1977) in what amounts to a feminist theatrical manifesto called 'Aller à la mer' ('Going to the sea', homonymically 'Going to the mother') that the only way women could legitimately go to the theatre would be as a political gesture aimed at changing theatre's means of production and expression, for otherwise, she stated, she and other women '[lend] our complicity to the sadism directed against [us and] assume, in the patriarchal family structure that the theatre reproduces *ad infinitum*, the position of victim'.[8] In her own 1976 play, *Portrait de Dora (Portrait of Dora)*,[9] Cixous takes issue with the patriarchal structure privileged by Freud, by questioning the key Freudian concept of infantile sexuality, particularly the problem of the daughter's desire. By implication she indicts the theoretical basis out of which the psychoanalytical establishment positions woman. Cixous reframes Freud's narrative of the Dora case and offers several possible versions of the seduction scene. In so doing she shows how Freud chose to ignore much of the information Dora gave him in order to interpret her coherently as an hysteric. At the end of Cixous's play, in an unambiguous gesture of refusal, the character Dora closes the door on Freud. She walks out into the world, while he is left to pick up the pieces of the life she has attempted to portray for him – pieces which become in his hands her 'case'.

Other writers and/or women of the theatre like many women historians and artists throughout the Western world – some calling themselves 'feminist', others not – set out to recover the lives and achievements of forgotten or undervalued women artists, thinkers, and activists. Anne Delbée, for example, in *Une Femme (A Woman*, 1982)[10] dramatises the life of sculptress Camille Claudel. Rejected by her mentor and lover Rodin, ignored by her brother the celebrated writer Paul Claudel, institutionalised for the last fifty years of her life, Camille had disappeared from history. In her play Delbée shows a complex and many-faceted personality, an artist who would have been commissioned to create what was to become

Rodin's 'The Doors of Hell' had the jury felt that a woman were capable of handling the project's hefty budget. In another instance of reclaiming 'foremothers' Ann Roche and Françoise Chatôt wrote and produced *Louise/Emma* (1982)[11] in which they pay tribute to the radical political daring of Louise Michel and Emma Goldmann.

Concurrently, women – with feminist critics at the forefront – 'discovered' Marguerite Duras who had in fact been writing plays since 1950. For a time she too aligned herself with a feminist agenda. Her dislocated texts, tortured women characters, and troubling themes of forbidden if realised passion, in for example her plays of the 1980s *Vera Baxter* (1980), *Agatha* (1981), or *Savannah Bay* (1982), and 1970s films *Nathalie Granger* (1973) and *India Song* (1973), permit readings which demonstrate her awareness of how society constructs gender and also represses what might be called 'feminine space'.[12] Duras, particularly in her films, images this space and with it something of the 'otherness' or subversive energy of woman, an energy she celebrates as positive.[13] Another and very fine example of theatre which defies commonsense notions about gender is Simone Benmussa's adaptation of George Moore's *La Vie singulière d'Albert Nobbs* (*The Singular Life of Albert Nobbs*, 1977)[14] which pictures character 'Albert's' nearly untenable situation of having to function as a man in a 'borrowed' body while thinking and feeling like the woman she is.

At the same time that readers were finding Duras's dispossessed characters emblematic of twentieth-century women, her contemporary Nathalie Sarraute, creator of sparse and mordant verbal dramas such as *Isma* or *Elle est là* (1978),[15] rejected any suggestion of an affinity with Duras or any woman writer who defined herself, first of all, as a woman. Before everything else Sarraute claimed her identity as writer. Fearful of ghettoisation – and not without reason given the history of literary criticism in France – Sarraute refused to accept that the condescending category of 'lady writers' had begun to lose its credibility.

On the other hand, established poets such as Andrée Chedid and Chantal Chawaf brought their lyric gifts to the theatre in order to create dramas based specifically in women's experience. These are delicate, ritualistic, and often choral, as for example Chedid's *La Déesse-Lare* (*The Goddess-Lar or Centuries of Women*, 1978)[16] which pits the character Gynna's happiness against ingrained notions of what her duties to the home must be, or Chawaf's *Chair Chaude* (*Warmth: A Bloodsong*, 1976)[17] which heralds the mother–

child bond. Even Boulevard theatre, that bastion of bourgeois and patriarchal values, found itself infiltrated by the comedies of manners of Loleh Bellon who in her play *Les Dames du jeudi* (*Thursday's Ladies*, 1977)[18] questions the primacy of the family and the inevitability of romantic love. Finally, an upsurge of women directors: Vivianne Théophilidès, Jeanne Champagne, Anne-Marie Lazarini, Françoise Chatôt, Brigitte Jacques, Simone Benmussa, Gilberte Tsai, and their younger colleagues Saskia Cohen-Tanugi and Sophie Loucachevsky, among others, dedicated themselves to finding and creating roles for actresses which correspond to the actresses' own notions about who they are. Théophilidès's work with Micheline Uzan in a rereading of Joseph Delteil's *Une fille â brûler* (*A Girl for Burning*, 1981)[19] is an excellent example of women working together to validate their own special rapport with the myth of Joan of Arc. In their explorations, these women directors speak to the same needs expressed by actresses who develop one-woman cabaret pieces. All seek to examine what it means to be a creative woman.

The concerns of women in French theatre, as indeed the work of women in theatre elsewhere in Europe and America fall, then, into several categories and practices: exalting values and experiences considered to be 'feminine' or women-centred, criticising the exploitation of women in patriarchy, dramatising the experience of forgotten women, questioning and revisioning the myths of the Western tradition, creating roles for actresses in which the performers do not feel they are playing out men's fantasies, and showing how gender is constructed through social interactions and expectations. To be sure there are women like Sarraute, who write and perform as though gender were not an issue. There are also women whose work can be understood as belonging to one of the categories or practices enumerated above who would not call themselves 'feminist', a term even more politically volcanic in French than in English. However, there are no women going into French theatre who have not on some level had to confront the issue of women's creative autonomy within the theatrical endeavour.

While this overview of contemporary women's activity in French theatre *does* indicate real progress, an overly enthusiastic assessment of the current situation of women's voices would be foolhardy.[20] As recently as 1985 at a conference on 'La Femme et la Créâtivité' (Women and Creativity) at La Criée Theatre in Marseilles,[21] theatre women lamented that not one woman is in a position of real power in any of France's state-subsidised theatres.[22]

They also angrily noted that out of the fifteen volumes of theatre studies – each one including about ten in-depth articles – published by the prestigious Group for Theatre Research of the Centre National de la Recherche Scientifique only two essays treat women artists. Moreover, they concluded that despite the financial difficulties of the French film industry it is still easier for women to find producers for films than for theatre: the recent film work of Agnès Varda, Yannick Bellon, Colline Serreau, and Diane Kurys attests to this. The consensus among Parisian theatre women interviewed in the fall of 1987[23] was that current theatre directors do, indeed, seek a 'woman's play' for their season. One play, however, is enough: tokenism governs programming in established theatres.

Contrasting the situation in France with that in North America and in Great Britain clarifies the distance yet to go in truly changing 'the production and expression', as Cixous puts it, of French theatre. In comparison with a total absence of networking in France, for example, there are over two hundred academic women involved in the Women's Theatre Program of the American Theatre Association. These women are involved in teaching theatre by or about women, and/or in producing such theatre. They support some fifty well-established regularly producing women's theatre companies active throughout the US, which in turn keep track of the others' work. Recently, there has been a plethora of new women playwrights in the Anglo-Saxon world – the Americans Beth Henley and Marsha Norman and the British Pam Gems and Caryl Churchill come immediately to mind. Their work is not only being produced in both countries by all the most important regional theatres but it can also be seen in main-stage London playhouses and on the Broadway circuit. Since 1975 there have been at least seven anthologies of plays by and about women published in the United States, while Michelene Wandor in Great Britain began an outstanding collection of new plays by women writers which has published volumes annually since 1982.[24] The only comparable activity in French drama by women can be found in Québec,[25] where, for example, women playwrights such as Denise Boucher and Antonine Maillet explode the stereotypes which have long oppressed women in French-speaking Catholic Canada (Boucher's *Les Fées ont soif* [*The Fairies are Thirsty*, 1978])[26] or celebrate minority cultures within the French community (Maillet's Acadian play, *Les Crasseux* [*The Rabble*, 1974]).[27]

Nevertheless, although there may not be a feminist or even a female horde storming the theatrical Bastille, and while those

Frenchwomen who do write do not constitute a movement or even a trend, there are a few writers and works which are so significant they stand examination on their own terms. Furthermore, these productions invite analysis of how women artists challenge fundamental notions about theatricality and the theatrical event. Whether or not this challenge is a feminist one is, in certain instances, debatable. What is not debatable is that these artists, unlike Quarton's crowned Mary, refuse to be silenced by patriarchal authority.

Four productions especially can be considered potential indicators of the future of women's voices in French theatre.[28] The first of these is Michele Foucher's 1976 montage *La Table: Paroles de Femme* (*The Table: Women-speak*)[29] in which Foucher problematises what the table means in Frenchwomen's lives. The second, Chantal Chawaf's 1976 *Chair chaude* (*Warmth: A Bloodsong*), a long and opaque dramatic poem, celebrates the mother–child dyad. The third, Marguerite Duras's 1977 *L'Eden Cinéma* (*The Eden Cinema*),[30] an autobiographical theatricalisation of Duras's growing up in Indochina, disrupts all the expected conventions of theatre and repositions the audience in terms of its rapport with the actors. The last, Hélène Cixous's 1987 production, *L'Indiade ou l'Inde de leurs rêves* (*The Indiad or India of Their Dreams*)[31] pictures the painful process of Indian independence and partition.

At the time of the creation of *The Table*, Michèle Foucher was an actress with Jean-Pierre Vincent's acclaimed Théâtre National de Strasbourg. She had grown tired of performing in plays in which the human condition, in her estimation, was portrayed strictly as the 'man's condition'. With her antic gifts and according to her leftist principles she set out to create an everywoman, a character who would speak for women, particularly lower-middle-class and working-class women, in contemporary society. She determined not to write the piece alone but, rather, to gather the words from real women by interviewing them about the central issues of their lives. To give her project and thus the interviews a focus she settled on the table as ubiquitous symbol of the Frenchwoman's rapport with her world. Given the role of food in French culture the choice turned out to be an excellent one, providing Foucher with some twenty hours of tape to edit into a two-hour show.

The resulting piece is comprised of twenty-six dramatic moments lasting from several seconds to as long as eight minutes each. The performed conversations run the gamut of accepted to contested notions about how a woman does and should relate to the home and to homemaking. For instance, vignettes explain how women should do the cooking at home but how only men can be great chefs. Others proclaim how a wife's duty is to figure out how to make ends meet even if her husband earns hardly enough money for the rent and, also, how men are right to beat unruly wives. Others, however, tell stories of resistance to accepted behaviour: how, for example, one man stopped going out with his 'work buddy' when he witnessed his violence towards his family. In a series of rapid comic and sometimes maddening juxtapositions the characters recount, for example, being scolded at the table or making love on top of it. The rhythm slows down for the occasional poignant story of abandonment or a triumphant one of revolt. The sketches tend to reinforce the image of woman as both nurturer and reproducer. Yet often by Foucher's editing as well as by the free-associating of her interviewees the texts contain a sardonic critique of this double image. Such is the case in the following exchange about eating horsemeat and going to a stud farm:

– You know, here, [in Alsace] we eat horsemeat. It's good! Really! With horse, you have to marinate it mmmm ... to go with a potato salad! [...] You have to marinate it in red wine [...] for three four four days! [...]

– But it's expensive, isn't it! Before the war, it wasn't expensive at all. Poor people bought it. It used to be the cheapest meat and now it's the most expensive. For a kilo of horsemeat you pay about 55 francs! [...]

– If you're weak, if you don't have any strength at all, you should buy a horsemeat steak, it'll build you up!

– You have to be careful not to eat too much!

– Yeah! I guess so! Boy, oh boy!

– Some of my friends and I went to a stud farm! We saw some horses, with a thing ... wow! like that! Yeah, it was that big!

All five of us went one morning. We had a little 'aperitif'. Then they brought out a stallion ... We said we couldn't miss that. So, we took a good look!

And He got ... like ... like ... that. Then he jumped a mare, well he sort of did this ... mmm ... and that ... mmmm ... , you know? And then, when he finished, it was on to the next one. So we were expecting to see his stuff again ... But it was over just like that! [...]

Afterwards, the mare, well she didn't want to get into the trailer.

Oh boy, you should of seen the ruckus she made ... The mare doesn't get much ... no, no it's over so fast! Everything's set up ahead of time.

Five to six times a day! ... the same stallion! And you have to pay for
it! But he's beautiful, so elegant. You know how much a horse like
that – a thoroughbred – is worth. 15 million old francs.
– They're beautiful horses. And the meat's good too, right?

Through their ribald conversation, the characters unselfcon-
sciously acknowledge the connection between sex and food. They
also invest this link with their own perspective. By the displacements in their unintentional parable, the women are the ones who
end up conquering, not to say cannibalising, the prize stud.

Foucher played all the roles in *The Table*, moving from one character to the next by changing a hat, a hand prop, a characteristic
gesture, or her position around one of the three tables that delim-
ited three separate playing areas. She transformed herself, for
example, from spinster to *grande dame* to frightened wife, thus establishing a multidimensional image of woman and her rapport
with her table. The tables in turn became hiding places, assembly-
line work tables, seductresses' dens, baby carriages, or school desks.

If the interviews she chose allowed Foucher to reflect both positive
and negative dimensions of the table in women's lives, the staging
permitted her to comment on the texts. In general rather than neu-
tralising it, Foucher's gestures destabilised the dialogue. Thus while
cataloguing the superstitions surrounding menses and the preparation of food, she knelt on the table in a very uncomfortable position
– conveying that there was something very wrong in connecting
spoiled mayonnaise with menstruation. In a vignette which dealt
with a woman's dilemma about what to do with a husband who
acted the tyrant at table, Foucher, with the awkward movements of
a little girl, played with a fork twice her size. The fork, like other
objects of the production invested with an emotional charge, sig-
nalled how the housewife is controlled by her environment rather
than being able to control it. Other sketches tore into the image of
the tranquil housewife by highlighting such characteristics as her
burlesque imaginative powers. Detailing her fairly banal daily
routine, for example, a character danced a sultry tango to her tran-
sistor radio. Throughout all this, one silent but constant on-stage
image – a caged bird at which Foucher glanced quizzically from time
to time – also made its statement about the woman's rapport with
her table. Although Foucher's production far from denied the sometimes spectacular personal resources of the French homemaker, this
caged bird and the last words of the play nevertheless indicated the

dangers of domestic imprisonment: 'I painted my table the same colour as my walls: white! That way they fade into each other, and when there's nothing on it, I'm really happy.'

By dint of the intratextual and gestural commentaries, by sympathetic characterisations alternating with distanced ones, and especially by the post-show discussions which followed each performance, Foucher's work encouraged her audiences to think about how the table constructs women's lives and creates 'meaning'. For certain members of her audience – those women whom she had interviewed and who had not, in many cases, ever been to the theatre before – just seeing their words given theatrical form made them re-evaluate their own possibilities as speaking subjects. *The Table* is, then, an excellent example of a kind of theatre which foregrounds considerations of social roles while at the same time appealing to a popular public.

Warmth: A Bloodsong, Chantal Chawaf's dramatic poem, can also serve as an exemplary piece, but in a very different sense. In it Chawaf seems to heed Hélène's Cixous's call in her polemical essay 'The Laugh of the Medusa' (1975)[32] for women's literature based in and written from the rhythms and passions of the female body, bathed, as Cixous would have it, in 'mother's milk'. In her own essay 'Linguistic Flesh', Chawaf speaks of writing in terms similar to Cixous's: 'Isn't the final goal of writing to articulate the body? For me the sensual juxtaposition of words has one function: to liberate a living paste, to liberate matter.'[33] Her aim is to realise the potential of words to free the unconscious, to regenerate woman's sensuality, to disintellectualise her body. Her work cannot and should not be read for its themes or story but rather for her phonic games, her syntactical and semantic inventions, and for the images she favours. Thus, for example, in her play *Warmth* she abolishes hardness, solidity, geometry, linearity – all those images commonly associated with masculinity or maleness. Instead, images of liquidity: of flowing blood, of spurting milk, of creamy butter fat abound. When she imagines impregnation, for example, she sees it in terms of nourishment rather than conquest: 'Man, drawn up by my vagina secretes the sticky substance that nourishes me. He impregnates me, oily, slippery, slow and he leans heavily and moves without haste and I take time to savour him. [...] and his mass spreads itself upon me in the rivers, hormones, plains, fields and forests of life's rich countryside.' In this and myriad other passages Chawaf assimilates the woman's body to the earth.

Chawaf gives voice through three 'characters' whom she terms 'The Mother', 'The Daughter', and 'The Heart Beat' – the last of these a choral character as suggested in the homophonic analogy 'coeur' (heart) and 'choeur' (chorus) – to the experience of pre-birth, birth, and after-birth as lived and felt in the female body. In her decidedly unusual focus of literary attention Chawaf transforms the functioning of the reproductive organs into poetic matter as, for example, in these lines by The Mother: 'Air penetrates my expanding tissues. Vermilion and scarlet matter harbours densely floating particles while soldered masses detach themselves from my walls. Life carried along in the flood descends and begins to emerge and our bodies reinforce each other's movements. My blood boils, my flesh explodes, forcing a passage, growing salty with milk, my blood cells, my plasma are electric, my belly, my breasts are stretched, engorged, overfilled.' Here The Mother follows the Daughter's passage through the birth canal by seeing her own body as if outside of itself and in the process of erupting into a wholly new universe.[34]

While Chawaf *does* indeed designate and ascribe lines to three characters, these appellations in fact only signal the places where the body's voice has momentarily settled. Mother, Daughter, and Heart Beat do not have distinct characterisations. Frequently they do not even directly pick up on each other's lines. They are, rather, a voice shattered and circulating, each intervention a rhythmic response to the one before. The voices therefore interweave and mingle, foregoing any kind of chronological ordering in their hymn to mother–daughter love and bonding.

Chawaf describes the desired space for the performance of her verses as uterine: warm and tender, 'crossed by the rhythmic poundings of life'. She would have the audience incorporated in this space as well. She imagines both an ahistorical and atemporal space, an undifferentiated magma all-encompassing and secure. She sees both the space of the production and the space that mother and daughter inhabit as what might be called a diary-garden association of body and nature, a feminine paradise protected from civilisation's incursions: 'a refuge in warmth, in the beginnings of the body'.

Warmth, as the quoted passages show, has none of the consciousness-raising intent of *The Table*. There is no built-in critical commentary nor is the staging meant to distance the spectators so that they think about the images being presented. Rather, the production expects to involve the audience in its rhythmic structures, to seduce it both through the pulsating light pattern suggested in the stage directions and by the vocal quality of the actors. The spectators should be overwhelmed by the flow of words, both hauntingly melodic and deliberately troubling. Chawaf, however, like Foucher, wishes to image a 'new woman',[35] a *speaking* woman – one who in Chawaf's case will create herself anew out of her body's energies. Her project, to abolish all distinctions between spirit and matter, to figure unmediated life on stage, rejoins that of Antonin Artaud, the twentieth-century theoretician who also sought a ritualistic and therapeutic theatre. Whereas Artaud, through participation and purgation, would reconcile human beings to the most dreaded and repressed elements in their psyches, Chawaf would sing that part of the repressed female psyche whose liberation, she believes, means empowerment.

Like Chawaf, Marguerite Duras, the best known and most prolific author of the four discussed here, writes plays dependent on voice. She, too, abolishes chronological ordering, creates a dream space, and develops her plays essentially according to rhythm rather than according to the dictates or necessities of conventional plotting. She does not, however, forsake a story, no matter how murky it may be. It is thus possible to consider 'what happens' in a Duras play without concluding that the question is bogus. Nevertheless, what happens is ultimately of much less importance than the onstage tensions Duras creates between the characters as they act out or tell of their love and paradoxically their need for separation.

In *The Eden Cinema* that story, as seen from the perspective of the character Suzanne whose memory dominates the piece, is one of separation from the mother. In her stage directions Duras calls this maternal character the 'object of the narration'. In the course of what might be termed the 'prologue', Suzanne and her brother Joseph accordingly *narrate* how the mother travelled to Indochina as a young girl, fell in love, had children, lost her husband, went to work as a pianist for silent films, used all of her savings to buy a worthless piece of land in hopes of developing a rice plantation, and muddied her mind trying to dam up the Pacific so that it would stop inundating her fields:

Joseph The mother was hard. Terrible. Impossible to live with.
(*The children go on kissing their mother's hands, caressing her body. And the mother goes on letting them do as they wish. She listens to the sound of their words.*)

> **Suzanne** (*Pause*) Overflowing with love. Mother of everyone.
> Mother of everything. Strident. Shouting. Hard. Terrible. Impossible
> to live with.

Throughout the first third of the play Joseph and Suzanne, reinforced by Duras in her stage directions, portray the Mother as elemental, inevitably catastrophic.

When the children reach the part of the Mother's story which
follows the fiasco of the destroyed seawall, all three characters
begin to vary the narration by miming and sometimes fully acting
out the sequel: how, so as not to have to worry about her anymore,
the Mother encouraged Suzanne to marry M. Jo, a rich planter's
son that the family met in a Ream café, how the family went to
Saigon to try and sell the sexual bribe, a diamond, that M. Jo had
given to Suzanne; how, unable to sell the ring to obtain enough
money to build another dam the Mother attempted to sell Suzanne;
how Joseph left mother and sister to follow an hallucinatory
passion; and finally, how the Mother died after Suzanne at last
made claim to her womanhood.

While *The Eden Cinema* is extraordinarily rich and can be examined from many perspectives, for instance an analysis of the theme
of incest or a study of the dramatisation of ageing,[36] of particular
interest are the problems the play poses to reception and
identification. Duras's *didascalia* as well as a familiarity with the
type of staging she sanctions or practises herself will help situate
these problems. As already implied, Duras eschews certain traditional dramatic components or dosages of these. There is little stage
action or movement, just as there is little dramatic action in the accepted sense, since the play takes place after the crisis. (The
mother's death, for example, is merely a *reconstruction* of her
death. The audience knows that she is dead when the play begins.)
The actors deliver nearly all of their lines from the apron, moving
just barely, sometimes lifting an eyebrow or slightly turning their
heads. There is almost no visual razzle-dazzle: the space of *The
Eden Cinema* is a square of light which can figure the Mother's
bungalow or the café in Ream or the hotel in Saigon. The usual
notion of dramatic progression is replaced by the ebb and flow of
on-going conversation and/or narration which at times is painfully
slow. And the characters – to use the term loosely – speak often as
though dispossessed of their words. Sometimes even off-stage
'voices' tell their story. There is, then, scarce opportunity for audi-

ence identification with a psychologically evolving character. Finally, there is almost no suspense of the 'what will happen next' variety. When compared to *The Eden Cinema*, the dramatic poem *Warmth* with its chorus of voices (which Chawaf suggests should also be dancers), its call to include the public within the dramatic space, and its throbbing lights, appears almost riotous.

The audience is, nonetheless, caught up in *The Eden Cinema* by techniques which run counter to the sensory pummelling of more 'theatrical' texts. Duras materialises the sensuality and rage of the family romance in pervasive transformative scenic configurations of twos and threes. These groupings convey the tension and desire between the characters. Suzanne, for example, can never completely leave the mother's aura and thus achieve total separation from her. She is as if uncontrollably pulled back to her mother's body, needing to touch her, seeking, it would seem, psychic wholeness. When Suzanne and Joseph dance together to the Mother's music they also seem bound up in her being.

Music, in fact, frequently replaces the dialogue – not commenting on the action or reinforcing the words but replacing the Mother's voice. Silences, too, speak her presence and convey the emotional currents passing between the characters. What is not representable in language finds its way into the pauses.

For the silences to work, however, as well as the stasis of the production as a whole, *The Eden Cinema* requires actors capable of projecting from the stage the charismatic density of Duras's characters. All of Duras's characters, and particularly Suzanne and The Mother in *The Eden Cinema*, live in an 'elsewhere' to which both other characters and the public are drawn. Vortices of desire, both seeking and projecting others' desire, the characters must be doubled by the actors playing them. Because of this, the actors are super-eroticised while, at the same time, the characters are 'deconstructed', that is they are shown to lack a stable identity. In *The Eden Cinema* Duras shows how identity is only rendered coherent through the process of representation. She therefore creates a radically different theatre piece which not only challenges notions of the theatrical but also images on stage a desiring woman who is caught not in the throes of passionate heterosexual longing but rather in the impossible desire for wholeness with a mother who is present only as memory.

Duras neither expressly prompts her spectators to see their roles as social constructs (as does Foucher) nor (as in the case of Chawaf) does she ritualise the most intimate and perhaps the most private of woman's experiences. She does, however, make tangible the many-layered world of memory and desire in which women (and men too) function – and she develops on-stage rhythmic and gestural patterns which manage to communicate the unsayable.

A fourth and yet again different manifestation of women's voices in contemporary French theatre is evident in Ariane Mnouchkine's and The Théâtre du Soleil's staging of Hélène Cixous's *The Indiad or India of Their Dreams*. This production, a sweeping historical drama recalling an eighteenth-century play of ideas, with a cast of some fifty characters, opposes two sets of ideals and the individual struggle of certain key figures to live according to them. Lengthy verbal confrontations between the two adversaries, the Indian Congress Party and the Muslim League, are juxtaposed with shorter, more pungent, often comic scenes depicting the ordinary people trying to make sense of their drama. As was true of the Mnouchkine–Cixous collaboration on *The Terrible But Unfinished Story of Norodom Sihanouk, King of Cambodia* two years earlier,[37] *The Indiad* is an epic-length and visually spectacular clash between interest groups and social classes which also provides a learning experience for the audience. It is therefore in a different theatrical vein from the intimist pieces – much more typical of theatre by women – of Foucher, Chawaf, and Duras.

The Indiad proposes a voyage to distant mentalities in order to contemplate better how one chooses to 'be' in the world. In *The Indiad* Cixous imagines the crucial period (1937–1948) in India's recent history when the predominantly Hindu Congress Party, fighting for independence, had to confront the Muslim League, combating for independence *and* partition. She positions the great men (and one woman) of the Congress Party, with their ideal of unity in a socialist secular republic, against the profound belief of Muhamed Ali Jinnah that a free society would mean second-class status for its Muslim citizens. And she shows how the two sides' stubbornness and amateurish strategising, as well as the pomposity of India's British rulers, helped lead to a brutal civil conflict. In the midst of and above all this she positions the Mahatma Gandhi.

Her play indeed becomes ultimately a homage to him and to his lifelong message of love. It is in this latter aspect that the text and especially the production might be read from the perspective of women's voices, because through Cixous's conceptualisation of Gandhi and the problematic of universal love – and in

Mnouchkine's scenic realisation – the author's earliest preoccupa-
tions with women's writing re-emerge. Many of Cixous's concerns
from 'The Laugh of the Medusa' are translated into theatrical
terms in the staging of The Indiad. It would seem that theatre,
by its potential for multiple transformations and, moreover, by
Mnouchkine's practice of these, valorises the techniques Cixous
sees as fundamental to woman's possibilities as writer.[38] 'When id
is ambiguously uttered – the wonder of being several – [woman]
doesn't defend herself against those unknown women whom she's
surprised at becoming, but derives pleasure from the gift of alter-
ability. I am spacious, singing flesh, on which is grafted no one
knows which I, more or less human, but alive because of
transformation.'[39]

A proper discussion of 'transformation' in The Indiad takes into
consideration an ensemble of features, the most salient of which
include: thematically, the notion of truth as constantly reworking
itself, thus the inability to arrive at one position regarding what
should be the 'true' future of India; scenically, the surging set
changes with the space being transformed before the audience's eyes
from one face of India (the starkly elegant opposing camps of the
central debate) to another (the nowhere land of the untouchables);
and textually, the constantly shifting registers from delicate lyricism
to commonsensical banter. In addition, the actors 'transform' themselves into characters directly in front of the public before the play
begins. They thereby maintain the awareness of the play of the real
while they also, through interaction and techniques of direct
address, pull the audience into the performance. Furthermore, communication is never centred for long in the written text. Movements
and especially music refocus communication in non-verbal aspects
of the performance.

Concentrating on three key figures – all three extensions or
materialisations of the vision which englobes the performance text –
will help demonstrate how transformation works in The Indiad.
These stage metaphors include: Gandhi, the prophet of love;
Moona Baloo, a dancing bear who is Gandhi's double; and
Haridasi, a Bengali pilgrim, the commentator who serves as the link
between the two political camps, between Ghandhi and his errant
followers, and between the actors and the audience.

Of all the transformative aspects of The Indiad these three contribute the most to the circulating and central concept of the
Mother and of mother love. Cixous insists in the programme notes

(and elsewhere) that 'the story which carries the fatal name of Partition is, in truth, an immense love story'.[40] And indeed, despite the violent quarrelling between the characters Nehru and Jinnah, despite the bloody massacres of a Muslim family and later their Hindu assassins, despite the bloody massacres of a Muslim family and later their Hindu assassins, despite the Shakespearean pile of corpses in the penultimate segment of the play, Gandhi's message of love weights and infuses the entire production. Such is the case in the following lines in which Gandhi pleads love as his defence against Jinnah's intransigency:

> There's no love without fear. And even, sometimes, no love without a kind of disgust, repulsion even. We human beings, Hindus, Muslims, men, women, we're so different, so strange. There facing me is the Other, and nothing's like me! For example, you and I, could anybody imagine anything more different. You, with your handsome head of hair, your fine tie, your suit, your polished shoes and all your teeth. And me without. Without anything. Without hat, suit, teeth, and with all my toes constantly chewing up the paths I walk on. What attracts us in this world? Mystery. The other sex, the other religion, the other being. If there are two leaves on a tree, they aren't identical but they do dance to the same breeze – that's true of the human tree, too. Let's allow time for human affairs to grow and ripen.
>
> (pp. 81–2)

The Indiad, then, suggests that if love does not conquer adversity today it can, if one believes, triumph tomorrow. While this thought may seem naïve in these cynical times, most people in their 'heart of hearts' *do* believe. Furthermore, when love is garbed in maternity – and Cixous makes patently obvious Gandhi's resemblance to the biblical mother pleading with King Solomon not to divide her child in two – it is exceptionally convincing.

But, as noted earlier, it is not just Gandhi who carries and conveys love's emotional charge but also the pilgrim Haridasi, witnessing and communing, extending and rendering immediate Gandhi's encompassing love, calling out to the public Peter Pan-like to 'believe in mankind'. And finally, in both its most complex and charming love is given form in the Dancing Bear. Cixous, in her essay 'The Bear, The Tomb, The Stars', portrays the human fascination with The Bear: 'How we love the innocence of living creatures, how we long for Paradise, and how we scratch at Heaven's gate each time we caress the Bear. But of course if by ill luck we are able to translate that bizarre tenderness as nostalgia for our own goodness, we take pains to place the Bear in a realm beyond the human. That human beings might define themselves as those who love others is something we ordinary Westerners hardly ever imagine, for such a thought does violence to the violence we're used to.'[41]

In *The Indiad* the Bear which enters to enliven the second half of the production doubles Gandhi's innocence and is sacrificed, as is Gandhi, at the play's end. Also like Gandhi, although indirectly in the Mahatma's case, the Bear paradoxically becomes a killer. This is because its innocence cannot resist the real beast shown to exist in humankind – a form of evil which refuses the divine or what Cixous also shows to be 'the Mother', that is 'the transcendent', in the human. In a sense what Cixous's and Mnouchkine's work in *The Indiad* suggests is that theatre, which gives birth, which permits – even insists on – multiple transformations and transgressions, is a maternal space in which spectators can find the divine, the heroic, and the courageous in themselves.

To conclude – although there is no proper conclusion to some-thing that has just begun – it is necessary to sound a cautionary note against understanding the conflation of Cixous's and Menouchkine's immense talents as necessarily 'female'.[42] One must not accept, without careful conceptualisation, the idea that their work is maternal. The experimental theatre of the 1960s, harken-ing to the theoretical formulations of Antonin Artaud, also prized techniques of metamorphosis and transmutation, of associative principles of connection and of organically evolving spaces. Likewise, one must be wary of confusing, as do some theorists, certain characteristics of post-modern theatre – such as multiple discourses, an absence of linear plotting, the inscription of silence on stage, or the impossibility of mastering discourse – as exclu-sively 'feminine'.[43] True, women playwrights do put to use many of these techniques. They forego traditional texts and conventional forms and attempt to alter the audience's experience of theatre. However, their goal in most instances is politically positive. They do not, as is frequent among many postmodern artists, evade politi-cal questions and play with the possibility of meaning. As they are finding their voices theatre women in France are also groping *towards* meaning. The usefulness and the excitement of their plural approaches, both to the future of society and to the future of theatre, depend now on a corresponding willingness in audiences to question the *status quo*.

From *Modern Drama*, 32:1 (March 1989), 5–23.

NOTES

[Miller narrates the emergence of feminist theatre in France, which although limited by French patriarchy, contains several strong women's voices and great possibility for the future. The author stresses the work of Michel Foucher, Chantal Chawaf, Marguerite Duras, and the Mnouchkine–Cixous collaboration. This piece makes a crucial contribution to the present volume by interrelating French theoretical feminism and theatre. Ed.]

1. See, for example, the overview of theatrical activity by women in the eighteenth century by Barbara G. Mittman, 'Women and Theatre Arts', in *French Women and the Age of Enlightenment*, ed. Samia Spencer (Bloomington, IN, 1984), pp. 155–69.

2. In fact, it was not until the sixteenth century that women were finally allowed on stage. Up to that point female players were almost completely excluded from the act of representation. Boys played women's roles, except for the role of the Virgin in medieval mystery plays. And in neighbouring Spain, to comply with decrees of the Church fathers, even that role remained 'unpolluted' by the presence of real women.

3. The following have been particularly helpful to me in in considering the question of feminism and the theatre: Sue-Ellen Case, 'Gender as Play; Simone Benmussa's *The Singular Life of Albert Nobbs*', *Women and Performance*, 1 (Winter 1984), 21–4; also Case's *Feminism and Theater* (New York, 1988); Teresa de Lauretis, 'The Technology of Gender', in *Technologies of Gender: Essays on Theory, Film, and Fiction*, ed. Teresa de Lauretis (Bloomington, IN, 1987), pp. 1–30; Elin Diamond, 'Brechtian Theory/Feminist Criticism: Toward a Gestic Feminist Criticism', *The Drama Review*, 117 (1988), 82–93 and 'Refusing the Romanticism of Identity: Narrative Interventions in Churchill, Benmussa, Duras', *Theatre Journal*, 37 (1985), 273–86; Jill Dolan, 'Feminists, Lesbians, and Other Women in Theatre: Thoughts on the Politics of Performance', *Themes in Drama*, 11 (1989); also Dolan's *The Feminist Spectator as Critic* (Ann Arbor, M1, 1988); Linda Walsh Jenkins, 'Locating the Language of Gender Experience', *Women and Performance*, 2 (1984), 5–20.

4. Monique Surel-Turpin, in 'La Prise de parole des femmes au théâtre', in *Le Théâtre d'intervention depuis 1968*, ed. Johny Epstein and Philippe Ivernel (Lausanne, 1980), pp. 56–78, discusses the Carmagnole troupe as well as other feminist agit-prop activity in the 1970s.

5. I spoke with representatives from La Théâtrelle at a conference on women and creativity at La Criée Theatre in Marseilles, 5 May 1985.

6. Christiane Makward, in an unpublished paper on women's theatre in France delivered at NEMLA, March 1985, reported on the number and characteristics of these cabaret pieces during the 1985 theatre season. Jane Moss, in 'Women's Theatre in France', *Signs*, 12 (1987), 548–67, reports in more detail on the theatre practices of Les Trois Jeannes and other cabaret-style women's theatre.

7. Personal conversation with me, 14 December 1984.

8. Hélène Cixous, 'Aller à la mer', trans. Barbara Kerslake, *Modern Drama*, 27 (1984), 546–8.

9. Hélène Cixous, *Portrait de Dora* (Paris, 1976).

10. Anne Delbée, *Une Femme* (Paris, 1982).

11. Françoise Chatôt and Anne Roche, *Louise/Emma* (Paris, 1982).

12. See Elin Diamond, 'Refusing the Romance of Identity', cited above, note 3; and Susan D. Cohen, 'La Présence de rien', *Cahiers, Renaud-Barrault*, 106 (1984), 17–36; Marguerite Duras, *Agatha* (Paris, 1981); *India Song* (Paris, 1973); *Nathalie Granger* (Paris, 1973); *Savannah Bay* (Paris, 1982); *Véra Baxter ou les plages de L'Atlantique* (Paris, 1980).

13. Here from the feminist journal *Sorcières* are journalist Xavière Gauthier's thoughts (trans. Erica M. Eisinger) on the subversive energy of women (see Elaine Marks and Isabelle de Courtivron (eds), *New French Feminisms* [Amherst, MA, 1980], p. 203): 'If the figure of the witch appears wicked, it is because she poses a real danger to phallo-cratic society. We do constitute a danger for this society which is built on the exclusion – worse – on the repression of female strength.'

14. Simone Benmussa, *La Vie singulière d'Albert Nobbs* (Paris, 1977).

15. Natalie Sarraute, *Elle est là, C'est beau, Isma, Le mensonge. Le silence* (Paris, 1978).

16. André Chedid, 'La Déesse-Lare', unpublished MS given to me by the author.

17. Chantal Chawaf, *Chair chaude, suivi de L'Ecriture* (Paris, 1976). All quotes from the text are in my and Cynthia Running Johnson's trans-lation and will appear in an anthology of plays by French and Francophone women writers edited by myself and Christiane Makward.

18. Loleh Bellon, *Les Dames du jeudi, L'Avant-Scène* (April 1977), pp. 5–32.

19. The play text for *Une fille à brûler* is unpublished. I was able to see the piece twice at the Avignon theatre festival in 1979 and also discuss the work with its director/adaptor Viviane Théophilidès.

20. Jane Moss's article, 'Women's Theatre in France', cited above in note 6, while correctly pointing to increased theatrical activity of women in France, doesn't examine the situation of this theatre in terms of the theatrical power structure from which it is still quite marginalised.

21. Anne-Marie Lazarini, Monique Surel-Turpin, Françoise Chatôt, and Anne Delbée addressed the question of women in French theatre during an afternoon panel which I attended, 5 May 1985.

22. Currently there are some twenty-five state subsidised theatres in France.

23. In Paris in the fall of 1987 I interviewed directors Brigitte Jacques and Judith Gershman, and actresses Cécile Cotté and Coco Felgeirolles.

24. See, for example, *The Women's Project: The American Place Theater*, ed. Julia Miles (New York, 1980) and *The Women's Project 2* (New York, 1986); *The New Women's Theatre: Ten Plays by Contemporary American Women*, ed. Honor Moore (New York, 1977); *Plays by and About Women*, ed. Victoria Sullivan and James Hatch (New York, 1973); *Plays by Black Women*, ed. Margaret Wilkerson (New York, 1986); and Michelene Wandor's *Plays by Women* volumes from Methuen (since 1982).

25. In Quebec, there is now a vital women's theatre movement. A glance through the catalogue of the Centre d'Essai des Auteurs Dramatiques indicates some two hundred titles of contemporary plays by women.

26. Denise Boucher, *Les Fées ont soif* (Montreal, 1978).

27. Antonine Maillet, *Les Crasseux* (Ottowa, 1973). For an overview of theatrical activity by women in Quebec, see Jane Moss, 'Les Folles du Québec: The Theme of Madness in Quebec Women's Theatre', *The French Review*, 57 (1984), 617–24. See also Paula Gilbert Lewis (ed.), *Traditionalism, Nationalism and Feminisms: Women Writers of Quebec* (Westport, CT and London, 1985).

28. Both the dramatic texts and the production texts serve as a basis for my discussion of recent women's voices. I had the good fortune to see three of these shows. The fourth, *Warmth*, was described to me in some detail by its author Chantal Chawaf in a personal conversation in the summer of 1979.

29. Michèle Foucher, *La Table, L'Avant-Scene* (October 1978), pp. 23–30. All quotations are from a translation by Christiane Makward and myself for an anthology of French and Francophone women's plays. I saw Michèle Foucher perform *La Table* in October 1980 at the University of Wisconsin-Madison. For more information on *La Table*, see Josette Féral, 'Writing and Displacement: Women in Theatre', trans. Barbara Kerslake, *Modern Drama*, 27 (1984), 549–63.

See also Michel Deutsch and Paul Guérin, '*La Table*: Connexion', *Travail Théâtral*, 16 (1979), 13–21.

30. Marguerite Duras, *L'Eden-Cinéma* (Paris, 1977). I saw this play in December 1977. All quotations appearing in this text are from an unpublished translation by Sonia Orwell and are to be included in the anthology of French and Francophone women's plays edited by Christiane Makward and myself.

31. Hélène Cixous, *L'Indiade ou l'Inde de leurs rêves et quelques écrits sur le théâtre* (Paris, 1987). I attended several performances of *L'Indiade* in November 1987. All translations of quotations from the play and from the theatre essays following it (*Quelques écrits sur le théâtre*) are my own.

32. Hélène Cixous, 'Le rire de la Méduse', *L'Arc*, 61 (1975), 39–54.

33. Chantal Chawaf, 'Linguistic Flesh', trans. Yvonne Rochette-Ozzello, in *New French Feminisms*, p. 177.

34. As my translation does not do justice to Chawaf's internal rhyme scheme and her powerful use of alliteration, I include here the original French: 'La matière du vermillion, la matière de l'écarlate se dilate, l'air est entré, les plaques flottent sur l'épaisseur, les blocs soudés se détachent, la vie entraînée pas ses poussées descend et les corps se renforcent, se chevauchent, prennent la position avec laquelle ils émergeront; je bouillonne de sang, la chair se bouscule, se fraye un passage, se sale de lait, les hématies, le plasma du sang se chargent d'életricité, le ventre, les seins se tendent, s'engorgent, s'hypertrophient, se déplissent.'

35. Chantal Chawaf, 'L'Ecriture' from *Chair chaude* (Paris, 1976), p. 77.

36. See, for example, Mary Lydon's essay 'Eden Cinema: Aging and the Imagination in Marguerite Duras', pp. 154–67 in *Memory and Desire: Aging-Literature-Psychoanalysis*, ed. Kathleen Woodward and Murray M. Schwartz (Bloomington, IN, 1986).

37. Hélène Cixous, *L'Histoire terrible mais inachevée de Norodom Sihanouk, roi de Cambodge* (Paris, 1985).

38. For a longer and more probing discussion of this, see Cynthia Running Rowe's PhD dissertation, 'Jean Genet and Hélène Cixous: Reading Genet Through the Feminine', University of Wisconsin-Madison, 1985. See also Cynthia Running Johnson's article 'Feminine Writing and Theatrical Practice', *Themes in Drama*, 11 (1989).

39. Hélène Cixous, 'The Laugh of the Medusa', trans. Keith and Paula Cohen, *Signs*, 1 (1976), 889.

40. Hélène Cixous, 'Préface a *L'Indiade*', p. 13.

41. Hélène Cixous, 'L'Ourse, la tombe, les étoiles', from *Quelques écrits sur le théâtre*, pp. 249–50.

42. Without labelling as 'feminine' or 'feminist' the cathexis of these two talents, I would suggest that their collaboration may herald a new epoch for *all* of French theatre. Cixous herself likens Mnouchkine's gifts to those of a modern 'Promothea'. See Hélène Cixous, *Le Livre de Promothéa* (Paris, 1983).

43. Compare, for example, Elinor Fuchs's 'Presence and the Revenge of Writing: Rethinking Theatre After Derrida', *Performing Arts Journal*, 26/27 (1985), 163–73 and Jeanie Forte's 'Women's Performance Art: Feminism and Postmodernism', *Theatre Journal*, 40 (1988), 217–35.

12

Male Ideology and Female Identity: Images of Women in Four Modern Chinese Historical Plays

HAIPING YAN

Modern Chinese historical drama emerged with the modern spoken drama in the May 4th New Culture Movement in the early twentieth century. The modern spoken drama, a Chinese imitation and appropriation of the form of Western modern drama which putatively began with Ibsen, was a radical negation of the Chinese traditional theatre represented by forms such as classical Peking Opera. Starting in 1917, *New Youth*, which launched by a group of young intellectuals and became one of the most influential journals of the New Culture Movement, vigorously criticised the traditional theatre in which 'no man speaks human language' and advocated a new drama about 'real people's real life'.[1] In their radical challenge to the traditional theatre, some of the young intellectuals argued that the genre of historical drama could not do anything useful but 'repeat the old habits and stories'.[2] Guo Mo-ruo, a radical activist and one of the founders of modern Chinese literature, had a different view on this issue. In his opinion, the long history of China contains 'the soul of the nation and indicates its future fate'. What he wanted to do, as he announced in 1923, was to project a living energy into the dead skin of history and to generate a new form of historical drama which combines the past and the present into an image of the future.[3] The trilogy named *Three Rebellious Women*

was his first dramatisation of this theoretical claim and, in a literal
sense, the beginning of modern Chinese historical drama.

The title – *Three Rebellious Women* – raises several questions:
Why did this man choose three women from the past to stage his
ideas concerning the present? What did he attempt to indicate
through the images of these women? And how do these images
figure in his representation of Chinese history? In short, what is embodied in this textual complex in which the past is recapitulated
and the present articulated through particular female images
dramatised by a male writer? These questions shall serve as the
focus of my analysis of Guo's trilogy and, moreover, as the starting
point in my examination of four twentieth-century Chinese plays
using historical female protagonists.

Zhuo Wen-jun,[4] the first play of the trilogy, was written in 1923.
According to the Han Dynasty historian Sima Qian (145 BC—?),[5]
Wen-jun was a young widow from a rich family who fell in love
with Sima Ziang-ru, a poor poet of genius. After Sima persuaded
her to elope with him, the father was outraged; but eventually he
weakened and gave a big sum of money to the 'shameful couple'.
Although the story had a happy ending thanks to the recognition
given by a father figure, the name of Wen-jun was still stigmatised
through literally thousands of years. Even as late as the time of the
Republic (1911–49), some 'moralists' still condemned Wen-jun as a
'bad woman'.[6]

Guo Mo-ruo's representation of the story in the 1920s was
clearly a challenge to the traditional moralists. Wen-jun in his
vision is a courageous woman who values her individual feelings
more than the order of the patriarchal society embodied by her
father. She does not go off secretly – that is, *elope* – with Sima as
Sima Qian recorded – and hence is immune from the pervasive
silence and implicit sense of guilt which are often associated with
the action of eloping. Instead, she declares her emotional attachment openly and opposes her father's will directly. More important,
she seems capable of articulating what she chooses to do with remarkable eloquence. When her father and her father-in-law order
her to commit suicide because what she does is absolutely disgrace-
ful and intolerable in their eyes, she not only refuses but gives a
solid rationale for her action:

> I have treated you in a way that a daughter and daughter-in-law
> treats her father and father-in-law; now I am treating you as an equal

human being. The old moral system made by You Men and sustained by You Old Men, cannot constrain us – the awakened young people, the awakened women – any more! ... My behaviour, I believe, will be praised by the people in future![7]

Between Wen-jun's choice not to elope with Sima and her open announcement with a particular value-conviction about her romantic attachment to Sima, one may argue, there is a moment of possibility opening up for interpreting or constructing the meaning of her attachment in its relation to a reconstituting of her identity. Yet this moment of possibility, as the above quotation indicates, soon disappears into Wen-jun's particular verbalisation which legitimises, moralises, and politicises her attachment to Sima in a specific discourse. In this long speech, there are several voices overlapping one another. We can hear, to begin with, echoes of Western humanism. People are *essentially* equals. Prior to social identities such as father and daughter, lies the universal human being with equal rights and independence. This ontologised image of Man with a capital M forms the point of departure for Wen-jun's rationalisation of her romantic feelings and, as the play unfolds, serves as the ultimate goal of her struggle. This ultimate goal, as I will discuss more specifically later, indicates that Wen-jun's attachment to Sima is based upon a type of humanistic consciousness which, while endorsing the truly liberating elements that the anti-imperial struggle contained for both Chinese men and women in the early twentieth century, also obscures and submerges the socio-historically bound anti-patriarchal dimension in women's struggle. Associated with this humanistic ontology, furthermore, the Western rationalistic concept of history as a process of necessary progress is also implemented in Wen-jun's speech. Made possible by the conceptualisation of time and underlaid by the conviction that the future is always universally and necessarily better than the past, such a concept, while in an important way functioning to endorse and privilege Wen-jun's struggle, points to a 'future' in which putatively all the undue differences between men and women should disappear into their ontologically shared humanity.

The questions one would naturally ask with regard to the ontologised Man and a totalised future are the following: What is contained in this image of Man for women as socio-historically bound human beings? What does such a 'future' specifically imply for women in their relationship with men? In the case of the play, what did Wen-jun, the rebellious woman, obtain through rebellion against her father? What would be Wen-jun's social status and identity in a 'future' such as is indicated in the play? It is important to note that the playwright, while being rather forceful in his rejection of the old patriarchal morality, is elusive about women's status in his paradisiacal 'future' of Man. In his appendix to the trilogy, Guo Mo-ruo writes:

> According to the old morality, our Chinese women have to strictly follow three principles of obedience: when she is a maiden at home, she shall obey her father; after she gets married she shall obey her husband; if her husband dies, she shall obey her son. Through all her life, a woman is always the dependant of men and never is allowed a moment of independence. These three principles have indeed crystallised the male-centred morality in a completely naked manner. ... Now, it is time for women to awake! They have been sinking under the male-centred morality for thousands of years and have sacrificed all their lives. They must first fight to be a real human being, then they will be able to ask for equal participation and competition in the society.

Guo concludes, 'Wen-jun is an excellent example of a challenge to the patriarchal order, and this is the most important motivation underlying my play'.[8] But what does this 'excellent example' choose to do to be a 'real human being?' The answer is very clear: She asserts herself as a 'real human being' by winning a husband. For the stage direction in the last scene Guo wrote, *Sima appears on the stage, gentle, rather tall and in a long white robe. Wen-jun looks up towards Sima, Sima comes to Wen-jun, holding her hands, looking down on Wen-jun with deep emotion for a long time.*[9] The tone here is very tender. After having gone through all the sufferings, the woman now is in safe hands – a good man's hands of course. Wen-jun loses her father who belongs to the past, but she does not lose the male endorsement dramatised in the image of her husband as the representative of the future.

The feminist dimension of the genuine dynamics contained in her rebellion against her father is not only implicitly appropriated into the androcentric humanistic discourse I have pointed out, but explicitly domesticated through her relationship with Sima. It is strongly suggested in this last scene that, in the mythologised humanistic 'future', Wen-jun is going to remain as an admiring and worshipping 'female' to the opposite of her sex – although the opposite this time of a 'new' and historically conditioned 'progressive' sex. The relationship between Wen-jun and Sima which has been highly romanticised throughout the play is hereby crystallised as being entirely unproblematic. This unproblematic relationship is accompanied and foregrounded by the distinct break between the father and daughter in the play. In the historical story recorded by Sima Qian, Wen-jun and Sima lived on her father's money happily ever after. In Guo's play there is no compromise between the Old and the New. The father absolutely refuses to accept this couple's relationship and Wen-jun hence makes an absolute break with her father in order to join Sima.

This ending is not accidental. Wen-jun's absolute break with her father and unproblematic union with her husband are highly suggestive of the author's desire. A significant shift has taken place between the historical model and its artistic counterpart when the play unfolds in such a way. The feminist dynamics contained in the conflicts between Wen-jun and her father have been finally resolved into a clear-cut dichotomy between the New husband–wife union and the Old father–daughter ties. The discontinuity between the two cannot obscure and in fact precisely reveals the continuity between the two – the continuity of male primacy. The conflict between the rebellious woman and patriarchal morality, in short, is displaced into the conflict between the Old Man and New Man. Wen-jun remains as an object to be essentially defined by her male companion rather than a self-defining subject. As we mentioned earlier, Guo's sympathy with rebellious Chinese women and their struggle against male-centred morality was clearly based on his general humanistic conviction. The difference between the humanistic conviction of universal human equality and the feminist struggle for equality[10] lies in the fact that the former is epistemologically universalised and the latter is socio-politically anchored. What are submerged in the claim of the universalised human equality, as manifested in the play, are the socio-historically bound particularities of humanity – the particularities that could be expressed through, for instance, the feminist discourse. The danger of such a claim, as I have pointed out in my above analysis and will discuss further below, lies in its intrinsic function to repress or erase genuine difference[11] in a given human society through its particular ideology. The notion of equality in the feminist agenda, on the other hand, insists on the specific conflictual dynamics of human relationships in historically conditioned processes and resists various essentialistic theoretical reductions, among which the humanistic discourse is an important type. What feminist practice attempts, as Michèle Barrett concisely articulates, is 'to break away from reductionism, and to locate sexuality and gender identity in the specificity of historical ideological processes'.[12]

Applying such an analysis to Guo's play immediately problematises the complex multiplicity of meanings which the image of Wenjun evokes. Such a perspective acknowledges both Wen-jun the Chinese woman who lived during the Han Dynasty, and Wen-jun the character of a twentieth-century drama – a drama in which she acts as spokesperson for the ontologised humanity formulated in the seventeenth- and eighteenth-century West. This complex matrix of images embodies a particular ideology which is humanistic by its nature and androgenic in its function. As an explicit challenge to the Chinese imperial moral order in the 20s, the humanist discourse does suggest a revolutionary alternative. The fact that the playwright does not follow the historically recorded story and changes Wen-jun's reconciliation with her father into an absolute break may be an indication of the degree of the author's desire to break away from the 'father-order', a desire that is so strong that he cannot see any possible presence of the Old in the 'future' of the New. As an assertion for a reconstruction of the male–female relationship, on the other hand, the androcentric 'high-argument'[13] of humanism reinscribes what it is used to undermine. Wen-jun's unconditional admiration for her husband can be viewed as an externalisation of the male desire to be not just followed, but worshipped by the ideal female. It is the authorial voice which speaks through Wen-jun and through the dramatisation of her story, the voice of a playwright who had an education in modern Western science,[14] was living at the turning point of modern Chinese history, and fighting against the imperial order characterised by its traditional patriarchy while promoting the Western humanistic ideology. In this image of a woman from the past lives the soul of a man, an author, struggling in the present.

This Self in Other, Present in Past, provides a revealing emblem of the social historical situation in China in the 1920s. Guo Mo-ruo projects an image of Wen-jun as a young rebel fighting against a particular 'father-order' – a fight which has important relevance to but cannot be identified with women's struggle against the inveterate Chinese patriarchal tradition. The historically conditioned complicity of Chinese men in such a tradition – the recognition of which does not replace the exploration of the absolutely crucial political, social and moral differentiations among them and the complexity of their radically differentiated relationships with women – appears absent in Guo Mo-ruo's dramatisation. The play suggests to us that the old imperial moral system as characterised by Guo could no longer hold people in the society together, and that the disintegration of such a system opens up possibilities for imagining different but nonetheless androgenic cultural alternatives. It also suggests that it was under such circumstances that the women's movement was recognised and praised by Guo Mo-ruo, among many other young male intellectuals, through a perceptible psychological displacement. In *Zhuo Wen-jun*, a Chinese woman is used as a symbolic and temporary advance guard in social transformation. Women's socio-political and economical marginality in an established male-dominated society made it more feasible for them to be appropriated as the symbols of the agents of social change, 'the first, temporary inhabitants of the future',[15] as Juliet Mitchell has put it. Such a coming 'future' as indicated through Guo's dramatic representation of a woman's present struggle, does embody a radical discontinuity with the past, but this discontinuity is not as thorough or complete as the playwright himself thinks; the continuity of the male gaze as materialised in Wen-jun's unconditioned admiration of Sima – a figure who is significantly different from her father but nonetheless a male providing leadership, morality, and security – is visible.

Wen-jun, this 'first inhabitant of the future', mediated in Western humanistic discourse as she is, indicates an important message for the development of modern Chinese history in the early part of this century. As Guo sees it, this message provides the moral ground for oppressed people to fight against their oppressors. From his many writings, one can see that Guo's cultural advocacy of women's liberation was also a derivation of his political rationalities about the oppressed social classes as defined by Marxism. Guo Mo-ruo's sympathy with the women's liberation movement was directed by his commitment to what he called 'the socialist revolution' in China in the 1920s. This commitment to a revolutionary social transformation enabled him to see in the women's movement a hope for a better society in the future from which both Chinese women and men would benefit. In his appendix to the trilogy,[16] he compared women's struggle against oppression by the patriarchal moral order with the worker's fight against the exploitation by the ruling social group:

Socialism means to raise class consciousness to start the class struggle; the feminist movement means to raise the consciousness of sexuality to start the struggle for women's liberation. The working class has been oppressed by the capitalist social organisation, they are asking for the equality of wealth, but the capitalists still treat them as inferior species. Women have been fettered under the male-centred morality, they are asking for the equality between men and women, but the supporters of the male-centred morality still view them as being widely arrogant and crush them down violently. . . Some people say that women are inferior to men, that they are different animals, and that the difference between women and men is similar to the difference between orang-utan and humans . . . It is the male-centred morality which has orang-utanised women! And after turning women into a kind of orang-utan, it has been turning men into the same thing. We Chinese men are deteriorating day by day and have obtained and developed all the bad qualities such as jealousy, suspiciousness, obedience, laziness, dependence, nasty gossiping, frivolity, knowing nothing outside of family, knowing nothing besides the tiny self, all these so-called 'feminine weaknesses' are fully manifested in our men's characters! We have already sunk to such an extent, really we don't want to try to save ourselves?![17]

The enthusiasm and a sense of devotion displayed by the author here towards the struggle of the oppressed people can hardly be over-estimated. A full recognition of its significance, however, does not prevent one from seeing that such an enthusiasm is gender-related but gender-blind. While pointing out the revolutionary core shared by the socialist transformation and feminist movement, and powerfully arguing that the male-centred morality not only oppresses women but also men, Guo seems to have entirely overlooked the different processes and mechanisms in which women and men have been 'orang-utanised' and the different implications and effects that the different processes exercise on men and women in a given historical time and place. It is interesting to see that Guo in his writing was unconsciously but clearly shifting his attention from women to men. By the end of the paragraph, Guo is in fact directly talking about men instead of women. Although he is acting as advocate for both men and women of the future and protesting against the 'Old Man' order, his emphasis is increasingly on the Old rather than on 'Man', let alone the intricate combination of the 'Old' and the 'Man'.

This gender-blindness embodied in Guo's articulation is not an isolated literary phenomenon; it is implicated in the general development of the cultural consciousness in the revolution that led to the founding of the People's Republic of China. It was believed that the theory of the class struggle provided by Marxism could solve the problems of the oppression of women. Indeed, Mao Ze-dong in his essay written in 1927, 'The Report on the Peasants' Movement in Hunan Province', insightfully points out that Chinese women in imperial China, while having to endure the oppression executed by the government in the name of divine gods and through the authorities of the local patriarchs, also had to endure the oppressive authority of their husbands.[18] But the nature of the authority of the 'husband' is simply termed 'feudal' by Mao and is concluded by Mao's followers and interpreters to be transparently the same as the oppressive authorities of the gods, the old government, or the 'feudal' heads of the local communities. It follows that the revolution which aims at the emancipation of all oppressed people through class struggle would necessarily and similarly liberate women as a part of the oppressed class. The intricate implications of and the problematic link among the four sources of the oppression for women which Mao suggested and the different forms in which the oppression of women may survive and operate under a different social structure, therefore, are not sufficiently explored. The questions concerning women's problematic situation under a newly constructed socialist economy and political system with a long patriarchal cultural tradition, in other words, are not quite opened up. Such an unproblematised view of gender indicates the underdeveloped aspects of revolutionary consciousness which are partially but not simply due to the historical constraints under which it was initiated and developed.[19] Moreover, the particular form of gender-blindness as representatively articulated by leading intellectual figures like Guo – the subordinate nature of women's struggle in its relation to the 'class struggle' – points to the theoretical limits of Marxism which, as Barrett points out, 'constituted as it is around relations of appropriation and exploitation, is grounded in concepts that do not and could not address directly the gender of the exploiters and those whose labour is appropriated'.[20] Such a gender-blindness gradually becomes explicitly problematic after the practical success of the 1949 revolution.

With the founding of the People's Republic of China in 1949,[21] the once young and rebellious Guo Mo-ruo became the president of the National Science and Social Science Academy. Together with some other former young male rebels of the 1920s and 30s, his works have figured as an important part of the cultural establishment for the new People's Republic. In 1959, he published another five-act historical play in which the central figure was again a woman – *Cai Wen-ji*. In this play, the oppressive father-figure has disappeared and the problematic relationship between old man and young woman has been replaced by a sublime harmony.

Cai Wen-ji, according to fragmentary records, was the daughter of Cai Tan, a prominent historian in the Han period (206 BC–220 AD). Her husband died in a war between Han China and the Xiongnu, a people living along the north-west border of China. She was captured by the Xiongnu army and became the wife of their khan. She stayed there for 12 years and had two sons by the khan. When Prime Minister Cao Cao finally gained control of China through military victories, he decided to ransom Wen-ji back in the hope that she would collect and edit her father's works which had been scattered and damaged during the war. The khan of the Xiongnu accepted the ransom and Wen-ji left her Xiongnu family, and returned to China alone. We do not know whether she actually fulfilled Cao Cao's expectations. What we do know is that she wrote a poem named 'Xiongnu Flute Song of Eighteen Verses', a long, passionate, and pathetic poem which expressed her feelings about the suffering she had endured. It was said that she finally married again with a civil official named Dong Si.

Guo Mo-ruo originally wanted to make this story into the third play of his trilogy *Three Rebellious Women* in the 1920s. He wrote in 1926:

> In her life, she [Cai Wen-ji] married three times – which is bad enough according to our Chinese morality, and the second time she was even married to a barbarian! In those moralists' eyes, she might very well be a gifted poet, but nonetheless a 'woman of shameless character'. Worst of all she did not commit suicide to keep her integrity as a Chinese woman after she was captured by Xiongnu! But such authoritarian judgements, in my opinion, are very dubious. I believe that the precondition for marriage is Love. Only those marriages based on Love are moral, regardless the beloved one is a 'negro', a 'barbarian', a whatever! Without Love, even if everything is done with perfect Chinese formality, a marriage is just a trade of bodies.[22]

Following his idea of Love, which apparently was derived from nineteenth-century Western Romanticism, Guo was convinced that Wen-ji loved the khan of the Xiongnu and would not have returned to China if the khan had not accepted the ransom. But the khan wanted the gold and sold her back to Cao Cao, thus Wen-ji realised that the khan actually did not love her as she had imagined. With deep disillusionment, she left her sons and returned to China. Guo Mo-ruo concludes in his essay: 'Therefore in my opinion, Wen-ji is entirely a classic Chinese "Nora" '.[23]

In Guo's play of 1959, the image of Wen-ji is strikingly transformed from Ibsen's Nora into an elegant woman civil official of the Weijin Dynasty. She begins with torn emotions over the conflict between her attachment to her sons and husband, and her moral commitment and devotion to her home country. After controlling her emotions, she finally reaches a sublime state of happiness in her total identification with a prosperous Han-China, an abstract entity symbolised by the image of Cao Cao. Sections of 'Xiongnu Flute Song in Eighteen Verses' occurring throughout the play are rewritten. The play opens with the first verse of the song. Wen-ji's original first verse was a denouncement of the chaotic situation in Han-China in which she suffered; Guo's first verse is a eulogy of Cao Cao's Han-China in which Wen-ji is presented as being highly pleased that Cao Cao is trying to ransom her back and at the same time as being saddened by the possibility of leaving her children behind. In the second Act, Guo does not change the original verses of the poem he uses and lets Wen-ji show more painful emotions through her singing. In the third Act, however, Wen-ji appears to have gained control of her feelings, put her 'small pains' in 'the right perspective', and to have followed the morally noble advice offered by Dong Si, the official sent by Cao Cao to accompany her back: 'Today's China under Cao is so different from the China you saw 12 years ago – it is now prosperous and peaceful and the common people are so much happier than before. Why don't you think about the nation's needs and the high expectations we all have for you to contribute to our cultural establishment instead of immersing yourself completely in your own personal feelings?'[24] The Wen-ji in the final act, logically, has become a civil official with a spirit of noble devotion to the country and a sublime sense of happiness. The 18th verse of the poem, used as the conclusion of the play, is changed from the original version – an uncompromising accusation against the merciless heaven, earth, and human world – into an ode to the Son of Heaven, Cao Cao.[25]

In his preface to the 1959 play, Guo Mo-ruo says: 'I want to declare one thing: My main purpose in writing *Cai Wen-ji* is to reverse a verdict that has been imposed on Cao Cao. Cao made great contributions to the development of our nation and of our culture. He is a great historical figure. However, since we have been trapped by the orthodox values dominant since the Song period, we have judged him very unfairly.'[26] In his essay on Cai Wen-ji's 'Xiongnu Flute Song in Eighteen Verses,' Guo says: 'From Wen-ji's life, we can see the greatness of Cao Cao. She was one among many saved by Cao Cao. . . . The decision to ransom Wen-ji back was based on lofty concerns for the nation's culture and not personal sentiments [for Wen-ji's father]. . . . Cao Cao should be viewed as a national hero.'[27]

When we put these lines written in the 1950s about Cai Wen-ji next to those of the 1920s, we might have difficulty believing that both are about the same woman and written by the same man. The difference between the 'main purpose' that Guo stated in 1959 and the 'major motivation' he described when he thought of writing this play in 1926, as I see it, shows that Guo's general view on a father-figure as the leader of a nation has in the 1950s changed into the opposite of what it was in the 1920s, when he was a rebel towards the established order embodied and controlled by its father figures. Indeed, the social and ideological implications of 'father figures' as national leaders in these two different periods in Chinese political history are of course profoundly and radically different, the complexity of the differences requires careful elucidation and has been generating articulations and rearticulations ever since 1949, as demonstrated in numerous scholarly and literary works in China. But the similarities between the two periods, intricately implicated in and at times inseparable from their difference, have been by and large submerged in all those elaborations and articulations – the similarities resulting from the long Chinese patriarchal tradition. It seems unproblematic to Guo, for instance, that the reconstructed moral order with its leading group of which he was a prominent member in the 1950s remained predominantly male in its constitution.

Guo in 1959 directly identified himself with his heroine Cai Wen-ji: 'Cai Wen-ji is me!', he says in his preface (echoing Flaubert's famous line about Madame Bovary). 'She is written in the image of myself.'[28] The following question then arises: In which sense is he Cai Wen-ji? He indicates in the same essay that by saying this he refers to his experience with his Japanese wife. They had three children and lived in Japan for ten years. When the War of Resistance against Japan started in 1937, Guo returned to China leaving his

Japanese wife and children behind. The feelings he projected onto Wen-ji, feeling split between devotion to her country and attachment to her family is indeed what he, as a man and husband, once experienced.

The traumatic memories of Guo's personal life in the 1930s and his view on the father figures of a new social order in the 1950s, both made their presence felt in this historical play. The literary patten in which the Self projects into the Other, the Present dramatises itself through the Past, reoccurred in this historical play with new implications. This time the woman, Wen-ji, was used not as a negation of the present and symbol of the future but to build up the present father figure as the centre of a positive social order.

From a more socio-historically oriented than biologically based feminist perspective, I should say that the shift embodied in Guo Mo-ruo's two historical plays about women in their relation to an established social order with its father figures, thirty years apart, is an ironical but highly complicated shift. It would be reductively formalistic to simply conclude that Guo finally arrived at what in the beginning he intended to break away from, that is, the traditional patriarchal order. The concept of 'patriarchy' as defined by the American radical feminism and psychoanalytical feminist theories appears to be insufficient to account for such a shift. Just as Michèle Barrett points out, 'a general problem with the concept of patriarchy is that not only is it by and large resistant to exploration within a particular mode of production, but it is redolent of a universal and transhistorical oppression. So, to use the concept is frequently to evoke a generality of male dominance without being able to specify historical limits, changes or differences.'[29]

Taking the specific historical changes and differences into consideration, one sees in Guo's case an intrinsic logical link but not a simple continuation between his absolute negation of the male-centred morality in the 1930s and his total identification with the father figures of the reconstructed social and moral order in the 1950s: He found himself in a total unity with the image of a 'good man' which had been part of his imagination thirty years before and had been an essential part of his motivation to fight the 'old rotten father figures'. Such a 'good man' who is in favour of women's liberation in the 1930s and becomes a positive father figure in the 1950s, as I discussed earlier, is pro-feminist in his social declaration but is humanistic in his ontologised epistemology. While standing for those Chinese women and men struggling against the imperial patriarchal order in the early decades of the century, the image of this 'good man' also has the potential function of erasing the irreducible particularities of historically conditioned and produced humanity such as that of gender. The fact that the two female protagonists in Guo's plays assert their moral choice and hence realise the meaning of their beings through men – Wen-jun through her total admiration for Sima and Wen-ji through her absolute gratitude towards Cao Cao – indicates a similar gender-blindness in Guo's understanding of the 'good man' in his relationship with women. Certain elements of the old male-centred morality that young Guo Mo-ruo consciously fought against make their presence felt precisely through these unconscious 'blind spots', registered in his dramatisation. Through those 'blind spots' and their development in Guo's later life and writing, one sees an interesting process in which the Chinese patriarchal tradition becomes reinscribed in a different form of cultural ideology.

This 'reinscription' does not just occur in Guo Mo-ruo's life and writing alone, it manifests itself in many important modern Chinese writers as well. Cao Yu, now the president of the Society of Chinese Dramatists, for instance, was radically opposed to the patriarchal order of the Chinese society in the 1930s. In his historical play written in 1979, in which the leading character is a woman – *Wang Zhao-jun* – Cao Yu follows Guo Mo-ruo's pattern in *Cai Wen-ji*.

The story of Wang Zhao-jun is part of Chinese folk literature. Compared to Cai Wen-ji, an aristocratic women poet, Wan Zhao-jun is much closer to the common Chinese people's heart. According to some historical records,[30] Zhao-jun, an extraordinary beauty, was chosen by the Imperial Palace as one of the concubine candidates for Emperor Yuan of the Han Dynasty. Since there were too many candidates, the emperor had to choose his favourites by viewing their portraits. The court painter thus obtained power over these women which he used to extract bribes. Those who refused to submit, and Zhao-jun was one, were portrayed as ill-favoured. For quite a few years, therefore, Zhao-jun had no chance to be seen by the emperor in person. When the chief of the Xiongnu paid his respects to the emperor in 33 BC and expressed his wish to marry a Chinese as a peace-making liaison, Zhao-jun, out of her deep sorrow and resentment towards the Han Imperial Palace, requested to be the woman to go to Xiongnu. Her request was granted by the emperor. When she appeared in the court for the first time to take her leave, the emperor was astounded to see how beautiful she was.

He wanted to make her stay but it was too late to do so. Zhao-jun left her home country alone and finally died of sorrow in Xiongnu.

As an innocent victim of the imperial patriarchal order, the beautiful, self-determining, and unhappy Zhao-jun has won Chinese people's sympathy and admiration one generation after another. In Cao Yu's play, however, although she initially feels resentment towards the living death of the concubine candidate's existence, she becomes a woman who shares the political motivation for the marriage. She even articulates this motivation in a poetic language which induces the emperor to exclaim: 'Oh, Wang Zhao-jun, Wang Zhao-jun, what you have said goes right to our heart!'[31] Zhao-jun leaves China with a noble smile and a clear purpose: 'I am the daughter of Wu mountain, an ordinary young woman. From thousands of miles away, the Son of Heaven dispatched me here, from thousands of miles away, you [the chief of the Xiongnu] welcomed me here. I have come, for the happiness of the peoples in Han-Chin and Xiongnu.'[32]

When he asked why he turned Zhao-ju into such a noble and smiling woman, Cao Yu answered:

> Why did I write a play for Wang Zhao-jun? Because this is a task that our dear Prime Minister Zhou assigned to me. I remember that was an afternoon in the 60s, in the meeting hall of the C.P.P.C.C.[33] the Prime Minister was talking with us. A comrade leader from Inner-Mongolia told the Prime Minister that in the area of Inner-Mongolia, in the Steel-City Bao Tou, the Mongolian young men had difficulty in finding fiancées, because the Chinese women do not want to marry them. Prime Minster Zhuo replied: We should promote marriage between Chinese women and minority men, we do not want Chinese chauvinism; in ancient time, there was a Chinese woman named Wang Zhao-jun who did this! Then the Prime Minister said to me: Cao Yu, you will write about Wang Zhao-jun, won't you? He also proposed a toast, to wish that the play *Wang Zhao-jun* might be born soon.[34]

Indeed, this is a historical play engendered by the concern of a man, the Prime Minister Zhou, about a portion of the male population in the People's Republic of China and written by a male playwright. But the central image of the play is a woman, a woman who lived thousands of years ago, a woman who, unlike Cai Wen-ji, did not leave any written words to us, and did not tell us anything about herself and what she actually went through in her life. She was a Chinese woman who married a chief of Xiongnu in the political interests of the Chinese as well as Xiongnu regimes, a woman who kept an absolute silence in Chinese history, as silent as her green grave in Xiongnu.[35]

The idea of opposing Chinese chauvinism in the interests of the ethnic minority that the Prime Minister Zhou advocated was certainly politically significant and socially progressive. The irony inherent in this socially progressive pronouncement, however, lies in the fact that is asserted by a Chinese man who was in an extremely powerful political position and appeared to have the authority not only to speak for Chinese women but to orient or even to organise their family lives. It is the Chinese political leadership which is predominantly male in its constitution and apparently has the authority to direct Chinese women's matrimonial arrangements that makes it possible to execute the socially progressive idea that Prime Minister Zhou advocated. The complexity of the power structure in which the Chinese male and female are engaged in different relationships with a particular minority male group, as manifested in this case, suggests that Zhou's idea to improve the relationship between the Chinese and ethnic minorities in China, although socially progressive in certain important dimensions, still resonates with the traditional patriarchal tonality in which women, a kind of social being differing from both Chinese men and the minority men in China, do not have their distinctive voice.

Cao Yu's *Wang Zhao-jun*, like Guo Mo-ruo's *Cai Wen-ji*, dramatises a total harmony or complete identification between a woman and an established social order with its father figures, and has the same if not higher literary beauty and elegance in terms of style. However, when *Cai Wen-ji* was staged in the 1950s it was a big success – the audience admired it; while *Wang Zhao-jun*, staged in the 1980s, was not an authentic success despite the newspapers' effusive praise. The Chinese audience found it almost impossible to feel sympathy or admiration towards this Zhao-jun. People seemed no longer to take the harmony and identification between a self-sacrificial woman and the political interest of an established order as something self-evidently sublime and beautiful; rather they found it contrived and artificial. Twenty years passed between the writing of *Cai Wen-ji* and *Wang Zhao-jun*; a twenty years process which is divided into two periods by the ten years of the Cultural Revolution. *Cai Wen-ji* belongs to the prime moment of the first period – the 'Golden 50s' and *Wang Zhao-jun* belongs to a beginning of another era – the 'Turbulent 80s'. As an elegant echo of

Guo Mo-ruo's *Cai Wen-ji*, Cao Yu's *Wang Zhao-jun* seems to be a belated birth.

In 1979, the same year in which Cao Yu wrote his *Wang Zhao-jun*, Chen Bai-chen, another important playwright in modern Chinese literature and currently the Vice-President of the Society of Chinese Dramatists, also wrote a historical play, *The Song of the Wind*, in which the leading figure was also a woman.

Chen's play draws on political events of the early Han Dynasty. According to *Shiji*, when Liu Bang, the Founding Emperor of the Han Dynasty, died in 194 BC, the Crown Prince Liu Yin was still too young to be a real ruler. Thus the Empress Dowager Lü was in fact in control of the court and the country for fifteen years until her death in 179 BC. This kind of situation in an imperial patriarchal structure was bound to produce political tension. During these fifteen years, the conflicts between the Empress Lü's family and the Emperor Liu's family were intense and at times potentially dangerous to the stability of the established order. The old high officials who were devoted to the dead Emperor were threatened by the possible political changes that might take place. They strongly supported the Liu's family line but could not directly oppose the Empress. After the Empress Lü's death, the old officials finally took military action, arrested some of the Lüs who were attempting to control the succession, and place Liu Yin on the throne.[36]

Chen Bai-chen's dramatisation has moralised the characters and the events with a particular ethical standard which, at first sight, is constituted of loyalty toward the Emperor Liu and the commitment to keep the established order stable. 'No one can be named as prince except those from the Liu-family' – the agreement reached between the Emperor before he died and his officials in order to avoid the possible shifts of power and political eruptions – is used in the play as the touchstone to divide characters. Those who attempt to violate it are presented as immoral characters, and those who defend it are presented as being highly moral. Empress Dowager Lü wants to name male members of her family as princes in order to strengthen her position, and the old officials oppose her in order to keep her from becoming too powerful. The conflicts between the two sides set up the basic dramatic situation of the play, and the characters' personalities are subtly portrayed as moral on the one side and immoral on the other. Virtues such as selflessness, honesty, integrity, and above all, loyalty toward the Emperor's will make those on the Liu's side appear noble and admirable; vices such as selfishness, dishonesty, cruelty, greed, and above all, disloyalty toward the Emperor's will make those on Lü's side devils.

Worst among those devils is the Empress Dowager Lü. As an Empress Dowager, she is a living part of the dead Emperor; as a woman with the surname Lü, she is the other to the Emperor. This particular dual identity enables her to do what she wants to grasp power but to be rewarded with a general resentment at a court which consists exclusively of the male loyalists of her dead husband. She imperceptibly and yet mercilessly strips the military power from the old high officials;[37] she puts her son Liu Yin on the throne and then forces her granddaughter to marry this young emperor who in fact is her uncle;[38] she secretly burns the Emperor's will because according to the will, Prince Zhao, the son of Lady Qi, a concubine of the Emperor, is appointed to inherit the throne.[39] Among all the malevolent things she does, the most terrifying is her treatment of Lady Qi. She first has Lady Qi's son, Prince Zhao, poisoned, and then she imprisons Lady Qi, has her arms and legs cut off, and names her a 'human pig'.[40] This appalling crime deranges the mind of the young emperor and the Empress Dowager finally gains control of the throne. The old officials are outraged but do not dare to do anything to stop her because she is the Empress Dowager in a patriarchal structure in which the present father-figure is missing. At the end of the play, after her death, the Lüs who have supported her fall from power and the fifteen year period under a cruel and amoral Empress Dowager comes to an end.

The Song of the Wind stirred the public when it was staged in Beijing in 1979. The response was very divided. Some were deeply moved by the play and viewed it as a courageous challenge to the Chinese patriarchal tradition of which the Empress Dowager Lü is the typical bad image. Some had more mixed feelings toward the basic tone of the play and pointed out that the sense of morality underlying the drama was itself orthodox and patriarchal. Some went a step further and argued that in Chinese history, whenever the patriarchal regime was disturbed, the women who were involved in it would be condemned and turned into scapegoats.

The divided opinions indicate that the implications of the play are not as transparent as people might think. In the play, we see that as a woman who was superbly empowered by a patriarchal structure due to her particular relationship with the father-figure of the structure, Empress Dowager Lü assumes a complicity in the patriarchal operation more than being its victim. The political identity of 'empress dowager' itself and the tremendous amount of power implied by it points to the intricate involvement in the imperial patriarchy that a Chinese woman could have. The complicated features of such a female's complicity in patriarchal power relations and her conscious exploitation of their mechanism can be further seen in Empress Dowager Lü's efforts to grasp the chance to be in the very centre of the order after her husband died. What she did was made possible by the way in which that particular power relationship functioned. The result of those efforts, as dramatised by Chen, shows that Empress Dowager Lü was no longer a marginal let alone victimised element as women usually were under the same order, but a powerful representative of the patriarchy. What Chen Bai-chen projected into such an image with a passion of resentment and critical insights, in short, was inseparable from certain vital characteristics of this political mechanism that Empress Dowager Lü embodied. By presenting her as a cruelly immoral character, Chen Bai-chen in fact revealed certain dark constituents of the political mechanism with which she was actively engaged. In his critical dramatisation of the Chinese patriarchal structure, Chen Bai-chen distinguished himself from Guo Mo-ruo and Cao Yu.

However, the dark constituents of a patriarchal mechanism in Chen's dramatic vision cannot overshadow the positive father-image. Empress Dowager Lü, in his eyes, was usurping power by violating an authentic patriarchal order and thus what she did was utterly illegitimate. In order to prove her illegitimacy, Chen Bai-chen calls upon the dead Emperor and makes him a symbol of an absent order. The sentiments attached to a positive political structure were carefully preserved in this absent male father-figure; and the hatred toward the negative exploitation of this same structure was fully expressed in a present female usurper. In other words, what happens in the play is an almost unconscious displacement: Chen Bai-chen displaces the positive male father-figure with a negative 'father-figure', the positive one is male and the negative one is a female. The male father-figure is absent from the immediate situation and hence forms a positive memory and conceptual entity, and the female 'father-figure' functions in the practical imperial politics and takes on a absolute negative character. In short, the woman here is used to embody a destructive and immoral political mechanism which should be utterly denounced; but for Chen Bai-chen this embodiment is a false representation of an essentially constructive and moral political order because she is simply a usurper. As I have pointed out, through the explicit image of an evil woman at the very centre of an operative power structure, Chen Bai-chen in fact conveys a strong criticism and denunciation of the patriarchal tradition implicated in this structure. But this criticism and denunciation are politically mediated and psychologically transferred through his conscious choice to hold a negative female historical figure – a false representation of this operative power structure – to be the immediate target.

This unconscious displacement, if not an intrinsic self-conflict in Chen Bai-chen's writing, reflects one of the paradoxical complexities of his generation; the generation which rebelled against the imperial patriarchal order since 1919 and meant to build up a fundamentally different new structure since 1949 found that the new establishment was not completely new and in some aspects still resembled its ancestors. Those who established this 'new' order see in it the harsh fact that they, the rebels of the old order, are also the very products of the old tradition; the 'new' society, unlike what they expected, appears to be in certain ways a continuation of the 'old'. They see themselves, shockingly enough, to a certain degree resembling their former enemy. Chen's preface to the play is permeated with this sense of tragic irony. Like Cao Yu, he also dedicated his historical play to Prime Minister Zhou; but this Zhou in the 1970s, unlike the Prime Minister of the golden 1950s that Cao Yu remembered, was engaged in a tragic struggle against the overwhelming political mechanism in which dark patriarchal features seem to be reincarnated and yet of which he himself was one of the essential elements.[41] It is not accidental that these features of the Self in Other which Chen Bai-chen refuses to recognise as a historical part of the Self, in the case of *The Song of the Wind*, should be dramatised through a negative image of woman.

Through this brief analysis of four major historical plays using female protagonists in modern Chinese literature, we may come to the following tentative conclusion: From the May 4th Movement in 1919 until the founding of the People's Republic of China in 1949, the established imperial patriarchal order embodied in particular father-figures was the direct target for rebellious young men who believed that they were the agents of a progressive future. Accordingly, as it was presented in such a historical drama as *Zhuo Wen-jun*, Chinese women were praised as being rebellious against Bad Man. After the historic year, 1949, the father-figure as it was presented in *Cai Wen-ji* and *Wang Zhao-jun*, took on a positive image. Consequently, Chinese women such as Wen-ji and Zhao-jun appeared to be either sublimely devoted to or totally identified with this positive father-figure, the Good Man. The intricate continuity between the two types of male ideology inherent in the two dramas reveals the extremely illuminating function of such Western feminist concepts as 'patriarchy' and 'male ideology'; the crucial discontinuity between the two plays, however, testifies to the limits of the feminist conceptualisation of the 'patriarchy' or 'male ideology' as it was initiated and developed in the West.

From 1980 on, the relationship between a father figure and the image of women, as dramatised in *The Song of the Wind*, began to appear further complicated. The destructive function of the Chinese imperial patriarchal tradition, which involves both men and women, was bitterly represented. But a positive father-figure was carefully preserved and his presence in the play is asserted by his very absence. Almost inevitably, the father-figure's other self, the woman who was placed in the position of the father-figure and functioned as such, was held to be fully responsible for the political destructions, i.e. the intrinsic products of the Chinese imperial patriarchal tradition. In its representation as well as critique of Chinese imperial patriarchal tradition, *The Song of the Wind* illustrates how much modern Chinese historical plays have transformed and developed since the 1920s. In this dramatisation the Chinese imperial patriarchy has been in fact severely criticised, but the criticism is conducted only through an explicit negative image of the marginal element – a woman – within the established power structure.

The complicated nature of Empress Dowager Lü's complicity in the imperial patriarchy as dramatised suggests to us that a reductive feminist reading will submerge certain important ambiguities inherent in women's engagement with the socio-political establishment. And yet the fact that a woman's image is evoked in criticising and denouncing the Chinese imperial patriarchy also indicates how much a fundamentally feminist analysis is needed. From this perspective, we may say that in the realm of critique of the Chinese imperial patriarchal tradition, the modern Chinese historical drama in the 1980s shares in what the May 4th Movement of the 1920s demonstrated: through the dramatic configuration of female images by male authors, one sees the self-critical reconstituting of male ideology. And the difference between the two, interestingly enough, lies in the fact that in the 1980s it is through a negative portrayal of a woman and in the 1920s it is through a positive portrayal of a woman that Chinese male authors realise their self-criticism. The images of women in these four major modern Chinese historical plays, in my view, indicate the tortuous journey that Chinese male intellectuals have undergone in constructing and reconstructing their own images by writing and re-writing Chinese social and cultural history. Through these dramatisations in which the female identity is positively and/or negatively reconstructed, one sees how the male ideology rooted in the Chinese socio-historical matrix is deconstructed, negotiated, transformed, and reinscribed. The historical plays yet to come will show us how such a fascinating writing and rewriting will continue and, hopefully, how such a cultural and ideological deconstruction and reconstruction can be substantially changed by women's conscious struggle to articulate their various experiences, assert their particular socio-historical identities, and construct their different images as essential parts of modern Chinese cultural consciousness.

From *Journal of Dramatic Theory and Criticism*, 8:1 (Fall 1993), 61–81.

NOTES

[The author traces social history and gender history in China as informed and inspired by poet/playwright Guo Mo-ruo, starting in the 1920s. After establishing this context, she moves to the history of gendered characters in modern, non-operatic Chinese dramas by men and argues that these plays achieve the self-criticism desired by their male authors by presenting positive portrayals of women. This piece is less obviously about 'feminist theatre', but is unique in suggesting the grounds on which a Chinese feminist theatre might be built. Ed.]

1. Qian Xuan-tong, 'Some Reflections', *New Youth*, 5:1 (July 1918).

2 Pu Buo-ying, 'How to Make the Drama Useful to the Situation of Our Country', *Drama*, 4:4 (August 1921).

3. Gou Mo-ruo, 'The Two Sons of Sir Gu-zhu – A Preface', *Creation Quarterly*, 1:4 (February 1923).

4. Due to the limited space and time, I will discuss only this first play of the trilogy.

5. Sima Qian, 'Biography of Sima Xiangru', *Shiji*, 1171 (Beijing, 1959), 2999–3074.

6. See Guo Mo-ruo, 'An Appendix to *Three Rebellious Women*', *Complete Collection of Guo Mo-ruo's Plays*, vol. 1 (Beijing, 1982), p. 193.

7. Guo Mo-ruo, 'Zhuo Wen-jun', *The Complete Collection of Gou Mo-ruo's Plays*, vol. 1 (Beijing, 1982), p. 118.

8. Guo Mo-ruo, 'An Appendix', p. 194.

9. Guo Mo-ruo, 'Zhuo Wen-jun', p. 121.

10. It is important to note here that feminism itself is of course not a self-evidently homogeneous system of theory. There are many different schools of feminism. But the differences within feminism should not obscure the crucial distinction between the specifically anchored feminist theories, different as they are from one another, and the ontologised humanist doctrines.

11. In the sense in which Derrida uses the word.

12. Michèle Barrett, *Women's Oppression Today: Problems in Marxist Feminist Analysis* (London, 1980), p. 53.

13. Cf. M.H. Abrams, *Natural Supernaturalism: Tradition and Revolution in Romantic Literature* (New York, 1971).

14. Guo studied modern Western medicine in Japan in the 1920s.

15. Juliet Mitchell, 'Reflections on Twenty Years of Feminism,' in *What is Feminism* (New York, 1986), p. 36.

16. The trilogy of which *Three Rebellious Women* is the first play.

17. Guo Mo-ruo, 'An Appendix', p. 189.

18. Mao Ze-dong, *Collected Writings of Mao Tse-Tung*, vol. 1 (Tokyo, 1972), pp. 235–6.

19. The bloody military conflicts during the revolution are often mentioned by Chinese contemporary historians to account for the almost exclusive concentration of the revolutionary theoreticians on the issues of class struggle in their works. But the culture critique as manifested in the works of such figures as Guo Mo-ruo indicates that the urgency to deal with the issues of class struggle as compelled by the military conflicts is not the sole reason for the pervasiveness and the persistence of gender-blindness in the development of revolutionary consciousness.

20. Barret, *Women's Oppression Today*, p. 8

21. Gong Ji-ming and Fang Ren-nian, *A Chronicle of Guo Mo-ruo's Life* (Tian Jin, 1982), p. 600.

22. Guo Mo-ruo, 'An Appendix', p. 197.

23. Ibid., p. 198. 'Nora': the heroine in Ibsen's play *A Dolls' House*.

24. Ibid., pp. 48–9. For conciseness, I paraphrase her rather than translate fully.

25. Ibid., p. 86.

26. Guo Mo-ruo, 'An Appendix', p. 4.

27. Ibid., p. 106.

28. Ibid., p. 3.

29. Barrett, *Women's Oppression Today*, p. 14.

30. See *The Collection of Materials for Chinese Contemporary Literary Studies*, ed. Department of Chinese Literature at Sichuan University (Sichuan, 1979), pp. 673–756.

31. Cao Yu, *Wang Zhao-jun: A five-Act Historical Play* (Chengdu, 1979), p. 59.

32. Cao Yu, *Wan Zhao-jun*, p. 103.

33. The Chinese People's Political Consultative Conference.

34. Cao Yu, 'The Eternal Charm of Zhao-jun', in *Cao Yu's Wang Zhao-jun and Others,* ed. Luo Kang-lie (Hong Kong, 1980), p. 50.

35. Her grave remains carefully preserved in the area today called 'Inner Mongolia' and continues to be visited by Chinese people.

36. Sima Qian, 'Biography of Empress Dowager Lü, *Shiji* (Beijing, 1959).

37. Cheng Bai-chen, *The Song of the Wind* (seven-act historical play) (Chengdu, 1979), pp. 48–9.

38. Ibid. pp. 34–6.

39. Ibid., p. 22.

40. Ibid., pp. 60.

41. See 'Preface to The Song of the Wind', *The Song of the Wind* (Chengdu, 1979), pp. 2–3.

Further Reading

FEMINIST THEATRE CRITICISM: BOOKS

Linda Bamber, *Comic Women: Tragic Men: A Study of Gender and Genres* (Stanford, CA: Stanford UP, 1982).

Janet Brown, *Feminist Drama: Definition & Critical Analysis* (Metuchen, NJ and London: Scarecrow Press, 1979).

Elizabeth Brown-Guillory, *Their Place on the Stage: Black Women Playwrights in America* (New York: Greenwood, 1988).

Sue-Ellen Case, *Feminism and Theatre* (New York: Methuen, 1988).

Jill Dolan, *The Feminist Spectator as Critic* (Ann Arbor, MI: UMI Research Press, 1988).

Helene Keyssar, *Feminist Theatre* (London: Macmillan, 1984).

Dinah Luise Leavitt, *Feminist Theatre Groups* (Jefferson, NC: McFarland, 1980).

Susan M. Steadman, *Dramatic Re-Visions: An Annotated Bibliography of Feminism and Theatre 1972–1988* (Chicago: American Library Association, 1991).

Michelene Wandor, *Understudies* (London: Methuen, 1981).

——, *Carry on Understudies* (London: Routledge, 1986).

——, *Look Back in Gender: Sexuality and the Family in Post-War British Drama* (London: Methuen, 1987).

——, *Drama Today: A Critical Guide to British Drama 1970–1990* (London and New York: Longman, 1993).

ANTHOLOGIES OF FEMINIST THEATRE AND CRITICISM

Enoch Brater (ed.), *Feminine Focus. The New Women Playwrights* (New York and Oxford: Oxford University Press, 1989).

Sue-Ellen Case, *Performing Feminisms: Feminist Critical Theory and Theatre* (Baltimore and London: Johns Hopkins University Press, 1990).

Helen Krich Chinoy and Linda Walsh Jenkins (eds), *Women in American Theater* (New York: Crown Publishers, 1981).

Lynda Hart (ed.), *Making a Spectacle: Feminist Essays on Contemporary Women's Theatre* (Ann Arbor, MI: University of Michigan Press, 1989).

Karen Malpede, *Women in Theatre: Compassion and Hope* (New York: Drama Book Publishers, 1983).

Elizabeth J. Natalle, *Feminist Theatre: A Study in Persuasion* (Metuchen, NJ: Scarecrow Press, 1985).

Judith Olauson, *The American Woman Playwright: A View of Criticism and Characterization* (Troy, NY: Whitston, 1981).

Phyllis R. Randall (ed.), *Caryl Churchill. A Casebook* (New York and London: Garland, 1988).

Susan Todd (ed.), *Women and Theatre: Calling the Shots* (London: Faber & Faber, 1984).

ARTICLES

Jessica Abbe, 'Ann Bogart's Journeys', *The Drama Review*, 24:2 (1980), 85–100.

G. Austin, 'Women/Text/Theatre', *Performing Arts Journal*, 9:2/3 (1985), 185–90.

Barney Bardsley, 'The Young Blood of Theatre: Women's Theatre Groups', *Drama*, 152 (1984), 25–9.

Susan Bassnett, 'Struggling with the Past: Women's Theatre in Search of a History', *New Theatre Quarterly*, 5:18 (May 1989), 107–12.

Carol Billman, 'Women and the Family in American Drama', *The Arizona Quarterly*, 36 (Spring 1980), 355–48.

Rhonda Blair, '*A White Marriage*: Rozewicz's Feminist Tragedy', *Slavic and East European Arts* (Winter/Spring 1985), 13–21.

Cornelia Brunner, 'Roberta Sklar: Toward Creating a Women's Theatre', *The Drama Review*, 24:2 (1980), 23–40.

Beverley Byers-Pevitts, 'Imaging Women in Theatre: Departures from Dramatic Tradition', *Theatre Annual*, 40 (1985), 1–6.

Charlotte Canning, 'Constructing Experience: Theorising a Feminist Theatre History', *Theatre Journal*, 45 (1993), 529–40.

Susan Carlson, 'Process and Product: Contemporary British Theatre and its Communities of Women', *Theater Research International*, 13:3 (1987), 249–62.

——, 'Issues of Identity, Nationality, and Performance: The Reception of Two Plays by Timberlake Wertenbaker', *New Theatre Quarterly*, 35 (August 1993), 267–89.

Sue-Ellen Case, 'The Power of Sex: English Plays by Women, 1958–1988', *New Theatre Quarterly*, 7:27 (August 1991), 238–45.

——, 'Gender as Play: Simone Benmussa's *The Singular Life of Albert Nobbs*', *Women and Performance: A Journal of Feminist Theory*, 1:2 (1984), 21–4.

—— and Ellen Donkin, 'FIT: Germany's First Conference for Women in Theatre', *Women and Performance: A Journal of Feminist Theory*, 2:1 (1985), 65–73.

—— and Jeanie K. Forte, 'From Formalism to Feminism', *Theatre*, 16:2 (1985), 62–5.

Irini Charitou, 'Three Plays by Deborah Levy: a Brief Introduction', *New Theatre Quarterly*, 35 (August 1993), 230–2.

Helen Krich Chinoy, 'Art Versus Business: The Role of Women in American Theatre', *The Drama Review*, 24:2 (1980), 3–10.

Scott Cummings, 'Seeing with Clarity: The Visions of Maria Irena Fornes', *Theatre*, 17:1 (1985), 51–6.

Rosemary K. Curb, 'Fragmented Selves in Adrienne Kennedy's *Funnyhouse of a Negro* and *The Owl Answers*', *Theatre Journal*, 32 (1980), 180–95.

——, 'Re/cognition, Re/presentation, Re/creation in Woman-Conscious Drama: The Seer, The Seen, The Scene, The Obscene', *Theatre Journal*, 37 (1985), 302–16.

Sandra Messinger Cyress, 'From Colonial Constructs to Feminist Figures: Re/visions by Mexican Women Dramatists', *Theatre Journal*, 41:4 (December 1989), 492–504.

Kate Davy, 'Constructing the Spectator: Reception, Context and Address in Lesbian Performance', *Performing Arts Journal*, 10:2 (1986), 43–52.

Elin Diamond, 'Invisible Bodies in Churchill's Theatre', *Theatre Journal*, 40 (1988), 188–204.

——, 'Refusing the Romanticism of Identity: Narrative Interventions in Churchill, Benmussa, Duras', *Theatre Journal*, 37 (1985), 273–86.

Maria R. DiCenzon, 'Charabanc Theatre Company: Placing Women Centre-Stage in Northern Ireland', *Theatre Journal*, 45 (1993), 175–84.

Glenda Dickerson, 'The Cult of True Womanhood: Toward a Womanist Attitude in African-American Theatre', *Theatre Journal*, 40 (1989), 178–87.

Jill Dolan, 'The Dynamics of Desire: Sexuality and Gender in Pornography and Performance', *Theatre Journal*, 39:2 (May 1987), 156–74.

——, 'Women's Theatre Program ATA: Creating A Feminist Forum', *Women and Performance: A Journal of Feminist Theory*, 1:2 (1984), 5–13.

Jossette Féral, 'Writing and Displacement, Women in the Theatre', *Modern Drama*, 27 (1984), 549–63.

Winona Fletcher, 'From Genteel Poet to Revolutionary Playwright: Georgia Douglas Johnson', *Theatre Annual*, 40 (1985), 41–64.

Maria Irena Fornes and Tina Howe, 'Women's Work: Tina Howe and Maria Irena Fornes Explore the Woman's Voice in Drama', *American Theatre* (September 1985), 10–15.

Joan French, 'Organizing Women Through Drama in Rural Jamaica', *Isis International Women's Journal*, 6 (1986), 104–10. On the Sistren Theater Collective.

Sharon Friedman, 'Feminism as Theme in Twentieth-Century American Women's Drama', *American Studies*, 25 (Spring 1984), 69–89.

Carol W. Gelderman, 'The Male Nature of Tragedy', *Prairie Schooner*, 49:3 (1975), 220–36.

Patti Gillespie, 'Feminist Theatre: Rhetorical Phenomenon', *Quarterly Journal of Speech*, 64 (1978), 284–94.

R. Gipson, 'Martha Morton: America's First Professional Woman Playwright', *Theatre Survey*, 23 (November 1982), 213–22.

Marianne Goldberg, 'Transformative Aspects of Meredith Monk's *Education of the Girlchild*', *Women and Performance: A Journal of Feminist Theory*, 1:1 (1983), 19–28.

Lizbeth Goodman, 'Feminist Theatre in Britain: a Survey and a Prospect', *New Theatre Quarterly*, 33 (February 1993), 66–84.

Mel Gussow, 'Women Playwrights: New Voices in the Theater', *New York Times Magazine*, 1 May 1983, 22–40.

Lynda Hart, 'Doing Time: Hunger for Power in Marsha Norman's Plays', *Southern Women Playwrights*, Special Issue of *The Southern Quarterly: A Journal of the Arts in the South*, 25:3 (1987), 67–79.

Noelle Janaczewaska '"Do We Want a Piece of the Cake, or Do We Want to Bake a Whole New One?" Feminist Theatre in Britain', *Hecate*, 13:1 (1987), 106–13.

Linda Walsh Jenkins, 'Locating the Language of Gender Experience', *Women and Performance: A Journal of Feminist Theory*, 2:1 (1984), 5–20.

Assunta Kent, 'The Rich Multiplicity of *Betsey Brown*', *Journal of Dramatic Theory and Criticism*, 7:1 (Fall 1992), 151–61.

Helene Keyssar, 'Hauntings: Gender and Drama in Contemporary English Theatre', *Englische Amerikanische Studien, Englisches Drama Seit 1980*, 3, 4 (December 1986), 448–68.

——, 'Drama of Caryl Churchill: The Politics of Possibility', *Massachusetts Review*, 24 (September 1983), 198–216.

Ann Gavere Kilkelly, 'Who's in the House?', *Women and Performance: A Journal of Feminist Theory*, 3:1 (1986), 28–34.

Karen L. Laughlin, 'Criminality, Desire, and Community: A Feminist Approach to Beth Henley's *Crimes of the Heart*', *Women and Performance: A Journal of Feminist Theory*, 3:1 (1986), 36–51.

Deborah Levy, 'Questions of Survival: Towards a Postmodern Feminist Theatre', *New Theatre Quarterly*, 35 (August 1993), 225–9.

Claire-Louise McCurdy, 'Feminist Writer Renée: All Plays Are Political', *Women's Studies Journal*, 1 (April 1985), 61–72.

R. R. MacCurdy, 'Women and Sexual Love in the Plays of Rojas Zorrilla: Tradition and Innovation'. *Hispania*, 62:3 (1979), 255–65.

Phyllis Mahl, 'Beyond Hellman and Hansberry: The Impact of Feminism on a Decade of Drama', *Kansas Quarterly*, 12:4 (1980), 141–4.

Joseph Marohl, 'De-realized Women: Performance and Identity in *Top Girls*', *The Modern Drama*, 30:3 (1987), 376–88.

Carol Martin, 'Feminist Analysis Across Cultures: Performing Gender in India', *Women and Performance: A Journal of Feminist Theory*, 3:2 (1987/1988), 33–40.

——, 'Charabanc Theatre Company: "Quare" Women "Sleggin" and "Geggin" the Standards of Northern Ireland by "Tappin" the People', *The Drama Review*, 31 (Summer 1987), 88–89.

Madonne Miner, '"What's These Bars Doin' Here?" – The Impossibility of Getting Out', *The Theatre Annual*, 40 (1985), 115–36.

Tony Mitchell, '"Scritture femminile"; Writing the Female in the Plays of Dacia Maraini', *Theatre Journal*, 42:2 (May 1990), 332–49.

Gaylen Moore, 'Ellen Stewart – the Mama of LaMama', *Ms* (April 1982), 48–56.

Jane Moss, 'The Body as Spectacle: Women's Theatre in Quebec', *Women and Performance: A Journal of Feminist Theory*, 3:1 (1986), 5–16.

——, 'Women's Theatre in Quebec: Choruses, Monologues and Dialogues', *Quebec Studies*, 1:1 (1983), 276–85.

Klaus Peter Müller, 'A Serious City Comedy: Fe-/Male History and Value Judgements in Caryl Churchill's *Serious Money*', *Modern Drama*, 3 (September 1990), 347–62.

Janice Paran, 'Redressing Ibsen: Directors Fornes, Near, and Mann Emancipate his Proto-Feminist Plays from their Victorian Bonds', *American Theatre* (November 1987), 14–20.

Vivian M. Patraka, '*Apple Pie* and *Signs of Life*: Contrasting Forms in Feminist Drama', *Women and Performance: A Journal of Feminist Theory*, 1:2 (1984), 58–72.

Sheila Rabillard, 'Absorption, Elimination, and the Hybrid: Some Impure Questions of Gender and Culture in the Trickster Drama of Tomson Highway', *Essays in Theatre*, 12:1 (November 1993), 3–27.

Maria-José Ragué, 'Women and the Women's Movement in Contemporary Spanish Theatre', *New Theatre Quarterly*, 35 (August 1993), 203–10.

Charlotte Rea, 'Women for Women', *The Drama Review*, 18:4 (1974), 77–87.

——, 'Women's Theatre Groups', *The Drama Review*, 16:2 (1972), 79–89.

Janelle Reinelt, 'Feminist Theory and the Problem of Performance', *Modern Drama*, 32 (1989), 48–57.

——, 'The Politics of Form: Realism, Melodrama and Pam Gems' *Camille*', *Women and Performance: A Journal of Feminist Theory*, 4:8 (1989), 96–103.

S. L. Richards, 'Conflicting Images in the Plays of Ntozake Shange', *Black American Literature Forum*, 17 (Summer 1983), 73–8.

D. Roll-Hansen, 'Dramatic Strategy in Christina Reid's *Tea in a China Cup*', *Modern Drama*, 30:3 (1986), 389–95.

Kavah Safa-Isfahani, 'Female-Centered World Views in Iranian Culture: Symbolic Representations of Sexuality in Dramatic Games', *Signs*, 6:l (1980), 33–53.

Ann Sargent-Wooster, 'Yvonne Rainer's *Journeys from Berlin/1971*', *The Drama Review*, 24:2 (1980), 101–18.

Jeannette Laillou Savonna, 'French Feminism and Theatre: An Introduction', *Modern Drama*, 27 (1984), 540–5.

Yvonnne Shafer, 'The Liberated Woman in American Plays of the Past', *Players*, 49:3/4 (1974), 95–100.

Beverly A. Smith, 'Women's Work – *Trifles?* The Skill of Playwright Susan Glaspell', *International Journal of Women's Studies*, 5 (March–April 1982), 172–84.

Jenny Spencer, 'Norman's *'night, mother*. Psycho-Drama of Female Identity', *Modern Drama*, 30:3 (1987), 364–75.

Susan M. Steadman, 'Comedy, Culture, Communion and Canvas: Breaking the Silence about Women Artists in Three Plays by Tina Howe', *Theatre Southwest* (October 1987), 12–19.

Judith L. Stephens, 'The Compatibility of Traditional Dramatic Forms and Feminist Expressions', *The Theatre Annual*, 40 (1985), 7–23.

Cynthia Sutherland, 'American Woman Playwrights as Mediators of the "Woman Problem "', *Modern Drama*, 21 (1978), 319–36.

Michael Swanson, 'Mother/Daughter Relationships in Three Plays by Caryl Churchill', *Theatre Studies*, 31–32 (1984–5/1985–6), 49–66.

Robert L. Tener, 'Theatre of Identity: Adrienne Kennedy's Portrait of the Black Woman', *Studies in Black Literature*, 6:2 (1975), 1–5.

Elean Thomas, 'Lion-Hearted Women: The Sistren Theatre Collective', *Race and Class*, 28 (Winter 1988), 66–72.

Yvonne Yarbro-Bejarano, 'The Female Subject in Chincano Theatre: Sexuality, "Race", and Class', *Theatre Journal*, 38:4 (December 1986), 389–407.

Michelene Wandor, 'Culture, Politics and Values in Plays by Women in the 1980s', *Englische Amerikanische Studien, Englisches Drama Seit 1980*, 3, 4 (December, 1986), 441–8.

——, 'The Fifth Column: Feminism and Theatre', *Drama*, 152 (1984), 5–9.

Ross Wetszteon, 'The Mad, Mad World of Tina Howe', *New York Times* (28 November 1983), 58–71.

'Where Are The Women Playwrights?', *New York Times* (20 May 1973), Sec. II: 1+.

Margaret Wilkerson, 'Diverse Angles of Vision: Two Black Women Playwrights', *The Theatre Annual*, 40 (1985), 91–116.

Sharon Wills, 'Hélène Cixous's Portrait de Dora: the Unseen and the Unscene', *Theatre Journal*, 37 (1985), 287–301.

Edwin Wilson, 'Separate and Subversive', *Wall Street Journal* (23 September 1987), 32.

Carole Woddis, 'Second Wave Dramatists', *Plays and Players*, 401 (February 1987), 30–1.

Notes on Contributors

Karen Cronacher received her PhD from the University of Washington's School of Drama in 1993. Her publications include a monologue in *Monologues For and By Women* (Heineman, 1994), a one-act play, *Traindreams*, in the journal *Numuse* (October 1994), and an entry on Ntozake Shange in *Contemporary Women Dramatists* (St James Press, 1994). Currently, she writes radio plays for National Public Radio.

Tracy Davis is an Associate Professor in Theatre and English at Northwestern University.

Barbara Freedman is Professor of English in the Honors Program at St John's University. She is the author of *Staging the Gaze: Postmodernism, Psychoanalysis, and Shakespearean Comedy* (Cornell, NY, 1991). She is currently completing a book on popular political resistance surrounding Shakespeare's theatres, entitled *Plays, Plague and Protest*, and a book on the screening of academic discourse, entitled *The Disembodied Theorist: Fetish, Film, Philosophy Machine*.

Jeanie Forte is an independent scholar, director and dramaturg living in Palo Alto, California. She has taught in Drama and English at the University of Tennessee and the University of California at Berkeley. Her publications include articles and reviews in *Theatre, Modern Drama*, and *Theatre Journal*. She has a book, entitled *Women in Performance Art: Feminism and Postmodernism*, forthcoming from Indiana University Press. Women's plays have been the centre of her work. In the future, she plans on continuing her dramatic and scholarly work on feminist theory and performance.

Deborah Geis is an Associate Professor of English at Queen's College, SUNY. She specialises in modern and contemporary drama and women's studies. Her works include *Postmodern Theatrec(k)s: Monologue in Contemporary American Drama* (Michigan, 1993), articles on Ntozake Shange, Adrienne Kennedy, recent female performance artists, and others.

Helene Keyssar is Professor of Communication at the University of California, San Diego. She has published extensively, examining feminist drama in two books (*Feminist Theatre* and *Feminist Theatre and Criticism*) and several articles. She has also written on the films of Robert Altman, *Robert Altman's America*, as well as a book *(The Curtain and the Veil)* and several articles on African-American drama. Currently, she is working on a socio-cultural history of theatre, film, and television and a television series modelled on the 1930s *Living Newspaper Theatre*.

Loren Kruger teaches drama and cultural theory at the University of Chicago. She is the author of *The National Stage* and translator of *The Institutions of Art* by Christa and Peter Bürger. She is currently at work on a book on drama and modernity in South Africa.

Judith Graves Miller is Professor of French at the University of Wisconsin-Madison. She has authored two books (*Theatre and Revolution in France Since 1968* (French Forum, 1977) and *Françoise Sagan* (G.K. Hall, 1988). Along with Christiane Makward, she has written a book entitled *Plays by French and Francophone Women: A Critical Anthology* (University of Michigan Press, 1994). She writes widely on contemporary French-language theatre and theatre production.

Janelle Reinelt is an Associate Professor of Theatre Arts at California State University, Sacramento. She is currently writing a book on Brecht and contemporary British Theatre. Her work has appeared in *Modern Drama*, *Yale/Theatre*, *Women and Performance*, *West Coast Plays*, *Theatre Journal*, and The *Brecht Yearbook*.

Patricia Schroeder is a Professor of English at Ursinus College, where she teaches modern drama, women and theatre, and American literature. Her publications include *The Presence of the Past in Modern American Drama* (Fairleigh Dickinson, 1989), as well as numerous essays on contemporary American playwrights and feminist dramatic theory. She is currently completing a book-length study of the feminist possibilities of stage realism.

Haiping Yan is Assistant Professor of Theatre and Comparative Literature at the University of Colorado at Boulder. She received her PhD from Cornell University. She is the author of a prize-winning historical drama (staged in Shanghai, Shenyang, and Hong Kong). She has published critical essays on modern Chinese drama, modern European drama, and gender and cross-cultural issues. She is currently compiling an anthology of Chinese drama from 1978 to the present.

Yvonne Yarbro-Bejarano teaches in the Spanish and Portuguese Department at Stanford University. She is the author of a book on seventeenth-century Spanish theatre, *Feminism and the Honor Plays of Lope de Vega* (Purdue). She has an article forthcoming in *Cultural Critique*, an essay forthcoming in the edited volume *Lesbian and Gay Issues in Hispanic Literature* (Oxford University Press), and also an essay forthcoming in the volume *Professions of Desire: Gay and Lesbian Studies in Literature*. She is currently working on a book on Cherríe Moraga and Gloria Anzaldúa (Texas).

Index

283